CULTURE, PLACE, AND NATURE
STUDIES IN ANTHROPOLOGY AND ENVIRONMENT

Devon Peña and K. Sivaramakrishnan,

Series Editors

CULTURE, PLACE, AND NATURE

Centered in anthropology, the Culture, Place, and Nature series encompasses new interdisciplinary social science research on environmental issues, focusing on the intersection of culture, ecology, and politics in global, national, and local contexts. Contributors to the series view environmental knowledge and issues from the multiple and often conflicting perspectives of various cultural systems.

The Kuhls of Kangra: Community-Managed Irrigation in the Western Himalaya
by J. Mark Baker

The Earth's Blanket: Traditional Teachings for Sustainable Living
by Nancy Turner

Property and Politics in Sabah, Malaysia: Native Struggles over Land Rights
by Amity A. Doolittle

Property & Politics
IN SABAH, MALAYSIA

NATIVE STRUGGLES OVER LAND RIGHTS

AMITY A. DOOLITTLE

UNIVERSITY OF WASHINGTON PRESS
Seattle and London

THIS PUBLICATION WAS SUPPORTED
IN PART BY THE DONALD R. ELLEGOOD
INTERNATIONAL PUBLICATIONS ENDOWMENT.

© 2005 by the University of Washington Press
Printed in the United States of America
Designed by Pamela Canell
12 11 10 09 08 07 06 05   5 4 3 2 1

All rights reserved. No part of this publication may be reproduced or transmitted in any form or by any means, electronic or mechanical, including photocopy, recording, or any information storage or retrieval system, without permission in writing from the publisher.

University of Washington Press
P.O. Box 50096, Seattle, WA 98145
www.washington.edu/uwpress

Library of Congress Cataloging-in-Publication Data
can be found at the back of this book.

The paper used in this publication is acid-free and recycled from 20 percent post-consumer and at least 50 percent pre-consumer waste. It meets the minimum requirements of American National Standard for Information Sciences—Permanence of Paper for Printed Library Materials,
ANSI Z39.48–1984.

CONTENTS

ACKNOWLEDGMENTS
vii

A NOTE ON THE TEXT
xi

INTRODUCTION
Powerful Persuasions:
Resource Control and State Rhetoric
3

ONE
Colliding Discourses:
Western Land Laws and Native Customary
Rights in North Borneo, 1881-1928
29

TWO
Redefining Native Customary Law in Govuton:
Struggles over Property Rights between
Native Peoples and Colonial Rulers
67

THREE
Resources, Ideologies, and Nationalism:
The Politics of Development in
Postcolonial Sabah
99

FOUR
Land Disputes in Tempulong:
Colonial Land Laws, Customary Practices,
and the Postcolonial State, 1950–1996
122

CONCLUSION
Imagining New Environmental Futures:
Alternative Strategies for Natural
Resource Governance
152

GLOSSARY
167

NOTES
171

BIBLIOGRAPHY
191

INDEX
213

ACKNOWLEDGMENTS

THE RESEARCH FOR THIS BOOK HAS ABSORBED MANY YEARS; ALONG THE way I have incurred innumerable financial and intellectual debts. The early stage of my research was supported by fellowships from the Yale Center for International and Area Studies and the Yale Council for Southeast Asian Studies. Nancy Peluso and Peter Vandergeest generously supported my archival research at the Public Records Office in Kew, England. Financial support for my dissertation fieldwork (October 1995–September 1996) was provided by Fulbright-Hays, Doctoral Dissertation Research Abroad Award; the National Science Foundation, Law and Social Science Program, Dissertation Improvement Award (no. SBR 9511470); and the Social Science Research Council/American Council of Learned Societies, Southeast Asia Program, International Doctoral Dissertation Award.

Many governmental agencies in Sabah were extremely helpful in providing me with access to information. I particularly want to thank the staff of the following offices in the Ranau District: the District Office, the Forestry Department, the Native Court, the Land Office, the Lands and Survey Department, and the Information Office. The friends I made in these offices dealt with my unending requests for information not only efficiently but also enthusiastically. The Sabah Parks Department and specifically Francis Liew, the director of research, generously sponsored my stay in Sabah and provided institutional support for my work.

I am grateful to John Beaman, who during my research was the director of the Institute of Biodiversity and Ecological Conservation at the University of Malaysia at Sarawak. Few botanists know Mount Kinabalu better than he does. I benefited tremendously from stimulating discussions with John Beaman and Gary Martin in their capacity as coordinators for the Kinabalu Ethnobotany Project; both their unflagging intellectual and personal support kept my spirits up in times of personal doubt. Jude Kissey and Joanna Kitingan-Kissey's hospitality whenever we were in Kota Kinabalu was gratefully appreciated.

Arun Agrawal, Michael Dove, Benedict Kiernan, Tania Li, K. Sivaramakrishnan, Nancy Peluso, and James Scott all provided excellent constructive criticism on my work, and each in varying ways has had a major influence on the formation of my ideas. I particularly want to express my gratitude to Nancy Peluso for her support of my project and her guidance during the early years of my research. The seeds for this research were planted in the fall of 1994 in Nancy's class on political ecology, where she introduced me to a whole new way of thinking about the relationships between people and natural resources and thereby changed the course of my academic career.

Jim Scott's Program in Agrarian Studies has been one of the highlights of my stay at Yale. The weekly meetings and the discussions of scholars' work have stimulated my thinking in productive ways that would not have been possible without the support of such a generous intellectual community. I have learned vast amounts about good scholarship, constructive criticism, and academic professionalism from the interactions that take place in the weekly meetings. Kay Mansfield, who keeps the Agrarian Program running smoothly, has always provided an understanding ear, and I thank her for that.

I owe special thanks to Michael Dove, who adopted me as his student in the final stages of dissertation writing. His criticisms have always been thoughtful, as he has continually pushed me to a finer level of analysis. He is a superb adviser who has provided me with critical professional advice.

My friends and fellows at Yale—Emily Harwell, Celia Lowe, Hugh Raffles, and Janet Sturgeon—have provided a tremendous support network through all stages of my research and writing.

An earlier version of chapter 1 was published as "Colliding Discourses: Western Land Laws and Native Customary Rights in North Borneo, 1881–1928" (*Journal of Southeast Asian Studies*, vol. 32, no. 1 [2003]:97–126). Bruce Lockhart and two anonymous reviewers helped me to strengthen the analysis significantly. Reed Wadley aided me in developing thoughts that are discussed in chapter 2 and the conclusion and that are included as a condensed chapter for a volume that he edited: "Controlling the Land: Property Rights and Power Struggles in Sabah, Malaysia, 1881–1996," in *Environmental Change in Native and Colonial Histories of Borneo: Lessons from the Past, Prospects for the Future* (Leiden: KTLV Press, forthcoming). An early version of chapter 2 appeared as "From Village Land to 'Native Reserve': Changes in Property Rights in Sabah, 1950–1996" (*Human Ecology*, vol. 29, no. 1 [2001]:69–98). I am grateful for the comments of three anonymous reviewers who helped by strengthening my argument. Portions of chapter 3 appeared as "'Are They Making Fun of Us?' The Politics of Development in Sabah, Malaysia" (*Moussons: Social Science Research on Southeast Asia*, vol. 4 [2001]:75–95). I am grateful for the comments of Bernard Sellato and two anonymous reviewers. I would like to thank Peter Vandergeest, who commented on an earlier version of chapter 3, and Tania Li, for sharing her unpublished manuscripts with me during my writing. Three anonymous reviewers and Lorri Hagman at the University of Washington Press have been enormously valuable in transforming my manuscript into a readable book. I appreciate the opportunity to be part of this new and important series "Culture, Place, and Nature."

I am fortunate that my husband is a wonderful photographer—he supplied me with all the photographs used in this study and reproduced them for presentation. His efforts saved me weeks of work. The maps were made by the technical artistry of Heather Salome at Metaglyfix from a compilation of historical maps and sketch maps made in the field.

Most important, the people who lived in the villages of Govuton and Tempulong made this study possible. They welcomed me and my family into their villages, generously shared the smallest details of their lives with me, tolerated my ineptitude in a foreign culture, and trusted me with their opinions and feelings about their land, its natural resources, and the processes of change and development. I want to thank them one and all for their participation. I hope that they benefited in some way from the year that my family and I spent with them.

Above all, I must thank my parents, George and Laura Appell. They introduced me to Borneo and to life in the field when I accompanied them on their fieldwork to both Indonesia and Malaysia. From them I learned many tricks of the trade that made my own fieldwork much more pleasant and prepared me for many of the surprises inherent in such work. Throughout the year of fieldwork in Sabah, they also supported my family and me with a steady supply of English novels and with constant feedback and advice on my work. I also want to thank my sisters, Laura and Charity, and my parents-in-law, Jerry and Gretchen, particularly for their support during our stay in Sabah.

And, finally, to Mike, Eliza, and Georgia, who make it a joy to leave my desk and be a part of their world, thank you for year upon year of sticking with me through this project.

A NOTE ON THE TEXT

THE PEOPLE WITH WHOM I WORKED SPOKE BOTH MALAYSIAN AND THEIR local Dusun dialect. It is not unusual for people to combine both languages in conversations. Although I relied mostly on Malaysian, I do know some Dusun and turned to a translator when I could not understand what was being said. The foreign words used in the book are all Malaysian, with the exception of those that are marked with a "D," designating them as Dusun words.

Dollar figures are quoted in two different currencies. In the colonial period, Straits dollars were used. According to Amarjit Kaur and Ian Metcalfe (1999), the value of the Straits dollar fluctuated during the nineteenth century. In 1904, it was pegged to the sterling at a rate of M$1.00 to 2 shillings and 4 pence (about US$0.60). In the mid-1990s, when I conducted my research, the currency was the Malaysian dollar (ringgit, or M$). At that time, M$1.00 was about US$0.40.

Following anthropological conventions, I use pseudonyms for the villages where I worked, for place-names within village boundaries, and for all my informants. For historical figures, I use their true names.

Property & Politics
IN SABAH, MALAYSIA

INTRODUCTION

POWERFUL PERSUASIONS

Resource Control and State Rhetoric

IN 1990, A PROMINENT POLITICIAN FROM SABAH, MALAYSIA, ANNOUNCED at an international conference on conservation and biodiversity that he intended to expand the boundaries of Kinabalu Park[1] to include an area that supported species-rich tropical forests and was known locally as Bukit Hempuen (Hempuen Hill).[2] Shortly after this announcement, two-thirds of Bukit Hempuen was burned to the ground, allegedly by local people. Prominent biologists and politicians were furious that local people could act so destructively. The plans to include the once-valuable forests in Kinabalu Park were dropped.

Both politicians and biologists were unable to comprehend why local people burned the area, in part because they did not give sufficient consideration to the social history of resource use and customary rights of access to Bukit Hempuen. The government never openly acknowledged the fact that, prior to the formation of the Kinabalu Park in 1963, local people for generations had hunted and collected forest products in the area. This is not to suggest that policymakers were *unaware* of the local uses of the area. In 1962, the following was written about the southern boundary of the then-proposed park, which bordered the town of Kundasang:

> It is uninhabited . . . though there is a Dusun path called Jalan Dili.[3] . . . [The area is a] rich breeding ground for animals. Jalan Dili is used by hunters, collectors of damar (gum of *Agathis*) and collectors of rattan. Pigs, barking deer,

and sumbar[4] were conspicuous. It is considered to be the chief breeding ground for large mammals around Kinabalu. . . . The question on hunting rights may be difficult. It may be necessary along the southern boundary to establish a buffer zone where pig and deer can be shot and where timber may be extracted for house building. At Kundasang there were signs of agitation among villagers, and new "rentis" (path) had been cut in the forest clearly as an endeavor to strike out claims before it might be too late.[5]

But during the formation of the park these customary rights were disregarded, the necessary buffer zone was never established, and all harvesting of timber, forest products, and game was strictly prohibited in the park regulations. Practices of resource use that local people had enjoyed for centuries became criminal acts under the new park regulations.

Present-day policymakers and government officials also ignored the fact that Bukit Hempuen had been *included* in Kinabalu Park when the boundaries were originally drawn in 1963. They overlooked the fact that in 1984 Bukit Hempuen had been *removed* from the park so that individuals close to the chief minister could log the forest for *Agathis* trees. After the valuable logs were removed and politicians abandoned the land, local villagers reclaimed sections of this region, as they slowly "encroached" on the boundaries of Kinabalu Park for shifting cultivation. And when the politicians wanted to take back the land again in 1990, people were angry. This entire history of informal and formal changes in the property rights and means of access to Bukit Hempuen was ignored when the politician from Sabah made what he considered a generous gesture indicating his dedication to the conservation of biodiversity.

For the people in this area, this political gesture was the last straw. They had given up the land to the Kinabalu Park in 1963. No one had publicly contested its removal from Kinabalu Park in 1984 for the benefit of political elites. None of the politicians had asked whether the local people needed the land more than did the already-wealthy politicians. And no one dared suggest that the rural population might need the land more than did the rare tropical plants. But when the government threatened to unilaterally take away land that local people needed and had reclaimed, the people acted. Burning the remaining forest seemed to be the only way that they could maintain control over the land. Ironically, it was the state's very project of resource and landscape protection that resulted in the burning of Bukit Hempuen.

Such destructive and violent acts are rare in Sabah. The rural population generally finds quieter and less obvious ways to assert and validate its control over natural resources. And in this way this story is a diversion, for I do not focus on this type of overt local resistance to state policies in the rest of this book. But I recount this story here because it dramatically illustrates processes that are continuously at play in Sabah, in subtle ways that require close analysis. In brief, this story highlights certain relationships that are ongoing between state agents and local people. And equally significant, this story illustrates the importance of understanding the broader historical, social, and political-economic circumstances that influence current land use strategies and property regimes in Sabah. Without this understanding, the actions of local villagers may seem unconnected, irrational, self-defeating, and illogical. Without this understanding, politicians and biologists fail to realize that a "simple" gesture of moving the boundaries of the park to include a single hillside could result in the destruction (at least temporarily) of that hillside.

This book explores changes in property relations and rights of access to land and natural resources in Sabah, Malaysia, from 1881 to 1996. Combining perspectives from anthropology, political science, environmental history, and political ecology, I explore how control over and access to resources are defined, negotiated, and contested by colonial state agents, the postcolonial Malaysian state, and local people. My analysis of changing property relations explores a sweep of history spanning more than one hundred years and analyzes data from both the state and local levels. Thus, this work is conceptualized as a multisited study in which colonial archives, rural villages, and government offices are examined as places of meaning and action, developing and shifting in relation to one another. I engage scholarly debates including the relationship between state and society, the role of legal pluralism under colonialism in the transformation of property rights, colonial and postcolonial discourses of rule and resource control, the multiple outcomes of state development projects, and the consequences of these actions for the future of sustainable resource use and conservation. Through two village-level case studies, I explore current conceptualizations of rights of access to resources, state-society interactions and power struggles, and modes of rule over native people and natural resources.

This study is grounded in methodological and theoretical advances in the field of political ecology. While political ecology is a broad field that draws from various different bodies of knowledge, it is characterized by studies that examine how social relations, at multiple levels and over time, shape the institutions and practices that surround resource use (Bryant 1992; Blaikie and Brookfield 1987). In other words, studies in political ecology stress that changes in the landscape and in resource use regimes cannot be understood outside of the context of local land use practices and the wider political, economic, and social systems that influence the land users' decision making. Rather than focus on the cultural and ecological relations only at a local site, a shortcoming for which human ecology has been critiqued (Goldman 1998), political ecology seeks to merge the traditions of human ecology and political economy by considering the influences of both micro- and macro-level factors on human-environment interactions. Practitioners of political ecology try to explain environmental conflicts in terms of the particularities of place, culture, and history. The field is predicated on the assumption that environmental problems are often common, but because their causes are complex and changing, solutions must be specific to time and place (Peet and Watts 1996). One of the major contributions of a political ecology perspective is its focus on the root causes of environmental degradation. This involves removing blame from the victims (typically perceived as the drivers of degradation) and exposing the underlying political, economic, and social forces that lead to resource degradation (Schroeder 1993:349). A key question that this book explores is, Who currently holds the power over influential narratives about appropriate resource use?

One of the central objectives of this study is to examine the ways in which power is mobilized and used as leverage in struggles over property relations and rights of access to valuable resources, both by representatives of the state and by local society. Therefore it is critical to investigate theories of the achievement and exercise of power; theories of property relations; the modes of official knowledge production by colonial and postcolonial officials about native people and their regimes of resource use; how this knowledge is crystallized in laws, policies, and development practices; and how the outcomes of laws and policies are ultimately challenged and revised in implementation and through everyday practices. One can think of these debates over who has the right to define what constitutes appropriate resource use as resting on a larger set of theoretical issues understood as "modes of governmentality"—that is, the political rationalities that support the expression of power (Foucault 1991a). Specifically, I am interested in the techniques of governmentality that control native people and their use of natural resources and how local property relations are shaped through the struggles over the exercise of power. Discourse analysis is effective for examining knowledge production, power, and politics because it assumes that power can be both coercive and productive, and, as a result, the differences between dominant discourses and subjugated knowledges are highlighted. Moreover, it draws attention to the role of human agency in social change as local peoples' responses to state interventions are expressed through accommodation, negotiation, and resistance. What is gained is a close analysis of the historical, political, and social/cultural factors that shape resource use on the ground. By bringing both state discourses of rule and the local peoples' responses to state rule into a single analytical field, this study provides insights that will be valuable in the formation of future policy on natural resource use.

POWER, KNOWLEDGE, AND DISCOURSE

Michel Foucault (1991b) has convincingly argued that people do not "have" power implicitly. Rather, power is a technique or an action that individuals can engage in. And wherever power is exercised, it will always produce other reactions or resistance to it. Foucault's conceptualization of power provides a critical way to understand state-society relationships. Specifically, one of the techniques of power, according to Foucault, is the use of bodies of knowledge to create "truths" as a product of discursive practices. These "truths" and discursive practices define the productive space for the state to exercise power and for society to respond, through individual expressions of power. Importantly, in contrast to Karl Marx, Foucault does not believe that power is held exclusively by the dominant ruling class. Instead power is made up of the various actions or techniques of conduct that all people can exert under various conditions, with varying outcomes. This study is concerned with both the political rationalities necessary to constitute a subject population and the reactions of society (the supposed subjects of domination) that are made possible by certain political rationalities.

In order to understand power in its materiality, one must focus on the level of practice, that is, the day-to-day operations of power relations (Dreyfus and Rabinow 1983:184–85). Foucault refers to this linking of technologies of power and modes of thought as "governmentality," arguing that it is not possible to study the technologies of power without an analysis of the political rationality underpinning it (Foucault 1977:27–28). Further, by defining government as "the conduct of conduct" the term governmentality covers the range of "governing others" to "governing the self" (Foucault 1982:220–21). Governmentality, therefore, explains how the modern state and the modern autonomous individual codetermine each other's emergence (ibid.). In other words, the exercise of power structures the field of possible reactions. As actions and reactions work in a reiterative way, one can conceive of power as being exercised in a spiral fashion, not as a unidirectional force that is exerted from "above" society (ibid., 222). Thus, the legitimizing of the nation-state (i.e., the ways in which the nation-state conforms to recognized principles and accepted rules) proceeds by the "constant reiteration of its power through what have been accepted as natural (rational and normal) state functions" (Cohn and Dirks 1988: 225).

Modes of governmentality can be understood as the "forms of calculated practices (inside and outside government) directing categories of social agents in a particular manner for particular ends" (Watts 2002:1315). In this study I am primarily interested in how power is exercised through the normalizing technologies of state rule. Normalization can be conceptualized as the molding of people into "normal" as opposed to "abnormal" forms and as the processes by which culture encourages people to regulate and achieve conformity with the established rules. Normalizing technologies of rule rely on the creation of knowledge to "define what is normal; at the same time, they define practices which fall outside their system as deviant and in need of normalization" (Dreyfus and Rabinow 1983:198). One of the rituals of power that serves to normalize society is the production of certain forms of knowledge about society, as well as the construction of discourses that legitimize state rule and constitute the subjects of rule. Through the actions of normalizing society, the state can attempt to exert control that renders subjects of rule docile, productive, and useful. By the state's creating knowledge about certain people and certain actions as to define them as "problems" or as "abnormal," the nature of government interventions to "correct the problem" becomes "self-evident." Any departures from the norm become the reason or justification for state intervention and regulation. In Foucault's own words, "There is no power relation without the correlative constitution of a field of knowledge, nor any field of knowledge that does not presuppose and constitute at the same time power relations" (1977:27–28). Following Foucault, this study examines the discourses of rule—or the ways in which knowledge is produced in order to set the limits, by both constraining and enabling the range of acceptable or "normal" behavior and discourse, and the strategies that are available for broadening or even defeating these limits (McHoul and Grace 2002:29–31). The type of discourse analysis that follows explores how human subjects are formed, how institutions attempt to normalize people on the margins of social life, and how the same people on the margins of social life respond to the exercise of power by the state. Writing on the inextricable link between discourse, knowledge, and power, Foucault (1980b:93) states:

> Relations of power cannot themselves be established, consolidated nor implemented without the production, accumulations, circulation and functioning of a discourse. There can be no possible exercise of power without a certain economy of discourses of truth which operates through and on the basis of this association. We are subjected to the production of truth through power and we cannot exercise power except through the production of truth.

Foucault also conceptualizes power as "a multiple and mobile field of force relations, wherein far-reaching, but never completely stable, effects of domination are produced" (1980b:102). Not exclusively the property of repressive states, power belongs to the weak as well as the strong (Dirks et al. 1994:5). Thus, in reaction to state rule one must expect a multiplicity of localized responses in the form of compromise, negotiation, collaboration, and resistance (Escobar 1984:331). By analyzing the exercise of power through state agents, one can also develop knowledge of various strategies that emerge at the local level in reaction to the practices of the state.

In the sense that power is exercised through everyday practices, much attention has been directed at "everyday forms of resistance" (Scott 1985, 1990). But in addition to everyday forms of resistance, this book explores the multiple ways in which local people collaborate and negotiate with the state in response to the exercise of power, in an attempt to exert their own power over the outcomes of state interventions. While it is compelling to think of the subtle ways in which local people through acts of everyday and overt resistance penetrate and manipulate elements of the dominant discourses of rule, it is equally important to explore the ways in which local people exercise their power through compromise, negotiation, and collaboration, strategies that ultimately alter the outcomes of state projects (Ortner 1995; Majid Cooke 2002). Focusing on the role of negotiation and collaboration is in fact a particularly useful way to explore Foucault's notions of power and knowledge since his work has emphasized the positive, productive role of power. Equally important, an understanding of local actions in terms of collaborations and negotiations, as well as resistance to state power, is key to crafting policies aimed at the sustainable use of natural resources. Ideally, a democratic and just state can be responsive to civil action aimed at correcting perceived inequalities, whether these actions are in the form of resistance or are attempts at compromise, negotiation, and collaboration. A failure to consider these social realities and expressions of agency in policymaking will result in social obstacles to the advancement of good policy (see Majid Cooke 1999), such as the unresolved disputes that surround access to and use of Bukit Hempuen described above. If the colonial and postcolonial states in Sabah had been more receptive to local struggles and actions in response to state interventions, possibilities of co-management of the resource-rich area in Bukit Hempuen might have been developed that would benefit both the conservation agenda and the local need for land.

Following Foucault, this study shows that power, exercised by state representatives in relation to local society, has the ability to create new forms of behavior, new modes of self-understanding, and new codes of meaning, as well as new ways to resist and oppose the ruling state (Foucault 1991b). Thus, state power and local resistance to power can have profound effects on social institutions such as property relations, no matter how unstable and subject to contestation and reformulation the state power is. At varying times and places one sees the relationship between state authorities and local society as characterized by contradictory forces. There are moments of state attention and moments of state neglect, moments of local acceptance and moments of local resistance, moments of collaboration between state representatives and local people and moments of discord. In this study, however, one generalization about state rule does emerge: the exercise of power and knowledge in Sabah, Malaysia, can be seen as a way to create a group of people who are classified as departing from the "norm" and to make them conform and contribute to the patterns of production necessary for a capitalist society. Thus, present-day state interventions and efforts aimed at correcting the "problems" of rural people and their livelihood strategies have deep roots in colonial history, as both colonial and postcolonial states turn to natural resources to fuel economic growth and modernization.

COLONIAL STATES AS REGIMES OF POWER

Colonialism throughout the world was made possible by cultural technologies of rule that created new categories and oppositions between the colonizer and colonized, modern and traditional, West and East, European and Asian (Dirks 1996:ix). An examination of the daily practices within the colonial state informs one's understanding of state power, technologies of rule, and the transformation of property relations. These include the ways in which colonial law was used as the primary tool for control over people and the territory and the ways in which the production and circulation of knowledge about indigenous peoples and their use of natural resources played a crucial role in providing external and internal legitimacy for colonial rule. Law therefore became a mechanism to demarcate the boundaries of state control and to exclude local people from certain areas, and the production of knowledge about native people and their shortcomings produced a stable knowledge base upon which colonial rulers could rest their claims to authority.

Colonial law, as a technology of rule and power, relied on several forms of knowledge production. These included gathering and classifying information about native peoples and their customary laws, selectively transforming that information to be compatible with Western legal principles, and finally turning the information into usable forms, through land codes, reports on land settlement, and the production of legal titles to land (Cohn 1996). Consequently, colonial intervention into native land matters relied on the ability of colonial knowledge to reinscribe the social and physical landscape through technologies of rule, such as creating administrative units, mapping and surveying the land, creating boundaries, writing land laws, delineating which areas could be used by whom, and creating land titles to legitimate people's use of the land (Vandergeest and Peluso 1995). This way of managing information epitomized the symbiosis of knowledge and power that was the basis for developing and ruling the territory through the colonial project (Watts 1995:48) and is the foundation of governmentality.

Colonialism typically involved the large-scale transfer of laws and legal systems from one society to another (Merry 1991:890). The importance of the transfer of European legal systems lies in the ability of law to legitimate certain visions of social order and to privilege certain modes of production over others (Hirsch and Lazarus-Black 1994:1). In reference to property rights, Western property laws equated landownership with the notion of "improving" the land through labor, a notion that can be traced back to Locke's "Second Treatise of Government" ([1690] 1963). Locke argues that the individual who works the land is given the right to claim private ownership over the land. Throughout the British colonies in Africa, Asia, and the Americas colonial officers attempted to reduce native customary rights to land to a system that vested a private title to the individual who could prove permanent and continuous cultivation of the land in the eyes of the colonialists. Variations in ownership—such as communally held village land that was redistributed to village members on an annual basis; the ownership of trees, separate from the land on which they stood; the importance of fallow lands in the swidden-fallow cycle; and village access to forested land for hunting and gathering, but not for agricultural purposes—were all overlooked by colonial officers, who were intent on establishing private and individual title only. And any land considered "idle" became state land, regardless of whether native peoples used it for hunting, gathering forest resources, fallows for the agricultural cycles, rituals, or watershed protection. Colonial law valorized Western forms of knowledge and thereby privileged the attendant property regimes, even when those regimes were difficult to enforce and were contested at various levels from within colonial rule and from the subjects of rule.

While colonialism relied on the large-scale imposition of Western legal principles, often these principles were adapted, albeit incompletely, to local situations. For instance, in many colonies the imposed European legal traditions were not meant to replace indigenous law, but instead were supposed to be integrated with the preexisting indigenous legal systems (S. Moore 1986a:19). These situations, in which two or more legal systems exist in the same social field—one set of laws for the colonizers and one set for the colonized—are defined as cases of legal pluralism (Merry 1988; Griffiths 1986). In Africa, the British and the French superimposed their law onto indigenous law, incorporating elements of "customary law" as long as it was not "repugnant to natural justice, equity, and good conscience" (Adewoye 1986:60; S. Moore 1992:18; Meek 1946) or "inconsistent with written law" (Okoth-Ogenda 1979; Meek 1946). In Southeast Asia, Dutch and British colonialists selectively codified elements of native customary law that would facilitate aspects of colonial rule—specifically the regulation of access to commercial resources. For instance, Charles Zerner has argued that the codification of Central Moluccan customary rules for agricultural production, and the subsequent imposition of these laws through the local authority of the raja, was a means of "creatively controlling the production and commercial management of agricultural and marine commodities as sources of income for local elites" (Zerner 1994:1087). By selectively recognizing specific elements of native law, such as revenue production, colonial rulers were able the build up traditional authorities as pillars of "indirect rule" (Okoth-Ogenda 1979). By acknowledging native authorities and establishing "native courts," colonial administrators were ensuring the complicity of at least some natives in their new structures of rule, simultaneously controlling the parameters and venues for local actions in response to colonial rule. In many places, indirect rule fostered highly authoritarian structures of power in rural areas, structures based ostensibly on customary law, but often underwritten by the colonial state (Mamdani 1996). Thus, power exercised through the legal practices of the colonial rulers was mobilized directly by local leaders who appeared, at least initially, complicit in the colonial project. Importantly, native leaders also used the colonial authority to enhance their own power at the local level (see, inter alia, S. Moore 1986b; Berry 1993; Peters 1994; Zerner 1994).

But equally important to ensuring the complicity of some natives in colonial rule, indirect rule was also a way to govern extensive territories, inhabited by scattered and diverse people, on a financial and administrative "shoestring" (Berry 1993; Black 1983). Thus, indirect rule was also a form of state simplification that expedited a bureaucratic reordering of property rights and facilitated revenue collection (Scott 1998, esp. chap. 1). In order to transform local property rights, with their complex bundle of property arrangements and land tenure, into a uniform and homogeneous system of "native customary land tenure," a simplification of local tenure arrangements was necessary. Locally distinct forms of rights to land and other natural resources became reduced to individual title. And with each parcel of land came a legal landowner and, hence a taxpayer, to bolster revenue collection necessary for colonial administration (Scott 1976, 1998; Vandergeest and Peluso 1995; Ranajit Guha 1963; Wong 1975; Sihombing 1989; Hooker 1980). The process of indirect rule, therefore, facilitated in multiple ways the extension of state power to the peripheries: it ensured the complicity of at least some natives in colonial rule; it created new institutions for the resolution of native disputes in the native courts overseen by native chiefs; and it was the most economically efficient way to collect revenue and inform natives about new policies regarding land settlement.

Indirect rule and land settlement also provided the space for radical reshaping of the native population by the colonials. In *A Rule of Property for Bengal* (1963), Ranajit Guha demonstrates the effects of several of the colonial techniques of rule on Bengali people and their resources during the period of East India Company rule in the late eighteenth century. In the following account can be seen the combined impact of the imposition of Western legal principles, simplification necessary to produce taxpayers, indirect rule, and the invention of "traditional" customs. Prior to interventions by the East India Company, the zamindar class was a group of elite peasants who were responsible for collecting tribute from the tenants or sharecroppers across a designated territory. The tribute was paid to the regional raj, or ruler, who controlled the use of the resources in the territory.

A new tenure system, imposed by British colonial rule, instituted permanent settlement, or the privatization of rights to land, in India in 1776. The consequences of imposing a new tenure system based on private property were far reaching. Under permanent settlement, the East India Company now vested the rights of private ownership to land to the zamindars. This created a new class of landowners with full rights of inheritance and sale of land where previously there had been no such class. And in turn, zamindars were now responsible for paying revenue to the East India Company. Therefore, they had to raise the amount of tribute that they demanded from tenants or lose their land to the East India Company. In many cases local tenants who could not meet the increased rent were evicted. Millions of laborers and tenants lost their customary rights of access to land and its products. Thus, the imposition of a new system of property rights in Bengal began a process of creating a new class of landed aristocracy who began to monopolize land and a new class of landless peasants. By changing the forms of rule, colonialism in Bengal facilitated the production of new local hierarchies, created new expectations of behavior among native peoples, and instituted new codes of conduct and meaning.

Despite the brute force that many colonialists used to expand their power and control vast resources, imposed colonial law was much more than a body of immutable rules, institutions, and procedures forged for indirect rule and revenue collection (Hirsch and Lazarus-Black 1994:8). Colonial law faced conflicts and challenges as the subjected populations responded to colonial rule, and, as a result, its reach was uneven in practice and diverse in form (Sivaramakrishnan 2000). A major challenge to the hegemony of the colonial state was local resistance to coercive policies (Scott 1985). As Edward Thompson, Douglas Hay, and other social historians have argued, one cannot necessarily equate law with complete, unstoppable power; just as Michel Foucault argues, one must focus on the relationship between a controlling state and local people's power to resist the control of the state, to negotiate with the state, or to use the law to their advantage against the state (cf. Thompson 1975; Hay 1976).

Following Foucault's notions of power as all encompassing and shaping the possibilities for response to power, the legal rules and procedures that were instruments of European domination were also tools of resistance, adaptation, and renewal for the indigenous peoples. For instance, the following chapters present evidence of how local leaders in Sabah used the British codification of customary laws to the advantage of the local community, in ways not anticipated by colonial lawmakers. Although the colonial rulers through their codification of native customary law set the parameters for local responses, they did not foresee all the ways in which local people could use the colonial laws to their own advantage. Law and power, consequently, are inextricably linked to both hegemony and resistance in the growth and emergence of a new nation-state.

In this dialectical relationship between the colonizer and the colonized, mediated by legal pluralism, European law was central to the colonial project, but in an ambiguous way (Merry 1988:891). By incorporating existing legal and social systems into their arena of power, colonial officials were able to extract land and services from indigenous people. Yet, at the same time, and in the spiral fashion in which power is exercised (Foucault 1983), legal pluralism also provided a way for local indigenous people to mobilize the ideology of the colonizers to protect their lands and to resist certain elements of colonial domination. In short, indigenous people, hardly passive and powerless, are able to resist and even change the nature of colonial domination, at times capturing and using state symbols of power (Synder 1981; Merry 1988, 1991). Sally Falk Moore describes the multiple systems of social ordering found in colonial states as a semiautonomous social field. The semiautonomous social field is a small field that "can generate rules and customs and symbols internally, but it is also vulnerable to rules and decisions and forces emanating from the larger world by which it is surrounded. The semi-autonomous social field has rule-making capacities, and the means to induce or coerce compliance; but it is simultaneously set in a larger social matrix which can, and does, affect and invade it, sometimes at the invitation of persons inside it, sometimes at its own instance" (Moore 1973:720).

By moving my analysis between an examination of colonial laws, both in discourse and practice, and native people's everyday practices surrounding property relations, I show how actions are the product of structures generated through the processes of negotiation, manipulation, and resistance and often diverge from the rules laid out by the state (Sivaramakrishnan 1999). Often the de facto practices become the basis then for a reformulation of the de jure laws and policies (Gururani 2000). As the following chapters show, this process of everyday actions reshaping laws and policies is under way in contemporary Sabah, as changes in property relations do not reach a stable end point but, rather, are continuously produced through ongoing power struggles.

In conjunction with the use of law as a technology of rule that legitimized and expanded colonial power, the production and circulation of knowledge about the colonized subject is an integral component of the exercise of power

(Foucault 1981; Said 1979). Rather than focus on the "truth" or "untruth" of specific discourses, it is important to see how language is used to structure power relationships. Historians have shown that colonial discourses are not a definitive set of texts, but are adapted to specific geographical locations and historical situations (see, inter alia, Spurr 1993; Memmi [1965] 1991; Thomas 1994; Said 1979). Nevertheless, broad generalizations can be identified in the terrain of basic tropes, conceptual categories, and discourses that emerge from the colonial experience. Two specific modes of colonial discourse are relevant to this examination of colonial law and native customary law in Sabah, Malaysia.[6] They are the call to create order and civilization in territories that had been purportedly engulfed in anarchy and chaos for centuries, and the desire to make the riches of natural resources, supposedly lying wasted and unclaimed, available to the rest of the world. Colonial administrators repeatedly invoked these ideals or "truths" to establish, legitimize, and justify their authority over native people and the territory (Spurr 1993:7–8). Focusing on these forms of knowledge and the power relations that they reproduced draws attention to the fact that law is never a neutral or benign institution used to regulate behavior. Instead, colonial law and the discursive practices that supported it are powerful elements of governmentality.

Early journals and the reports of administrators and explorers in Sabah illustrate how specific discourses were employed to justify colonial control over the land and the people. For example, in 1885, Lord Walter Medhurst, one of the founders of the North Borneo Chartered Company (the colonial power in Sabah until World War II), described the Company's objectives as "the reclamation of a vast and fertile tract of country from a state of primeval savagery, and its utilisation as a source of commercial wealth and progress for the benefit of the world in general" (Medhurst [1885] 1983:91).[7] In this brief sentence, Medhurst wiped away all notions of local management of the land for subsistence use and emphasized that, by commercializing natural resources, the colonial rulers were providing a service for the good of all mankind.

Similarly, Lord Brassey, director of the North Borneo Chartered Company, legitimized colonial rule through rhetoric that drew attention to the ability of colonial rulers to "create order" in a "savage" world through the international commodification of resources. Lord Brassey wrote in 1889:

> Gradually, and by the most peaceful means, it [the North Borneo Chartered Company] is establishing order in a savage country. It is opening to the teem-

ing multitudes of China a new field of labour. It is giving to the congested capital of Europe, without distinction of nationality, another outlet. Every flag is welcomed in its ports on equal terms. The property of a country thus administered is a benefit to mankind. (Lord Brassey, as cited in *Handbook of British North Borneo* [Government of British North Borneo Chartered Company 1890], 167)

And in reference to the natural resources, the colonial rhetoric suggested that these resources belonged rightfully to the colonizers who would utilize them more "profitably" and "rationally" than to the indigenous people who inhabited the land. This discourse was apparent in the *Handbook of British North Borneo* (ibid., 103), which stated that

> fruits occur in abundance in the forest; in a good fruit season it is astonishing what a lot of fruit trees are apparent; wild duriens, rambutans, pulusans, langsat, lychees, mata kuchings, &c. abound . . . fruits that fall to the ground yearly are more likely to continue to fatten orang-utans, monkeys, elephants, rhinoceroses, squirrels, and pigs, than to be turned to any more profitable account.

This colonizing trope of resource waste takes for granted the notion that the land and its resources belonged to those who are best able to exploit them according to Western commercial principles, not to the original inhabitants of the territory and their subsistence and trade practices (cf. Spurr 1993:31).[8] This rhetoric also rested on the notion that resources mobilized for "benefit of mankind" were superior to local peoples' use of resources. This pattern of representation privileges European interests at the expense of natives' interests and privileges the commercial exploitation of resources over local subsistence use of resources.[9]

To summarize, colonial legal practices and discourses were critical elements of colonial governmentality and, as such, facilitated colonial control over the indigenous people and their land. The imposition of Western law—justified under the rhetoric of order, citizenship, governance, and the commercialization of resources—was a means to strengthen colonial power and legitimize colonial authority over people and the territory. Importantly, these discursive fields of power detracted attention away from the other effects of colonialism, namely, the privileging of European people over indigenous populations and appropriation of natural resources from the colonized for the benefit of the colonizer. The value in identifying the recurrence of imagery and tropes in colonial discourse is that it serves to denaturalize categories of knowledge that may have come to be accepted. Through such a critical examination of colonial rhetoric one can see that the effect of colonialism continues in present-day Sabah as new logics of governmentality are invented to serve the same purpose: elite control over marginalized people and their resources by making them and their resource use systems the target of critique through economics and science.

POSTCOLONIAL STATES AS REGIMES OF POWER

Postcolonialism does not simply refer to the time period following the breakdown of colonial rule. Nor is the condition of postcolonialism in South Asia, Southeast Asia, Africa, and South America experienced in a universal way by those ruled or by the rulers.[10] Postcolonialism emerges as a continuation of global processes of domination, defined by Western systems of power and the accumulation of normalizing technologies (Escobar 1984:393). Of concern here is how elements of colonialism, specifically forms of rule based on the invention of knowledge, have been reconfigured into a new system of postcolonial rule that is experienced by marginalized people in a manner remarkably similar to the colonial rule.

Many postcolonial states have both expanded and transformed the basic institutions of colonial law and administration (Chatterjee 1993; Vandergeest and Peluso 1995). But in countries where conservative authoritarian regimes have taken over from colonial authorities, colonial administrative structures are often maintained (Mamdani 1996; Anderson 1990). This is the case in Malaysia. National elites, who took the place of the British colonial elites, were and still are invested in maintaining the same systems of rule. The postcolonial project then is defined by the ambition and fears of a dependent political class trying to come to terms with a global condition where the rules were set by someone else (Abraham 2003:406).[11]

In postcolonial Malaysia, as elsewhere in Southeast Asia, state interventions into rural people's lives have come to be framed through a discourse of backwardness and the need for development.[12] The imperative of rural development in many postcolonial nations is linked to regimes of capitalist growth and state legitimization, as a new class of ruling elite takes over from colonial rulers. Like many of the colonial administrative policies introduced under the umbrella of law, the notion of development in postcolonial states draws its inspiration from Western conceptions of progress and modernity. Michael Cowen and Robert Shenton (1995:29) argue that "the modern idea of development is necessarily Eurocentric because it was in Europe that development was first meant to create order out of the social disorder of rapid urbanization, poverty and unemployment." And like the colonial notion that it was the obligation of Europeans to create order and productivity out of the primitive state of chaos and wasting resources, postcolonial notions of development are embedded in the belief that visions of modernity and progress are universal. Too often development is presented as a natural process with commonsense objectives, its connections to power veiled and unknown (Sivaramakrishnan and Agrawal 2003). But poststructuralist critiques of development have increasingly come to see development efforts as central strategies of power. Development, therefore, becomes a crucial tool in the process of state formation (Ferguson 1994). In order to better understand the power of development, Arturo Escobar (1984:384) urges an examination of the production of discourses and the workings of normalizing techniques that produce systematic ways in which development is deployed to manage, control, and even create marginal or peripheral people.[13]

Development initiatives rely on the production of knowledge that shapes reality into categories that make sense to planners, nutritionists, demographers, and economists (Ferguson 1994; Pigg 1992). People on the peripheries are placed into categories that define their problems and their treatment—the poor, the malnourished, the illiterate, pregnant women, the landless (Escobar 1985:214). Thus, the creation of knowledge about marginal communities is linked to the exercise of power—specifically state-sponsored interventions are aimed at "correcting" the problems of marginal communities as they have defined them (Escobar 1984) and, in doing so, producing governable subjects. Consequently, development becomes an instrument of state power that allows its makers a degree of control over marginal populations by classifying problems, formulating policies, and passing judgment on people and visualizing their future—to produce a regime of truth and norms about development (Escobar 1984:387–88). Building on these ideas of development as one of the current arenas in which the state exercises power, I treat development projects in Malaysia as the modern state's attempt at self-fashioning rule. And, it is evident, just as in the early colonial state, the accomplishment of rule in postcolonial Malaysia is always fragile and contingent, depending on the how state rule is received and reconfigured on the ground.[14]

A focus on the forms of knowledge that development produces and the power relations that it underwrites and reproduces (Crush 1995) emphasizes that development initiatives are not benign attempts to "help the poor." Instead, development projects can be understood in terms of the side effects that they produce. In his path-breaking analysis of international development programs in Lesotho, James Ferguson (1994) demonstrates that the most powerful side effects of development projects are the expansion and entrenchment of bureaucratic state power. In other words, although development often fails to alleviate poverty, it succeeds in penetrating, integrating, managing, and controlling marginal populations in increasingly detailed and encompassing ways (Escobar 1984:388). A globalized radical critique of development that has begun to take shape suggests that the very processes that were "supposed to deliver humanity from oppression and injustice may be at the core of continuing dependency and exploitation" (Sivaramakrishnan and Agrawal 2003:26).

But the side effects of development, according to Ferguson, "occur unconsciously, behind the backs or against the wills of the 'planners' who may seem to be running the show." Thus, drawing on Foucault, Ferguson argues that the outcomes of planned social interventions can come together into powerful constellations of control that were never intended and in some cases were never even recognized by the planners of development (Ferguson 1994:19–20). Other scholars of development point out that state agencies and officials are political beings, and therefore it is important to consider the possibility that the entrenchment of state power and the extension of the capacity of state agencies are the *intended* effects of development (Sivaramakrishnan and Agrawal 2003:30 *n*101). And, in fact, Ferguson's own analysis begs the question, How can development erase politics (or depoliticized development projects such as "neutral" interventions of aid) while simultaneously pursuing the very task of expanding bureaucratic power (Skaria 2000; Li 1999a)? It is my contention that development, in fact, can accomplish both the depoliticizing of state interventions and the expansion of state power. As development projects focus on the technical aspects of modernization, such as building specific infrastructure, they fail to examine the political-economic inequities that underlie poverty and thereby depoliticize development. The state rarely, if ever, suggests that what is needed is political and economic reform to restructure histories of inequalities; such work is far too political to undertake easily without upsetting the status quo. Thus, while the root causes of poverty are depoliticized in neutral development interventions, development can simultaneously extend bureaucratic power to the peripheries in multiple ways.

By exploring the particularities of a development project in Malaysia, I seek to expand Ferguson's and others' critiques of development by suggesting that at times development can be intentionally used as a tool of state bureaucratic control. In the context of rural development in Malaysia, there is evidence that both the state officials and the local people are aware that development serves to extend state bureaucratic control as much as it alleviates rural poverty. In Malaysia some political leaders knowingly deploy development strategies not only to change the rural standard of living but also to extend control and to ensure the continued domination of the ruling Malay-Muslim elite. Since local people are also aware of the political nature of development, at times they are able to expropriate state interventions in creative ways, demonstrating that marginal people are not just subjected to development plans but can also be involved in altering the final outcome (Agrawal 1995; Pigg 1992). Just as the colonial practice of imposing a new legal system on local society must be understood not simply as an act of domination but also as a site for local action, local agency in response to the postcolonial practices of rural development must also be acknowledged. While state practices surrounding rural development in postcolonial Sabah serve as a crucial vehicle promoting the expansion of state power and appear to constrain the actions of local people, they simultaneously provide the forum in which local society has regular interactions with representatives of the state. The development projects of the state, therefore, are fragile, incomplete, and open to contestation, negotiation, and resistance.

This tension between the homogenizing effects of development, aimed at imposing a single cultural model on the world, and the local reaction and resistance to development projects, which produces a multiplicity of localized variations of development, is the subject of recent scholarly debate (Sivaramakrishnan and Agrawal 2003).[15] In brief, this debate emphasizes that, instead of conceptualizing development as a "homogenizing juggernaut of domination," the focus needs to be on the dynamic and conflictual interactions between the planners and the subjects of development. Likewise, the cultural variations in nation-states need to be acknowledged and the multiple ways in which modernity and development are experienced at the local level need to be attended to.[16] This study addresses these issues by looking at the shape of postcolonial development projects in Sabah, at local reactions to these projects in one village, and shows how the process of development attempts to leave its homogenizing imprint of modernization on rural villagers and their landscape in Sabah, an imprint that also carries expectations of behavior and agricultural practices specific to the conditions of Malay-Muslim rule in Malaysia. The expectation would be that in other nations development initiatives would not look exactly the same, even if the state's supposed goals of modernization and economic commercialization of resources were the same.

To summarize, the practices and discourses surrounding rural development in postcolonial nations are employed in the service of power by state officials. They work to extend state bureaucratic control on the margins and to create a rural population that is governable from the center by attempting to regulate the way people live their lives (Li 1999b). Development policies—justified under the rhetoric of poverty alleviation and modernization—are a means to strengthen state power and legitimize state authority. By specifying the ways in which "modern" people rely on resources for economic growth, development policies often have the effect of destabilizing local control over resources. For instance, by emphasizing commercial production of a single crop over subsistence production of multiple crops, development projects simultaneously change the local production and consumption patterns and influence land use regimes and property relations. But local agency must also figure into an understanding of the practice of development. By resisting, negotiating, and collaborating with state-sponsored development projects, local people find ways to mobilize state ideologies to their advantage in disputes over land use and ownership. Not merely passive subjects of development, local people find multiple ways to assert agency though development plans, either as individuals or as groups.

By focusing on the technologies of rule employed by the state and the ways in which discourse is used to obfuscate the intentions of state policies and actions, postcolonialism appears to resemble and perpetuate key aspects of colonialism.[17] In both periods the production of forms of knowledge and the practices or technologies of rule that extend from that knowledge become a major legitimizing force of the nation-state over society. Continuities between colonial and postcolonial rule in Malaysia demonstrate how crucial the invention of knowledge is to the exercise of power. This understanding of the similarities in governmentality between colonialism and postcolonialism owes much to Foucault's notions of power. It is through the careful examination of how specific knowledge, techniques, and discourses are formed and practiced that their relationship to the practice of power becomes apparent (Foucault 1979).

Inasmuch as Foucault suggests that discourses are historically contingent and discontinuous, this study diverges from Foucault by emphasizing the ways in which discourses of rule overlap and intersect as they simultaneously perpetuate power structures from the past and change to meet contemporary needs, particularly in respect to the treatment of rural agriculturalists and their resource use regimes (cf. D. Moore 1999). The unraveling of the discourses and practices associated with colonial and postcolonial rule in Malaysia is valuable because it tells of the enduring mechanisms of state building, even when the ideological stances of the states differ significantly.

PROPERTY RIGHTS AS SOCIAL RELATIONS

As colonial and postcolonial power operated and continues to operate at the local level, it shapes the limits of local actions. Since the focus of this study is on resource use and property relations, it is important to understand how people maneuver within institutions of rule in different places and at different times to alter daily practices surrounding property relations. In identifying property relations as one of the multiple sites in which social actions in response to state power are revealed, the fragility and the strength of colonial and postcolonial rule are highlighted, and the productive ways in which society tries to broaden and redefine what it perceives as unjust state control over resources can be identified.

Anthropologists and property rights theorists have long acknowledged the social nature of property rights (MacPherson 1978:3). Property rights are relationships between people with respect to things, not between people and things, and are constructed around issues of power, wealth, and meaning. Consequently, multiple aspects of social institutions influence configurations of property relations (Peluso 1996:513). Property relations are thus social terrain where struggles over the exercise of power are enacted. For instance, the formation of property rights can be influenced by conflicting sources of legitimate authority, as in colonial states when contradictions between customary and colonial legal institutions foster entirely new property relations (Merry 1988:875; see also Fortmann 1990). The relationship between customary law and statutory law is a complicated one, with no predictable or universal outcome, because as expressions of local power these types of law are in part contingent on temporal and geographic contexts. In different times and places, colonial statutory law criminalizes native rights (Peluso 1992, 1993, 1996; Neumann 1998), selectively codifies some aspects of native rights (S. Moore 1986a; Ranger 1983; Chanock 1985), or "invents" customary laws to serve the colonial agenda (Burns 1989; Ranger 1983; Synder 1981; Zerner 1994). The ways in which local people respond to these laws and institutions of state rule are, therefore, contingent on the ability of state power to enable and constrain the actions of civil society.

Regardless of whether the state criminalizes, selectively codifies, or invents customary law, local institutions of access to and ownership of natural resources often persist in everyday practice, with or without official recognition from the state. The relationship between customary law, statutory law, and everyday practices is central to this study as it untangles the various influences these institutions and practices have on the contemporary landscape and on local decision making about resource use. In brief, following the understanding of broader power struggles, the colonial state power significantly reduced the nature and extent of the property relations that natives enjoyed through customary law, while at the same time created a space for new forms of local property relations to emerge. In what follows, how "traditional" customary property rights and Western forms of property rights are used strategically in struggles over access to resources is seen. What is not seen is a unidirectional evolution of native customary law to statutory law in this system based on legal pluralism. Instead, various ways in which the two systems are intertwined in efforts to assert control over resources are observed. This finding breaks apart any remaining dichotomies between traditional institutions and modern institutions, or customary laws and statutory laws, and draws attention to the contingent nature of the transformation of property relations. This nonevolutionary model of social change is one that is very difficult for politicians and nongovernmental organizations to understand and incorporate into policies because it requires a close understanding of each locality and no "blueprint" of transformation of property relations is available. By exploring the specific contexts and histories of communities and their natural resource management regimes, this study provides a detailed analysis that policymakers can use to produce site-specific resource management strategies in Malaysia rather than rely on generic strategies adopted from other contexts (cf. Brosius, Tsing, and Zerner 1998).

Politics, discourse, and institutions surrounding conceptualizations of community, identity, or gender also alter the means of access to resources within the landscape (Li 1996:503; see also Peluso 1996; Schroeder 1993). Struggles over negotiated systems of cultural meaning, social identity, and community are one of the ways in which property relations are changed through action.[18] For instance, Tania Li has shown how in Sulawesi contests over the distribution of land are articulated in terms of competing representations and divergent images of "community" (1996:508). As individuals seek legitimacy and empowerment through varying definitions of social identity and collective community, they are also striving to address generations of misdistribution of access to valuable resources. Thus, struggles over property rights and struggles over identity are often mutually constitutive, as changes in the boundaries of one social institution will also alter the boundaries of another.

Bina Agarwal (1994b) has shown how women's struggles for land rights in South Asia are part of the larger struggle for gender equality in a male-dominated society. Shifts from patriarchal power, embedded in control over land, require major shifts in other social institutions. But decades of collective and individual resistance among South Asian women have begun to draw attention to the connections between the politics of gender and the politics of distribution; exclusive male control over land is being questioned. Again, drawing on Foucault's conceptualization of power, legitimacy of action is built through constant reiterations of power. And as women in South Asia work to gain access to land and enjoy small successes, they are also restructuring broader gender imbalances in society.

The formation of property rights can also be influenced by a person's position in society, that is, their membership and relative autonomy or power in different social networks (Blaikie 1985; Berry 1993; Suryanata 1994). Thus, a person may defend or gain access to land through participation in various social, political, or economic networks that control the rights over land, capital, and the mediation of land disputes (Berry 1993). In brief, the varying ways in which these issues of power, wealth, and social meaning can come together to influence property relations are as unique as each social setting. A recent upsurge in nuanced analyses and interpretations of property relations has drawn attention to these contingent and unique shifts in social relations and property relations. Most important, studies focusing on the fluid social nature of property relations demonstrate that the politics of distribution (access to resources) are always intertwined with the politics of recognition (cultural identity) and the politics of power and wealth (both discursive power and material power). As Michael Watts aptly points out: "Rights over resources such as land or crops are inseparable, indeed isomorphic with, rights over people" (Watts 1992, cited in Schroeder 1993:349).

Several studies from Africa (S. Moore 1986b; Berry 1993; Peters 1994; Schroeder 1993) and Indonesia (Peluso 1992, 1996; Li 1996, 1999b) have emphasized that access to resources and the transformation of property rights are shaped not only by the incorporation of rural areas into the colonial and national political economy but also by local and regional conflicts over cultural meaning, social identity, and power. Importantly, these studies all situate changes in property relations at the intersection of local, small-scale events and large-scale political and economic factors that influence the local social setting. This study contributes to knowledge about the social nature of property relations and the ways in which property relations are formed at the intersection of state power and discourse and local agency in two ways. First, it expands previous studies on property relations by explicitly viewing from the same vantage point the forms of rule employed by the colonial and postcolonial states. In so doing, it simultaneously seeks to denaturalize the colonial project as a unique moment in the history of state-society relationships and denaturalize the postcolonial project as a significant break with the past. What emerges is the notion that the state structures that constrain and enable the formation of property relations at the local level endured across the nineteenth and twentieth centuries in ways that might not have been predicted based on knowledge of the different ideological platforms of each state.

Second, this study brings into question the idea that indigenous people have strong cultural bonds to "traditional" customary laws and ways of relating to the environment. Although advocates for natives and their rights to land and resources may have found the concepts of *indigeneity, community, custom, tradition,* and *rights* useful in promoting possibilities for local empowerment in national and transnational policy discussions (Brosius et al. 1998: 159), local people rarely share the same understanding of these concepts. While some native people in Malaysia may have deep ties to a prior lifestyle, when they enjoyed greater autonomy, others seek a future outside their current agrarian lifestyles. The latter see customary laws as an instrumental means to an end—that is, as access to or control over valuable resources. Thus, for many natives, attachment to traditional social institutions rarely stems from a romanticized view of a better time, but rather it derives from a larger group of social relations and power struggles. This finding should provide a warning for anyone interested in reinvigorating native customary laws in order to promote cultural autonomy and local control over resources. First, local reactions to such representations must be considered. And, second, it should be anticipated that altering one set of social institutions will have wide-ranging influences on other social processes and may destabilize the community in unexpected ways.

The daily actions on the periphery that are the focus of the two village-level studies in this book are actions of compromise and negotiation, rather than acts of everyday or overt resistance. This study requires a focus that breaks down the binaries of state dominations versus local resistance and demonstrates the subtle ways in which marginal populations work to exercise their power, no matter how limited, to alter the outcome of state projects that are not in their interest. Furthermore, through ethnographic richness, the internal politics of village life are revealed, showing variations in the intentions, desires, and fears (cf. Ortner 1995:190) of the actors involved in struggles over power and property. By filling in the details of complex and sometimes contradictory actions, the internal conflicts within society become apparent. Ultimately this approach shows interplay of power in the relationships *within* society and *between* society and the state surrounding control over natural resources. By exploring property relations as a site of agency and power, I hope to put to rest any notions that property rights are simply a set of rules. Instead, property relations must be understood as coded power relations that are expressed in discourse or language of rule, the actions and reactions to rules, and struggles over livelihoods and power relations. Property relations therefore serve as critical markers of individual and community identity and autonomy (or lack of autonomy) in resource-related decisions within the structures of state rule.

This study of two ruling states and their interventions into local property relations and land management between 1881 and 1996 will be valuable for future policy initiatives surrounding natural resource use and management. Spaces can be found between national and local institutions and their power relations where positive dialogs can occur to foster local governance and control over natural resources within the economic and institutional shelter of supportive nation-states. Devolution of authority to the local level, supported by larger national institutions, is a particularly salient form of resource control at a time when institutions concerned with natural resource governance are caught between the opposing trends of global intergovernmental treaties and bodies designed to monitor natural resource use and governments that are decentralizing the control of natural resources, often in response to civil action. Both ends of this spectrum, intergovernmental treaties and devolution of authority to resource users, have strengths and weaknesses in terms of equitable distribution and long-term management of natural resources. The following historical account of shifting power relations, transforming property relations, and divergent views of "appropriate" resource use in Sabah, Malaysia, will be valuable if it moves governments, nongovernmental organizations, academics, and practitioners one step closer to understanding the complex web of factors that currently limit the ability to achieve distributional equity and long-term sustainable management of natural resources.

ONE

COLLIDING DISCOURSES

Western Land Laws and Native Customary
Rights in North Borneo, 1881–1928

> Our readers are so well acquainted with the outlines of the enterprise which has been entered into by the [Company] . . . that it is unnecessary to recapitulate the struggles for possession, the difficulties of planting a young Government firmly on its feet, and the endeavors to introduce usages, laws and institutions of a civilised nation into a country which tradition tells us was formerly only a *happy hunting ground for pirates and the orang utan.*
> — BRITISH NORTH BORNEO HERALD, January 1, 1886 (emphasis added)

THE IMPOSITION OF COLONIAL RULE IN NORTHERN BORNEO UNDER THE North Borneo Chartered Company (hereafter referred to as the Company) brought major changes to the landscape as the logic of Western-based property rights and economic rationality replaced indigenous rights to resources and local patterns of resource use. The supposed "happy hunting ground for pirates and the orang utan" was gradually reordered and "normalized" according to the legal and economic principles of the colonial state, aimed at transforming the land into a marketable commodity based on plantation agriculture. Western-based land laws and revenue production systems became significant sources of colonial power, legitimizing their control over the people and natural resources in North Borneo.

Native peoples and their laws, customs, and land use practices are explored in this chapter through the views of colonial administrators. Natives

MAP 1. Borneo, 1878. © Metaglyfix.

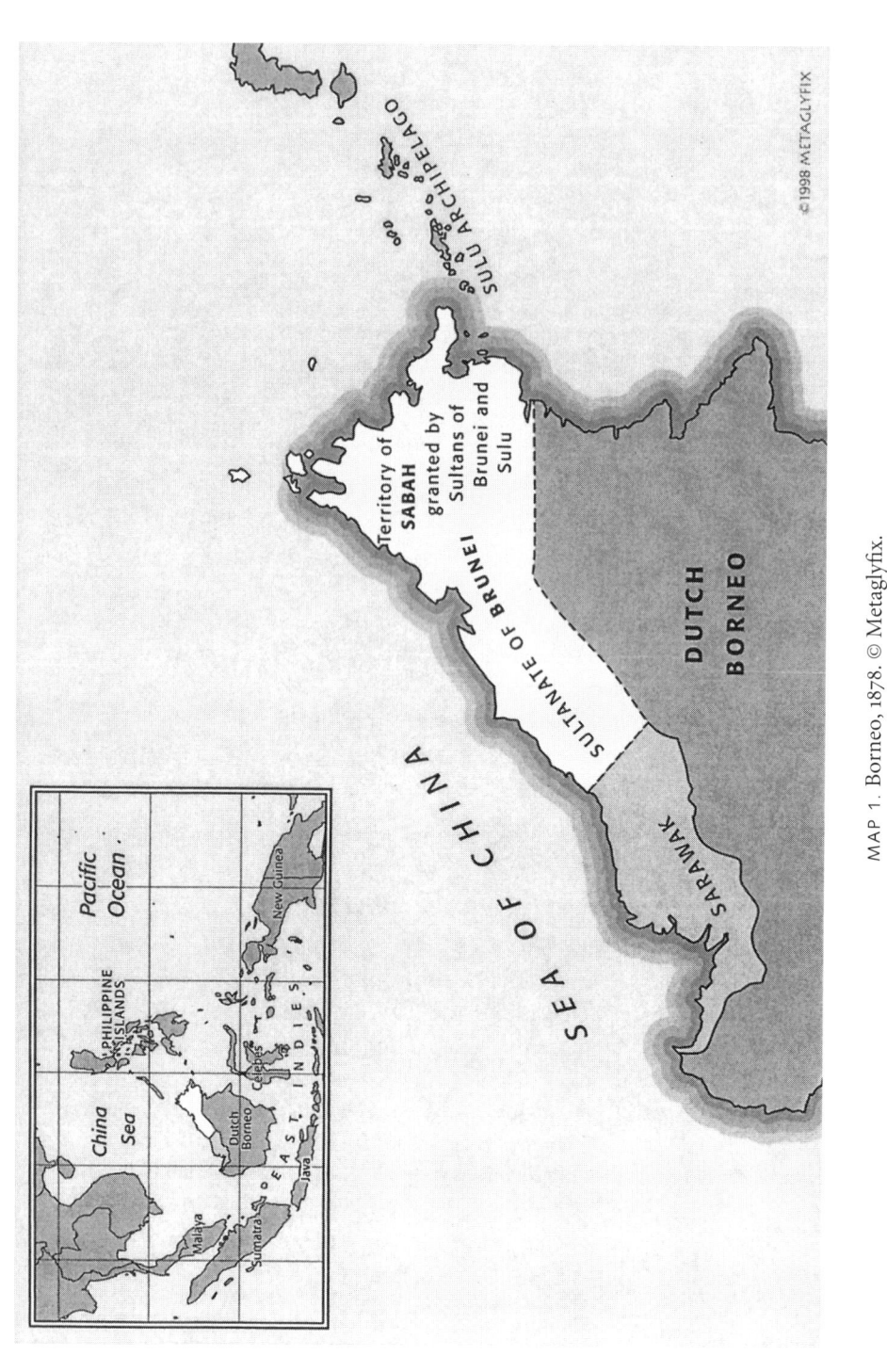

did not write voluminous minutes, memorandums, and reports as did Company officers. Administrators saw natives as consumers of natural resources, actual or potential taxpayers, and a backward, lazy population in need of a "strong and just Government" (Treacher 1890:112). This way of categorizing indigenous peoples was part of the technique of rule that enabled the Company to shape the local inhabitants into governable subjects. Colonial power as expressed through land laws and resource taxation was fragmentary and open to contestation, as are all colonial projects. Yet there is no denying the impact that land laws and related policies had on the landscape and the indigenous people. Native rights to land were incrementally diminished with each new colonial law and policy, whereas European rights to land were increasingly privileged. Since the available fragmentary evidence rarely gives a clear picture of how colonial policies were received at the local level during the period prior to World War II, the focus in this chapter is primarily on the attitudes and policies of the Company in North Borneo.[1]

THE BEGINNINGS OF THE NORTH BORNEO CHARTERED COMPANY, 1877–81

In 1877, the acquisition of North Borneo by the Chartered Company was negotiated on two fronts. The sultan of Brunei controlled the western areas of North Borneo, and the sultan of Sulu claimed ownership of the eastern side (see map 1). Both sultanates had been longtime participants in the lucrative trade in nontimber forest products with China. But by the late nineteenth century, these sultanates were suffering from weakened authority and were impoverished as a result of European commercial competition.[2] The Brunei sultan and his court were largely bankrupt, lacking the necessary revenue to pay retainers and maintain their influence over northern Borneo, and therefore welcomed British interest in the territory (Tarling 1978).

On December 29, 1877, Baron von Overbeck, an Austrian businessman from Hong Kong, met with the sultan of Brunei, Sultan Abdul Mumin, and one of his chief ministers, Pengiran Temonggong. Overbeck had financial backing from his past employers, Alfred and Edward Dent, heads of a prominent British trading company in Shanghai and London. The object of Overbeck's and the Dents' involvement in North Borneo was to "form a British Company somewhat, though on a smaller scale, after the manner of the ... East India Company, the main desire being to develop the agricultural resources of the northern part of Borneo" (Tarling 1978:193–94).

William H. Treacher, the acting governor of Labuan (the British island colony in the mouth of Brunei Bay), supervised the negotiations between the sultan and Overbeck (Black 1983). For a yearly sum of Straits $12,000 paid to the sultan and Straits $3,000 paid to his minister, Overbeck and the Dents became rulers over a large section of North Borneo (Black 1983:1). The territory transferred was impressive—nearly twenty-eight thousand square miles—but the jurisdiction of Brunei over northern Borneo had long been merely nominal, and the sultan of Sulu also claimed a large part of the territory (Galbraith 1965:108). To remove any doubts to the title, Overbeck sailed from Brunei to Sulu to acquire the rights in North Borneo claimed by the sultan of Sulu.[3] An additional yearly sum of Straits $5,000 was paid to the sultan of Sulu, Sultan Jamal ul-Azam (Tarling 1978:196).

In 1880, Overbeck sold his shares in North Borneo to the Dents, who then sought financial backing for their commercial venture from businessmen in England. Although the Dents were considered in England to be highly respectable merchants and bankers, "respectability" was not enough to attract serious investors. So the Dents sought British approval of their venture in North Borneo and British protection against the intervention of any foreign power (Galbraith 1965:111). Alfred Dent argued to the Foreign Office and the Colonial Office that North Borneo was important because of its commercial potential and strategic location in the East and South China seas, between India and China.

Sensing more sympathy from the Foreign Office than the Colonial Office, Alfred Dent spent two months in 1878 preparing a statement for his case. The proposed North Borneo Chartered Company, Dent assured the foreign secretary, was and would remain British. It would seek no monopoly, trade would be free subject to customs and duties, and slavery would be abolished (Galbraith 1965:116). To accomplish these ends, Dent sought a Royal Charter for the Company, which would enable it to exercise effective jurisdiction and would afford it protection from Britain against intervention by other European states (ibid., 117).

Finally, after two years of delays, the British government granted Alfred Dent a Royal Charter in November 1881. At this time, there were only two other British chartered companies: the East India Company and the Royal Niger Company (Galbraith 1965). The final impetus on the part of both the Foreign Office and the Colonial Office to grant the charter was the fear that Dent, without official sanction from Britain, would face bankruptcy and be forced to sell his interest to another European power (Galbraith 1965:120–23). As with the British involvement with the Malay states on the peninsula, the fear that Britain's informal control over the region might be challenged by other European powers was the only impetus that the British government needed to take action and extend its informal control over the region.[4] Such an informal, cost-effective way to expand Britain's control in the region was attractive to the Foreign Office. Leigh Wright, a historian of British colonial policies, summarizes the Foreign Office's position on the matter:

> While Britain could hold a veto and thus control over the direction and nature of the development of North Borneo, no responsibilities for administering the territory would devolve upon her Majesty's government. Yet the world would be assured that the project was a British venture, and by virtue of a charter British position along the eastern flank of the South China Sea would be strengthened. (As cited in Leong 1982:42)

CONFLICTING RESPONSIBILITIES OF THE COMPANY

The North Borneo Chartered Company had a dual mission in North Borneo, reflecting both the economic and moral tone in nineteenth-century England. The first concern was the economic growth of the Company through the exploitation of North Borneo's natural resources. The 1881 charter authorized the Company to improve, develop, and cultivate any land in the territory and to acquire additional lands if desired. It further authorized the Company to settle the territories, to promote immigration, to grant mining and timber concessions, and to grant land leases for agriculture for limited terms or in perpetuity (McT. Kahin 1947:43–65). Owen Rutter, a longtime officer of the Company and later a plantation owner in North Borneo, described the importance of financial growth for the governor of the territory:

> He [the governor] is responsible to the Court of Directors, and the Court of Directors is responsible to the shareholders that dividend-making revenue is produced. He is responsible for the progress of the country, but that *progress is apt to be gauged in terms of revenue rather than in terms of development.* (Rutter 1922:158; emphasis added)

This preoccupation with revenue production provides insight into the motives that lay behind the imposition of Western legal principles in North Borneo. The principles of individual ownership of land titles and a system of taxation were all crucial to the production of revenue based on the commodification of land.

The second concern of the Company was its obligation, stipulated through the Royal Charter of 1881, to respect native rights and customs. This concern over native welfare and customs was raised at the insistence of individuals in the British government who were opposed to the rule of British territories by the Chartered Company (Black 1983:31). The section of the charter titled "Administration of Justice to the Inhabitants" required the Company to pay careful attention to

> the customs and laws of the class or tribe or nation to which the parties respectively belong, especially with respect to the holding, possession, transfer, and disposition of lands and goods and testate or intestate succession thereto, and marriage, divorce and legitimacy and other rights of property and personal rights.[5]

There were inherent conflicts between these two considerations. Although the Company had a legal responsibility to protect native customs and rights, in practice the Company's policies and regulations that were aimed at revenue production often restricted native rights, particularly in respect to land. In fact, these two conflicting responsibilities, the economic development of the territory and the protection of native customs and rights, proved to be the crux of many future administrative conflicts in North Borneo.

The primary tool through which the Company supported economic growth based on plantation agriculture was the introduction of a Western legal system. The political-economic role of this legal system was to transform land into a commodity and to produce revenue for the state. However, the introduction of a Western legal system was a complicated process, often encumbered by the mandate to respect native rights and customs. Many of the governors of North Borneo found themselves in a bind; the very property rights and native legal institutions that they were charged to respect soon became significant obstacles to the expansion of commercial agriculture. As a result, the Company instituted a system of legal pluralism in which some native customary laws were supported, while those that hampered the commercial exploitation of land were replaced with Western legal concepts. Over the ensuing decades of Company rule, conflicts emerged not only with the native people, who felt that their rights were being impinged on, but also from within the Company administration as to the best way to honor native rights and to achieve economic growth. The years 1881–1928 were characterized by the rapid imposition of new laws and major changes in the ways in which natives could claim their rights to land. During this period, there were nine different governors of North Borneo, each with a different agenda and style of rule. This chapter focuses on three pivotal periods in the debates and controversies over native customary rights to land. Each period resulted in further diminishing native rights to land and resources, the inevitable outcome of state activities that simplified complex local institutions and agricultural practices in order to produce governable subjects. The following examination of the formation of colonial knowledge about property rights and native peoples focuses not only on the laws and policies but also on their practical application on the ground. By concentrating on the points of knowledge production, codification of land laws, and practices of land settlement, one sees the uneven and location-specific ways in which colonial laws were applied.[6]

THE EMERGENCE OF LAND LAWS: DEFINING "NATIVE RIGHTS"

"Protecting natives from their own improvidence"

Land administration becomes intertwined with broader issues of agriculture, revenue production, stable local means of production, and state control over people. Thus, a key issue that slips into the processes of knowledge production about appropriate land management is the practice of governing. The Company's policies about land, land settlement, land administration, and land use ultimately are concerned with furthering state control over people and territory and the production of revenue that flows from the control of people and territory.

William H. Treacher, the first governor of North Borneo, devoted much of his attention to the abolition of slavery there. His preoccupation with this matter was in large part due to the urging of the court of directors and the antislavery lobby in Britain. Consequently, he gave scant attention to formulating land laws (Black 1983:55–60).[7] The first two pieces of land legislation that Treacher introduced, the Proclamation of December 23, 1881,[8] and the Land Proclamation of 1885,[9] entirely failed to incorporate any aspects of native customary rights to land (see table 1.1 for a summary of the land laws discussed in this chapter). The only mention of native rights to land occurred in Articles 26 and 27 of the Land Proclamation of 1885, in which Treacher placed the ultimate authority over land with the state by refusing to allow natives to buy or sell land to foreigners, unless such transactions took place through the state. According to these articles of the 1885 proclamation (emphasis added):

26. All dealings in land between Europeans and Chinese and other foreigners on the one hand, and the natives of the country on the other hand are hereby *expressly forbidden,* and no such dealings shall be valid or shall be recognised in any Court of Law. . . .

27. A foreigner desirous of purchasing land from a native shall address his application to the Governor through the Commissioner of Lands, and the Governor, if he sees fit to sanction such purchase, shall, if the native owner consent [sic], acquire the land on the behalf of the Government, and shall fix the premium at which the same shall be leased by the Governor to the applicant. . . .[10]

In many ways the first article of the 1885 proclamation did more damage to native rights to land than future, more comprehensive and inclusive legislation did. This first law set the stage for later laws and established unequivocally that the state was the ultimate authority over land. On the basis of this proclamation, native rights to land would subsequently have to be mediated by the state and made compatible with the broader state agenda of commercial development of the territory. These colonial land laws also established a fundamental distinction between natives and nonnatives. Just as Mahmood Mamdani (2001) found with colonial practices in Africa, rights belonged to the European colonizers and not to the natives. Although this legal code over landownership clearly draws on Western forms of land privatization, British officials believed that they were simply replicating the native systems of land tenure. Resident W. E. Maxwell, the British overseer in Selangor, wrote a well-regarded statement on Malay land tenure (1884). He cited Hugh Raffle's understanding of the principles of the sovereign's land tenure in Java to make the statement that "property in the soil is vested in the Raja of the country" and that "the occupier has only the usufruct (*usaha* in Malay, *hak ulayat* in Javanese) to the right of possession as long as the land is kept under cultivation, [and] the usual taxes paid" (cited in Peluso and Vandergeest 2001:777). Considered at the time an elaborate and systematic study of indigenous land tenure, Maxwell's theory of Malay land tenure played a significant role in the development of land laws in Malaya under Britain (Wong 1975) and presumably in North Borneo under Company rule.[11]

In 1888, Governor Charles V. Creagh, who had seen a version of the Torren's system of land registration in operation in Perak and other Malay states, replaced Governor Treacher (see table 1.2 for a list of the governors of North Borneo during this period).[12] He urged the adoption of the Torren's system in North Borneo and called for urgent measures to protect

TABLE 1.1. Key Land Laws in North Borneo from 1881 to 1913

1885 Land Proclamation, introduced by W. H. Treacher. Articles 26 and 27 deal with native rights to land:

"26. All dealings in land between Europeans and Chinese and other foreigners on the one hand, and the natives of the country on the other hand are hereby expressly forbidden, and no such dealings shall be valid or shall be recognised in any Court of Law unless the dealings shall have been entered into and concluded before the 16th day of January, 1883."

"27. A foreigner desirous of purchasing land from a native shall address his application to the Governor through the Commissioner of Lands, and the Governor, if he sees fit to sanction such purchase, shall, if the native owner consent [sic], acquire the land on the behalf of the Government, and shall fix the premium at which the same shall be leased by the Governor to the applicant." (Anonymous, "Land Regulations, North Borneo," 1885, 158–63).

1889, Proclamation III "Native Rights to Land," introduced by C. Creagh. Summarized below is section 5, which determines the type of lands and the mechanisms by which natives could claim rights to land:

(1) land under cultivation or land being used for housing, (2) land planted with fruit trees at the rate of twenty or more per acre, (3) isolated fruit trees if enclosed by a fence, (4) grazing land stocked with animals, (5) wet and dry padi land so long as it was cultivated for at least three years prior to registration, (6) burial grounds, and (7) rights of way.

It was the duty of the District Officer and the Native Chief to determine all native rights on land earmarked for foreign concession. Either native lands were "reserved" from the foreign concession or natives were given a cash settlement.

1913, Land Laws, introduced by C. Parr. Three main changes were made to Proclamation III of 1889. They are summarized below.

1. The settlement of native claims to land were compulsory.

2. Once native rights were settled, they could receive a Native Title. This was a permanent, heritable title, with a reduced annual rent of Straits $0.50 cents an acre. Natives were forbidden to sell their lands to nonnatives.

3. Foreigners could lease state land under a Country Lease. Country leases had a one-time premium of Straits $42.00 per acre and an annual rent of Straits $2.50 an acre. The leases last for 99–999 years.

native rights to land (Black 1983:109). The resulting legislation, "Native Rights to Land," Proclamation III of 1889 put in place both the Torren's system and a new legislation concerning native land rights.[13] Proclamation III of 1889 primarily focused on how native rights to land would be settled when applications by foreigners for "Government waste land" were received. The legislation states that as soon as the boundaries of the land application were defined, it was the duty of the district officer to inform the native chiefs in the area about new foreign concessions. Native chiefs, as part of the colonial administration by indirect rule, should then inform the district officer of all native claims that existed in the area of the application. The district officer was expected to forward the native claims to the government secretary, who would compile the register. Once this process was complete, native lands could be surveyed and boundaries marked.

This proclamation was much more inclusive than the previous one and acknowledged multiple ways in which natives could claim rights to land. According to section 5 of the 1889 proclamation, natives could claim rights to the following: land under cultivation or land being used for housing; land planted with fruit trees at the rate of twenty or more per acre; isolated fruit trees if enclosed by a fence; grazing land stocked with animals; wet and dry padi land, so long as it was cultivated for at least three years prior to registration; burial grounds; and rights of way.

Once native rights were determined to be legitimate by the district officer, they could be settled in one of two ways, both requiring government sanction. The land could be "reserved" from the foreign concession for the native owners through the clear demarcation of native holdings. If possible, a consolidation of native holdings was attempted by moving isolated natives to grants of land close together. The second method to settle native claims to land was by a cash payment as compensation, based on the agricultural value of the land. By overlooking the multiple ways in which people could have ties to the land (e.g., cultural, ritual, familial, or historical), the Company's policies highlight the strength of their convictions in economic rationality, a belief that underscored much of the colonial activities in North Borneo.

Proclamation III of 1889 was the first land law that made any attempt to recognize the nature of native rights to land and to provide the mechanism by which natives could formalize these claims according to the Company. Although broader in scope, this proclamation was also similar to the previous land laws in that all native rights had to be sanctioned by the colonial state before they were given official recognition. Unfortunately, even though

TABLE 1.2. Governors of North Borneo, 1881–1930

William Hood Treacher	1881–1887
W. M. Crocker	1887–1888
Charles Vandelleur Creagh	1888–1895
Leicester Paul Beaufort	1895–1900
Hugh Charles Clifford	1900–1901
Ernest Woodford Birch	1901–1903
Edward Peregrine Guertiz	1904–1911
Francis Robert Ellis	1911–1912
James Scott Mason	1912
Cecil William Chase Parr	1913–1915
Aylmer Cavendish Pearson	1915–1922
Sir William Henry Rycroft	1922–1925
John Lysseter Humphreys	1926–1929

native rights were recognized on paper in this proclamation, time would show that Governor Creagh and subsequent governors of North Borneo were unable to uphold fully the letter of this law. With fewer than thirty Company administrators and £30,000 for annual expenses (Tregonning 1956:50), the administration found itself unable to settle native claims to land adequately.[14] Furthermore, although this proclamation made attempts to acknowledge native rights to land, native ownership and uses of non-timber forest products were ignored. The pervasiveness of the colonial emphasis on private property regimes and commercialization of resources over all other forms of resource ownership and use is seen in the disparaging remarks of one colonial officer who, in referring to natives, wrote:

> The main reason why so little advantage of these resources has been taken hitherto is that matters have been in such a disorganized and anarchical state that it was impossible [for natives] to store up the slightest wealth without someone more powerful than the possessor coming and seizing it, by force of armies if need be. It is useless therefore . . . for anyone to do more than provide for his immediate want; and so much has this grown to be a habit, added to the natural laziness of the Malay character, that the bulk of the people simply have, even now, no thought for tomorrow. (Medhurst [1885] 1983:99)

By describing native resource use as disorganized and anarchical and native people as lazy and short-sighted, the language of the colonial administration served to produce weak and disorganized people who needed legal and economic order placed on them by the supposedly superior colonial state. By categorizing natives and their property regimes as lazy and disorganized, Company officials created a "self-evident" target of colonial interventions. This categorization also defined who the agents of this intervention or exercise of power were: district officers and the Lands and Survey Department. Although the Company began to register native claims to land as early as 1889, by delineating native rights on land earmarked for foreign concessions, it was not until the introduction of the Land Laws of 1913 that the registration of all native claims to land became compulsory. Governor Cecil W. C. Parr, the first governor intent on demarcating and taxing all cultivated land in the state, issued a comprehensive set of land laws in 1913 that required the registration of native claims to land (Black 1983:216).

In the Land Laws of 1913, different categories of land grants were established for natives and nonnatives, called "native title" and "country lease," respectively. Native title was the formal mechanism under which natives could gain state recognition of land to which they had customary rights. Native customary rights were defined under the Land Laws of 1913 in essentially the same way that they had been in Proclamation III of 1889. The only change was that now natives could claim rights not only to isolated fruit trees but also to sago, rattan, and other plants of economic value that they could prove they had *continuously kept and managed*.[15] Although this was an important concession in the legislature, in practice colonial officers almost never found the time or the manpower to survey and issue titles to the native claims to fruit trees and forest products. With the registration of land under native title came the initiation of land taxes; the owner was required to pay Straits $1.00[16] per acre to cover survey fees and an annual quit rent of Straits $0.50 per acre.[17]

Country lease was the mechanism by which nonnatives could lease state land. Country lease had a one-time premium of Straits $42.00 per acre and an annual quit rent of Straits $2.50 an acre.[18] Furthermore, a country lease was leasehold, limited to a term of years, anywhere from 99 to 999 years. Most important, a country lease allowed the owner the right to sell the lease to a third party at the will of the original lessor, during the period of the lease. Native title was considered a more generous title (by the Company) since it was free from premium, had an annual rent of only Straits $0.50 an acre, and was a heritable and permanent title. But the cost was dear: natives could not sell or transfer titles without permission from the government;

those rights were only available to nonnatives. The notion behind this restriction was that natives were not experienced enough in commercial transactions in land, and if they were not "protected from their own improvidence," they would sell all their land to foreign land speculators and be left with no land to cultivate.[19] The apparently paternalistic motivations of the Company glossed over the colonial goal of transferring ownership of as much land as possible out of native hands and into the government's and creating a subject of "native" that required close governmental supervision (cf. Mamdani 2001).

Slow to recognize native rights to land legally, the Company took nearly thirty years (1885–1913) to establish clear land laws that provided natives with a state-recognized title to their land. Yet, once native rights were given some measure of formal recognition in land laws, Company administrators still failed to put this legal recognition into action. This failure was due in large part to the lack of Company officers and to insufficient finances. But another major obstacle in the settling of native land rights was the debates within the Company administration over the actual implementation of the land laws. While the land laws may have unambiguously defined what constituted native customary tenure according to Company rule, in practice Company officers had a great deal of latitude in how they settled these claims. As a result, many natives never obtained title to the land that they used in their agricultural cycle. Land that natives cultivated for fruit trees, forested areas they used for forest products, and land they left fallow were lost to foreigners before they could be registered.

Freedom in the interpretation and implementation of the land laws occurred in the administration at two levels. The first was the level at which policy documents (usually in the form of minutes, memorandums, circulars, and notifications) were created by the governor of North Borneo. At times, the governor created policies in direct defiance of the letter of the land laws. The second was the local level, at which Company officers were often faced with complexities of native life that defied the types of simplification required by the land laws and policies. In the Company's history, confusion over the implementation of the land laws repeatedly came to a head, and colonial administrators debated the definition of native customary tenure. With each debate the primary outcome was further restriction of native rights. Thus, the imposition of Western land laws and the fragmentary attention paid to native legal institutions illustrate how colonial law was a tool of control over people and land that slowly eroded native customary rights and institutions. Law and land settlement became the language of control that the Company used to defend its actions against natives and their lands.

The three pieces of legislation and their implementation explored in detail below provide insight into how the enforcement of statutory laws diverged significantly from the laws' original intention, with outcomes of debates expressed through colonial administrative discourses and practices.

The Duty of a Landholder: Punctual Payment of Rent

When land settlement in North Borneo began in earnest in 1913, colonial officials hoped to increase revenue through taxation of native holdings. In his "Report on Administration, 1911," Sir Richard Dane[20] pointed out that in Peninsular Malaya significant revenue was derived from native quit rents, the annual rent paid to the state for use of the land. He argued that in North Borneo these potential rents were being lost. Commenting on the ineffective land settlement under Governor Birch's administration (1901–3), Dane urged the survey and settlement of all indigenous land holdings and the collection of rent on them.[21] But land settlement not only determined the amount of native rents; it also allowed the Company to determine which lands could be deemed as "waste lands" and made available to foreign plantation owners for commercial agricultural development. The Company was pinning its hopes for profits on large agricultural concessions and the export of agricultural products.

Despite the fact that Proclamation III of 1889 and the Land Laws of 1913 recognized various ways in which natives could claim land, the primary objectives of demarcation of native land rights in the period from 1913 onward were the surveying and registration of land kept under *permanent* cultivation only.[22] Land settlement officers found the demarcation of native rights other than for permanent agriculture far too confusing to undertake. As the commissioner of lands, G. C. Woolley reported in 1915: "At present the state of affairs with regard to titles other than those for native-owned rice fields is somewhat chaotic."[23] But this confusion existed only in the perceptions of Company officers, as natives themselves never considered their customary land laws as chaotic.[24] Consequently, Company administrators found it convenient to describe land in fallow or secondary forests as unowned, empty, waste, abandoned, or useless. Land classified in this manner was far easier to appropriate and transfer to other uses than if such land were viewed as integral components of native agricultural and land tenure systems (cf. Dove 1983).

Natives were asked to clear the boundaries on their permanent agricultural land to assist the Company in the settlement of their lands. But obstacles plagued the district officers whose job it was to oversee land settlement. Cooperation was not forthcoming from the natives who were negatively affected by land settlement. In the words of one district officer who was attempting to survey native claims:

> To all intents and purposes the *kampongs* [villages] were deserted. After much shouting and the sending of the few old women and small boys, that were about, to search, the headman deigned to put in an appearance. [In] his non-appearance earlier he excused on the grounds of *"Oh sahaya potong rentas lagi tuan"* ["Oh, I have been clearing *more* boundaries, Sir"]: I have underlined the word *"lagi"* [more] on purpose as there were . . . already apparently over 100 acres rentased [cleared], whereas 50 acres should have been the maximum.[25] Hereupon commenced a lengthy discussion. I tried the arts of persuasion but without success; I mentioned possible penalties only to be met with stony silence. I have emphasized the point that the Government's *"hukum-an"* [trial or penalty] would, in spite of opposition, be carried out, only to receive such replies as *"Baik la tuan, jikalu Prentah kasi masok jail tidapa, kalu mati, tidapa juga."* ["Fine Sir, if the Government puts me in jail, never mind, if I die, also never mind."].[26]

There are numerous accounts in the Company papers detailing the district officers' struggles with land settlement, which was constantly impeded by the local population. The letters describe many instances of both passive and active resistance on the part of the natives.[27] It was not unusual for inhabitants of a village to fail to be present on the assigned day that the surveyor was available for boundary marking[28] or even to remove the wooden boundary pegs once the survey was complete.[29] These actions reflect the local perception of the survey process as inherently disempowering and unjust. Unable to stake fully their claims through their presence, they resisted by making themselves absent. Peasants' passive resistance to rulers' coercive actions, which they felt were unjust, is well documented in Southeast Asia (Adas 1981; Scott 1976; Dove 1985; Peluso and Vandergeest 2001) and not surprising in this context where the Company officers felt entitled by birthright to make unilateral changes to native customary practices.

Company officials hoped to overcome native resistance to land settlement by gaining the cooperation of the native chiefs. In order to achieve this goal, native chiefs were made exempt from the payment of land rents.[30]

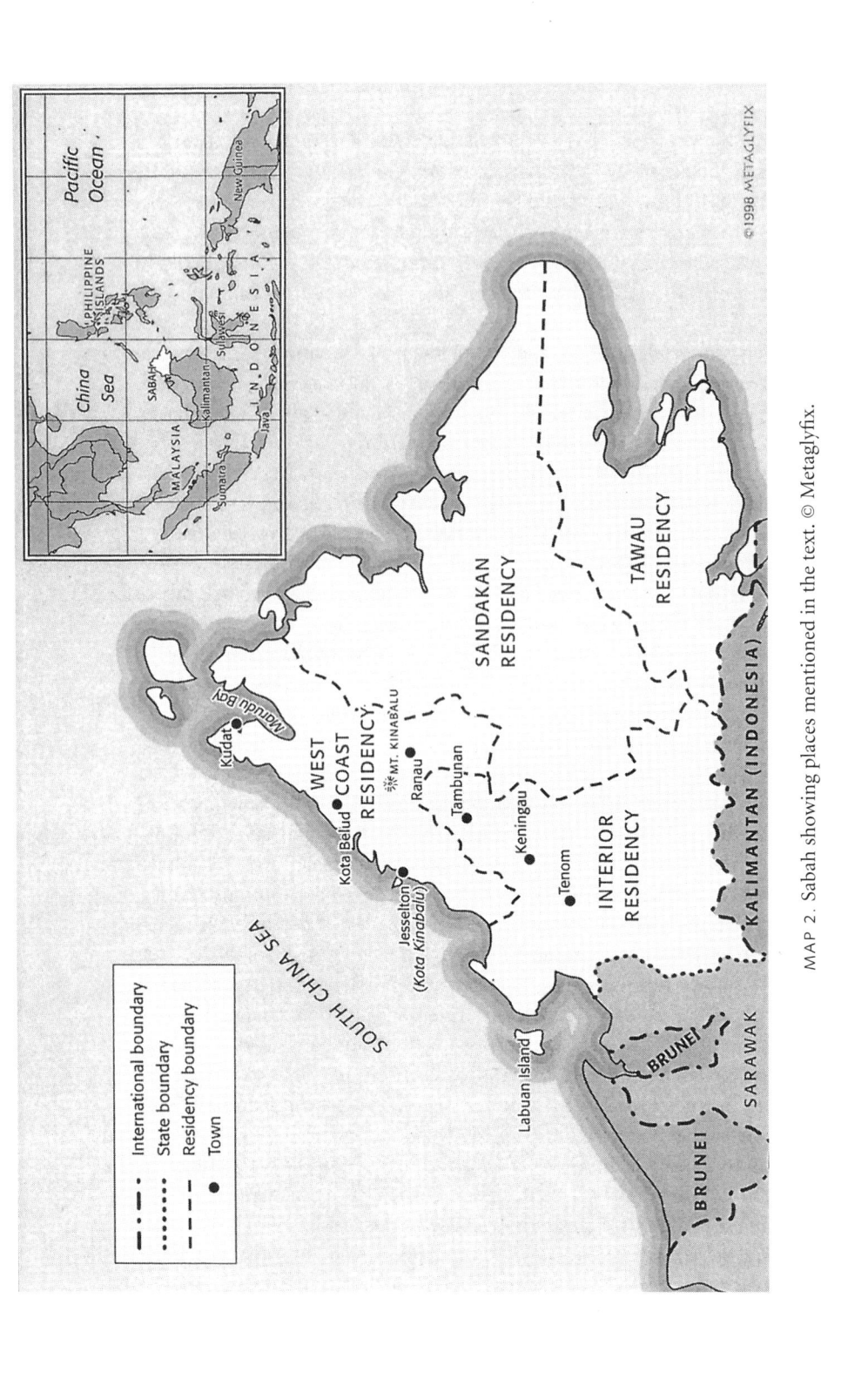

MAP 2. Sabah showing places mentioned in the text. © Metaglyfix.

In return for this tax exemption, native chiefs would be held responsible for the compliance of natives with the land settlement plans.[31] But even that was apparently not enough incentive for native participation. For example, the assistant district officer from Keningau (in the Interior Residency, see map 2) expressed his dismay over the lack of compliance from the native chiefs. In his report, he wrote:

> Paid chief Sebayai at Tambunan was arrested and detained until his people pointed out their lands. Sebayai was subsequently dismissed [from government service]. This year an attempt was made to roughly mark out and register native lands. With the exception of two paid Government chiefs all the natives refused to point out their lands. . . . Much of the cultivated land is common land or used by others than the customary owner.[32]

As illustrated in the final sentence of the above quote, one of the primary difficulties that Company officers faced as they grappled with native rights to land was their inability, or perhaps unwillingness, to understand the native system of land tenure. In their understanding, natives were classified as "nomadic," moving from place to place to cultivate jungle land, rarely staying on one piece of land and "improving" it, in a Western sense. To many Company officers in North Borneo, this suggested that the natives were "squatters" on land and not owners of it.[33] Furthermore, the notion of the village holding common rights over agricultural land, as opposed to an individual farmer holding these rights, frustrated the officials who were insistent on simplifying indigenous claims and settling individual rights only. Finally, the notion that the ownership of some resources, such as fruit trees, could be held by one individual (or a group) irrespective of the ownership of the land was a complicated arrangement of rights that collided with the rigid view of individual property rights held by the British (Appell 1990, 1992, 1995:32–56).

The result of land settlement prior to 1915 was that Company officers focused on settling permanent native holdings while other types of native property were ignored. To acknowledge these rights to fruit trees, swidden fallows, and forest resources and to draw boundaries around them would take up vast amounts of land that the Company wanted to sell to European planters. Company officials quickly realized that it was easier to settle with a single monetary compensation for claims to isolated fruit trees destroyed by plantation owners than to give natives title to the land surrounding the trees, thereby prohibiting plantation owners from acquiring it.[34]

Moreover, by settling native claims to permanent holdings, the British could meet Dane's recommendation of collecting land taxes and, they hoped, significantly increase land revenue for the Company.[35] The following statement illustrates the rigid thinking on the topic of land registration and taxation:

> They [the natives] should be educated gradually to realise that they can no longer with impunity acquire land by the hitherto accepted custom of merely settling on it without any reference to Government and must be taught under the new regime the punctual payment of rent will be considered by Government the first duty of a land holder.[36]

And, in fact, the registration of permanent native holdings rapidly began to produce the expected revenue. In 1914, the rent roll for indigenously held land produced approximately Straits $6,000; by 1920, the amount had risen to Straits $32,605 (Black 1983:218). Yet, not surprisingly, this figure of Straits $32,605 represented only a tiny amount of the overall yearly budget for the Company.[37] In addition to the financial aspects of land registration, notions of making order out of territory perceived to be in a state of chaos, creating rational, governable subjects through the imposition of law, and making the resources of North Borneo available for the benefit of all people were important in legitimizing Company rule in North Borneo.

"Ancient Native Customary Laws" or "Native Profiteering"

By 1919, Company officials appeared to be winding down their efforts to demarcate and settle native claims to land under permanent cultivation. In the Tambunan District (in the Interior Residency, see map 2), the district officer reported, "Land settlement was finally completed in 1917."[38] In the annual report of the Land Settlement Department, 1919, the commissioner of land wrote, "No large area of Native holdings now await demarcation."[39]

While many Company officials felt that they had sufficiently demarcated and settled native holdings to land under permanent cultivation, others realized that the demarcation of village communal reserves, forest reserves, and land used for shifting cultivation and isolated fruit trees had been neglected. But to most Company officers it did not seem urgent or practical to demarcate these rights. For example, in 1919, the acting commissioner of lands, C. F. Macaskie, reported, "In practice I do not think that it would be possible to mark or register such rights as isolated fruit trees." Later in the report, Macaskie stated that he saw no urgency in the demarcation of communal reserves.[40] He concluded his report, recommending that these rights be dealt with only when conflicts arose if foreigners applied for the same lands.[41] These statements reflect that some Company officers, while recognizing the *validity* of native claims to land and resources other than those held under permanent cultivation, doubted the *practicality* of trying to demarcate those rights.

Although the Company was less concerned with native access to valuable nontimber forest products and to common territory, these rights were integral components to the livelihoods of local peoples. This is not to suggest that the colonial officials did not recognize the economic value of nontimber forest products, which were indeed a significant source of revenue to the Company in the early days. Birds' nests, rattan, cutch, damar, and other "minor" products provided regular income to the Company in the period prior to extensive timber harvesting. While many colonial states in Asia did overlook the value of what they considered "minor" forest products in comparison to the valuable timbers (Tucker 1998; Bryant 1997), the Company built on the extensive trade route and collection points that had been established by local ruling chiefs, or pengirans, to extract as much revenue as possible from these forest products.[42] Like the colonial states of the United East India Company in Java and the Brooke regime in Sarawak (Peluso and Vandergeest 2001; Majid Cooke 1999; Kaur 1998), the Company emphasized the importance of taxes and trade permits on nontimber forest products for revenue. By categorizing native rights to isolated and diverse resources as difficult and lacking urgency to demarcate in the colonial laws, the Company was effectively assuring that these rights would ultimately come to the state.

Acting on the reports that land settlement was near completion (and ignoring statements that many aspects of native customary tenure had *not* been demarcated), Governor A. C. Pearson issued a memorandum in February 1920 informing district officers that in the future the Company would be under no obligation to grant natives land under native title.[43] Pearson argued that since native title was supposed to be the recognition of "ancient native customary rights" to land, once settlement of native claims was complete, natives should have no future claims to land based on native customary rights. All claims based on customary tenure were considered to have been settled or to have lapsed by default.[44] Customary laws would effectively be replaced entirely by statutory laws. Governor Pearson recommended that since land settlement was completed, natives looking for new land would have to acquire it under "a Country Grant, and the terms would be the same whether the applicant was a Native, Chinese or other alien."[45]

What Governor Pearson found most objectionable about natives claiming state land under native title, once the settlement of native customary rights had been completed, was the loss of potential revenue to the Company through native "profiteering." Pearson explained:

> It had hitherto been regarded by Land Officers as an accepted state of affairs that any Native of a district, provided he has a few dollars, has the right to select from any vacant land in his district and acquire it on "native Title" [sic], in other words free from premium, with a permanent rent of 50 cents per acre. An alien applying for the same land pays ... an enhanced rent of $2.50 ... and a premium of $42.00 per acre.
>
> After careful perusal of part IV Land Laws, I am still of the opinion that ... part IV was intended to apply exclusively to land held under "Customary Tenure." I fancy it was probably adapted or adopted from the F.M.S. [Federated Malay States] Laws. ... If the view is correct, the "Settlement" of any area closes that area to any future application on Native Title.[46]

C. F. Macaskie (the acting commissioner of lands) advised Governor Pearson that the Land Laws of 1913 clearly *did* allow natives to apply for state land under native title based on customary law, even if the use of the land was established after the start of Company rule. Macaskie wrote:

> I am of the opinion that under the Land Law:
> (ii) Any native who wishes to take up State land may apply for a native title (section 56) but the grant of refusal is at the discretion of the Collector [of Land Revenue].[47]

Pearson suggested that the Land Laws of 1913 be amended to restrict natives from applying for state land under native title, since land settlement of native customary rights was completed, in order to restrict the use of native title to his interpretation of native customary tenure. Under the amended land laws, native land grants would be subjected to the same premiums and rent as foreigners.[48] Pearson sent a draft of this amendment, Circular 14 of 1920, to his district officers. The proposed amendment evoked a heated debate within the Company administration over the validity of restricting the rights of natives to acquire land under native title, demonstrating that the Company was not a monolithic hegemon, but open to internal contradictions.[49]

One of the first officers of the Company to respond to Circular 14 was the land settlement officer, Maxwell Hall. Hall argued that because land settlement was *not* complete the state could *not* bar future applications for native title. In a letter to the government secretary he explained that "our settlement was not a full settlement. We dealt with claims which *brought rent,* but rejected others. We omitted sago swamps, village and grazing lands and hill lands. I think that there is no area which may be considered closed by settlement."[50]

Further opposition to the governor's proposed amendment came from the district officers.[51] One of the most vocal district officers was A. B. Francis, who had served in North Borneo since 1902. On the question of whether land settlement of native rights was complete, Francis wrote:

> No native titles had been issued except for padi lands; orchards, house sites, grazing lands, timber reserves, sago, reserves for expansion have all been excluded from the settlement, mainly . . . because they were *not assessable with rents* or with only small rents.[52]

Francis further argued, "The whole tenor of the land law is to allow natives certain priority and preference over aliens."[53] He could see no reason why Governor Pearson objected to natives making a few dollars in the entrepreneurial sale of land.

District officer Barraut echoed Francis's sentiments, stating, "I don't see the harm . . . if they [natives] do speculate in land, it opens up the country if they take fresh land up and plant it, and they will know they can make money by cultivating it. I should have thought it was a good thing to encourage."[54]

Not all opposition to Pearson's policy of a more strident approach to land settlement and tax collection was based on a paternalistic or moral stance toward the natives. Other officers were more concerned with potential violent uprisings if natives were forced to comply with unfavorable Company laws and policies. One resident wrote to Governor Pearson: "In no uncertain terms . . . strict adherence to this procedure would result in trouble and probable loss of life . . . [it is] necessary to go to work slowly and with great tact."[55] Many of the officers who worked closely with the native population realized the depth of local antipathy toward the land laws and were fearful that there might be open conflicts like those experienced in 1915, when several rebellions broke out after natives protested what they felt were unfair and coercive land policies and taxes.[56] For the Company agents working closely with the native population and responsible for maintaining order and stability, the proposals from the governor to curtail customary rights were seen as a reason for concern.

This debate illustrates the tensions in Company administration in North Borneo between the more paternalist administrators who worked intimately with the native population and knew the strength of native opposition to Company rule and those who were more concerned with order, the supposed supremacy of colonial rule, and the importance of revenue production. Competing obligations to the natives and to the Company's shareholders left individuals in the administration with mixed motives and ambitions in their political and administrative actions. Additionally, different departments within the Company had different mandates, creating conflicting agendas of rule.[57] For instance, the welfare of native people was the concern of the district officers. Consequently, it is not surprising that some district officers, such as Francis and Barraut, felt a paternalistic duty to the natives and acted on the premise that natives should be given priority over foreigners in land matters and be encouraged in entrepreneurial activities, even at the expense of increased state revenue. However, although Francis and Barraut were considered paternalistic in comparison to other Company officers, British officers in neighboring colonial states saw very little evidence of the classic British paternalism in the majority of the Company's actions. In Sarawak, for example, the Rajah Brooke regime had a far different approach in its ruling of the native population, often categorized by its commitment to native peoples' welfare, regardless of the fiscal costs to the state. One resident from Sarawak criticized the fiscally driven policies of the Company for being those of "an association of European capitalists whose every motive in native eyes is the acquiring of wealth and the disregard of native religion, custom, and happiness."[58]

Other officers, such as Governor Pearson, who represented the upper echelon of Company rule, felt a stronger responsibility to the shareholders of the Company. It was the governor's mandate to ensure the financial viability of the Company. In fact, one of the founders of the Company, Lord Medhurst, commented that revenue and expenditure "must always be regarded as a test of the progress or otherwise of a territory" (1885:105). Taking this mandate seriously, Governor Pearson's primary concern was the loss of the Straits $42 premium per acre that resulted when a foreigner bought land from a native rather than from the Company. In fact, Pearson was concerned that the "Chinamen" and natives were acting together to defraud the Company of land revenue. He was worried that natives were acting as agents for foreigners by acquiring land free from premium under native title and then selling it to foreigners for less money than the foreigners would have to pay the state in the form of land premium, actions that make sense under the economic rationale that underscored many Company practices.[59]

The governor, who was most concerned with his obligations to the shareholders, was not able to rewrite the treatment of native customary law in statutory law to meet his objective of increased revenue. District officers who recognized that land settlement was not complete, who supported native entrepreneurial activities, and who recognized the potential danger of inciting natives to the point of rebellion over unfavorable policies successfully opposed Governor Pearson's proposed amendment to the land laws. Natives were able to continue acquiring land from the Company under native title for at least another two decades. In 1928, however, Governor John L. Humphreys renewed the debate over native rights to land and succeeded in limiting their rights where Governor Pearson had failed.

"Free Civilizing Intercourse": The Effects of a Superior Civilization on the Depraved Habits of the Natives

One of the original goals of the land laws was to recognize formally lands that a village used in common, to be called "native reserves" or "communal lands," as well as permanent, individual holdings. However, there were no official procedures in the land laws or in policy documents for determining which lands were communal lands or for granting title for native reserves. As a result, land settlement officers were reluctant to go into the field and demarcate these complex rights.

In some cases, communal lands were marked as native reserves on survey office maps, but no formal title was issued and no ground survey was completed.[60] Other times, communal lands were legally gazetted as native reserves and the headmen or native chiefs were appointed as the trustees of the lands for the village. However, even when village lands were demarcated and gazetted as native reserves, this provided no long-term security of ownership to the village.[61] The case of the native reserve in the village of Tenom (in the Interior Residency, see map 2), described below, illustrates this point.

In 1928, Governor Humphreys considered the agricultural development of Tenom to be the key to the continued economic growth of North Borneo. At this time, Tenom signified the "frontier" to the interior of the state. Although it was connected to the capital city of Jesselton[62] by railroad, previous governors had restricted foreigners from applying for land in this area.[63] Tenom, and other areas in the interior, were considered "native areas,"[64] or

> neighborhoods where under present conditions and circumstances there is an objection to the presence of aliens in any considerable numbers. The reason for this objection may be based on one or more of a number of factors, e.g. congestion of ownership, the nature of the country and its inhabitants, danger to the aliens, distance from a Government station.[65]

Humphreys felt that the designation of Tenom as a native area was no longer useful, particularly since the Chinese immigrants nearby were eager to acquire land from the state. In reviewing the question of foreign concessions for land near Tenom, Humphreys found that a large area (more than three thousand acres) had been demarcated on Tenom maps as native reserves,[66] yet natives had failed to make claims on the land set aside there for them. The district officer in Tenom reported on the apathy of the natives, who, when called on to make their claims on the land, placed claims for a total of only seventy-five acres.[67] At the same time, the district officer had received nearly two hundred applications (totaling about two thousand acres) from the Chinese for this same land. Since the district officer understood that the land was to remain set aside for the native population only, he had refused the applications from the Chinese. Yet, in a letter to the governor, the district officer expressed the opinion that the designation of the area in Tenom as a native reserve was, in fact, an impediment to "progress."[68] In response to this report from the district officer, Governor Humphreys wrote to the president of the Company. Arguing that "free civilizing intercourse and economic development has always been the aim of the Court [of Directors]," Humphreys suggested that the time had come to abolish restrictions on foreign landownership in the native areas.[69] He also expressed the opinion that land development, in the hands of the Chinese, would benefit the native Murut population around Tenom. Humphreys wrote:

> It may also be not unreasonably suggested that the depraved habits of the Muruts and such wasteful barbarism as excessive *tapai* [rice wine] drinking, shifting cultivation, and nomadic villages, are actually fostered by denying [them] contact with people of a superior civilization whose example would hasten their disappearance.[70]

Using his executive powers, Governor Humphreys published Notification 24 of 1928. This notification removed all agricultural restrictions in Tenom by abolishing the native reserves and opening up these areas for settlement by foreign agriculturists.[71] Additionally, Humphreys called for all "districts to be opened to applicants for land without distinction of nationality."[72] At home in London, the court of directors applauded the actions of Governor Humphreys. The court felt that Humphreys was finally "sweeping away barriers to alien penetration of the Interior" and saw his actions as a "significant step in the land policies" in North Borneo.[73]

The Company had long encouraged Chinese immigrants and farmers to establish themselves in North Borneo, believing that Chinese were far more industrious than the native population. For instance, in 1883 a liberal policy toward Chinese gambier and pepper planters was adopted, offering them a ninety-nine-year tenure to land, without premium. For the first three years they were charged no rent, after which a rent of $0.10 per acre was charged.[74] And according to William Treacher,

> Experience in the Straits Settlements, the Malay Peninsula and Sarawak has shewn [sic] that the people to cause rapid financial progress in Malayan countries are the hard-working, money-loving Chinese, and these are the peoples whom the Company should lay themselves out to attract to Borneo. [Once we get them] . . . the financial success of the Company would, in my opinion, be secured. (Treacher 1891:148; as cited in McT. Kahin 1947:57)

To encourage Chinese migration further, by 1892, the Official Regulations stated that each Chinese male might be granted five acres of uncleared government land. This land would be provided rent-free for the first five years. In addition, the Government would grant advances for the first six months at the following rates per month: Straits $6.00 for married men with children, Straits $5.00 for married men without children, and Straits $3.00 for single men.[75] Colonial officers in Sarawak and the Malay Peninsula shared the belief that the Chinese were more successful agriculturalists than the natives, and it was hoped that encouraging Chinese immigration would provide a significant source of revenue to the Company.[76] Such financial incentives were never offered to natives. In fact, (as previously shown) natives were often discouraged from commercial agriculture under Ordinance V of 1928, which allowed them to acquire land under native title for *subsistence cultivation* only, and not for *commercial cultivation*. If natives wanted to cultivate their land with commercial crops, they needed to acquire the land under a country lease and pay an increased rent to the state.[77] This situation is not unique to North Borneo. An analogous colonial policy in Peninsular Malaya encouraged native production of rice for subsistence use but not rubber cultivation for commercial use (Nonini 1992).[78]

The archival records indicate that as the native reserves in Tenom were opened up to the Chinese population for development and ownership and obstacles were placed in front of native commercial agriculturalists, only one Company official spoke out against these actions. The lone voice belonged to G. C. Woolley, the Company expert on native laws and customs, who argued that Humphreys was too willing to sacrifice the interests of the natives for "material progress."[79] Woolley suggested an alternative plan for development, arguing that the Chinese could sublease the land from the Muruts for a limited period. In response, Humphreys called Woolley's proposal "fantastic" and concluded that only by opening the lands to Chinese and abolishing the native reserves would there be a "sound base for agricultural development" in the Interior.[80]

Humphreys' actions demonstrate how the Company paid only token regard to native welfare in the codification of native customary laws. In his vision of land development for North Borneo, agricultural growth needed to expand unimpeded, and this required the disposal of any native land rights that might obscure that vision. If elements of native customs and social institutions appeared as obstacles to the commercial exploitation of land, they were slowly eroded in colonial law and in the practice of land administration. Humphreys seized a window of opportunity to limit native rights and provided increased rights to nonnatives. This opportunity arose as native populations became more compliant (there had been no active rebellions in thirteen years), and there was an increasing optimism that agriculturalists, particularly the industrious Chinese, could open up the interior of the territory for the Company and begin a new period of agricultural development there.

THE DISCOURSES OF APPROPRIATE LAND USE: PITTING SHIFTING CULTIVATION AGAINST "ROTATIONAL" PLANTATION AGRICULTURE

In stark contrast to the treatment of native rights to land, and motivating restriction of native rights to land, was the Company's drive to identify, demarcate, and market land for sale to European investors (Cleary 1992). In an age when plantation agriculture was exploding in parts of Southeast Asia, the Company used liberal land leases and promises of large tracts of land to attract investors from other areas. In contrast with Deli (Sumatra), where tobacco planters were hampered by heavy taxation and a lack of suitable land, the Company established less restrictive regulations and easy terms to welcome prospective agriculturists to North Borneo (Government of British North Borneo Chartered Company 1890:91; John and Jackson 1973). The Company's discourse surrounding tobacco plantations as a highly scientific and economically rational land use illustrates how it justified its treatment of native customary rights. The following examination of how European planters were viewed and treated by the Company during the years 1880–1930 complements the previous discussion of the treatment of native agriculturalists during the same period.

In the late 1880s, with enthusiastic encouragement from the Company, tobacco estates in North Borneo multiplied rapidly (John and Jackson 1973:94). During this period, the Company's policies toward land can only be characterized as laissez-faire. It was prepared to grant European planters concessions of up to forty thousand acres at an initial premium of Straits $0.30 per acre, free of quit rent, for 999 years. Export duty on estate tobacco was charged at a maximum of Straits $0.01 per pound for a period of twenty years, computed from five years after the initial crop. These incentives proved to be so attractive that applications for land grants were received for two hundred thousand acres of land in 1887 alone, forcing the Company to adopt more conservative land polices. In 1888, the minimum premium was raised to Straits $1.00 per acre, and by 1890, it stood at Straits $6.00 per acre (ibid., 93–94).

A booming market in land for tobacco plantations characterized the period of 1887–90. The value of tobacco exports rose from Straits $1,619.00 in 1885 to Straits $396,314.00 five years later,[81] when the government began to charge a small export fee on tobacco. By 1895, the value of tobacco exports reached Straits $1,176,000.00.[82] At the height of the boom in land grants, the Company received more than Straits $200,000.00 in revenue from land leases for three years in a row, peaking at Straits $256,183.00 in 1889.[83] With total revenue for 1889 standing at Straits $507,785.00, land leases to Europeans alone were responsible for more than 50 percent of the Company's yearly revenues.[84]

Although the boom in land concessions to tobacco planters provided much needed revenue to the Company, it also caught the Lands and Survey Department totally unprepared. In the rush to grant concessions, large areas of land later recognized to be under native ownership were leased to European planters. Resident Daly of the West Coast reported in 1888:

> I find that large blocks of land, enclosing native homesteads, villages and even rivers themselves, regardless of all Government reserves, have been alienated . . . and paid for at so much an acre by lessees, one of whom [an European] on the Bingkoka river actually claims the right of stopping all navigation in the river so far as it passes through his property, as he maintains that he has paid for that river as the area of its surface was computed in the 11,170 acres granted to him.[85]

At this time the Company made no attempt to guarantee native claims to land before making concessions to foreigners, and as a result, by 1889 land disputes between natives and planters were on the rise. In response to these disputes, Governor Creagh issued Proclamation III, which defined native rights to land and the mechanisms by which they should be settled. According to the legislation, district officers, with the help of native chiefs, were responsible for determining native claims to land in areas that were earmarked for foreign concessions. The legislation, however, was vague as to whether native rights should be settled before or after the concessions were granted to the European planters. It emphasized only that natives must be compensated, by having their claims excised from the foreign concession, by being resettled to land of equal size, or by receiving cash payment. In practice, native rights were often settled *after* European planters received their grants and began cultivating the land.

Given the vast amount of land in the territory, the small number of Company officers, and the contradictions within the Company's mandate, it is not surprising that district officers had significant latitude in how they negotiated land disputes, despite the regulations outlined in Proclamation III of 1889. The land dispute between Count Gelose d'Elsloo, a Dutch tobacco planter, and the Dusun natives on the Kudat Peninsula (see map 2) highlights the tensions between the paternalistic and economic motivations of the Company. It also clearly demonstrates that natives and their agricultural systems were seen as scientifically and economically inferior to the Europeans and their systems, which therefore justified Company restrictions on natives' access to land.

Count Gelose d'Elsloo consistently acted in a high-handed manner with both the government and the natives (Black 1983:111). By 1888, the count owned thirty square miles along the southern end of Marudu Bay.[86] He wrote that the "unexpected difficulty arising from native rights" on his tobacco estate annoyed him.[87] G. Davies, the district officer in the Kudat district, was responsible for settling disputes between the count and the local population. Regarding native claims to the land, Davies wrote to Count Gelose d'Elsloo in 1889: "There will be great difficulty in settling 'Native Rights' . . . if we proceed on the plan of cutting out the land to which [native] people are entitled under Proclamation No. III of 1889."[88] Davies added that if they did cut out all the land from the count's estate that natives claimed rights to, the best land in Marudu Bay would cease to be available for Count Gelose d'Elsloo's tobacco company.

To remedy the situation Davies came up with an alternative scheme that would allow the natives to remain on the land that had been sold by the government to the count. He was proposed that the natives would "carry out their *little* planting operations as in the past, subject to the understanding that *they shall always give way to the tobacco planters,* when both want to use the same piece of land during the same season" (emphasis added).[89] He further suggested that natives be encouraged to plant on the land that the count had previously used to grow tobacco, paying the European planter 10 percent of their crop for the privilege of using the land. Additionally, the natives were "ordered before cutting any jungle to apply to the manager of the estate near where they lived . . . to find out whether the place they proposed to plant will be required by him [the estate manager] during the next two . . . seasons."[90]

Count Gelose d'Elsloo was not satisfied with this arrangement and responded, "I told you that the planting by natives on land where jungle is growing would certainly not enrich the land and also deprive us of the timber grown on it required for building."[91] To appease Count Gelose d'Elsloo on this point, Davies suggested that the "native shall not be allowed to cut down valuable timber suitable for posts of houses . . . so long as there is sufficient land cleared or land with small trees on it."[92] This concession seemed to satisfy the count, and Governor Creagh supported Davies' settlement of the native claims to land on Count Gelose d'Elsloo's tobacco estate.[93]

This exchange of letters between Davies, the count, and the governor took place only five months after Governor Creagh issued Proclamation III of 1889, detailing native rights to land. Yet native claims to the land on the tobacco concession were not settled according to this proclamation. Native claims were not surveyed and set aside for native ownership, nor did the natives receive any cash settlement. Instead, they were required to pay a tax to the estate holder for the use of the land, and they were confined to using land that had previously been used by the estate. Furthermore, they had always to apply to the estate manager for the use of land and had to cultivate the land according to the needs of the estate, not according to their own land claims. None of these restrictions were part of the land laws. Despite Proclamation III of 1889, native claims to land were not recognized when they interfered with income-producing plantation schemes. In practice, the needs of plantations, which were equated with economic progress and growth, were given precedence over native needs because the Company needed revenue. Again, nonnatives became the right-bearing citizens under Company rule, whereas natives were denied equal rights in practice, even when token attention had been paid to those rights in legal documents. In the particularities of Company land management with regards to both natives and Europeans, the unstable nature of colonial rule is evident. Although the land laws were set in place to define a universal code of property rights, their implementation was contested by native peoples, the terrain of their implementation was uneven as a result of the complexities of local life and the demands of European planters, and they were ultimately reshaped in policies and practices that did not adhere to the letter of the law.

Throughout Company rule in North Borneo, administrators continually expressed their disapproval of the wasteful native practice of shifting cultivation. In his description of Labuan, an island off the shores of Brunei, Governor Treacher reported in 1890 that valuable timber trees had been destroyed "chiefly by the destructive mode of cultivation practiced by the Kadyans and other squatters from Borneo, who were allowed to destroy the forest for a crop or two of rice, the soil . . . not being rich enough to carry more than one or two such harvests under such primitive methods of agriculture as only known to natives" (43).

Despite the Company's alarm at the native practice of shifting cultivation, it recognized the similarities between tobacco plantations and rice swiddens and made no effort to try and conceal these similarities. District officer Davies, mentioned above, reported that the native "people of Marudu Bay, *like the tobacco planters,* use the land and then leave it for ten years before returning to it again" (emphasis added).[94] Treacher confirms this in another region of North Borneo, stating, "So long as there remains any untouched land on his estate, the [European] planter rarely makes use of land off which a crop has been taken" (1890:81).

But in perhaps the most telling comment, Treacher, who, in a letter to the chairman of the Company, stated, "Fears have been expressed as to the bad effects tobacco planting would have in using up the country, *as only one crop is taken from the land, and fresh land is therefore opened every year*" (emphasis added).⁹⁵ The Company, however, viewed tobacco plantations not as a commercial variety of shifting cultivation but, instead, as a distinctive type of plantation agriculture (John and Jackson 1973: 88), for tobacco planters paid land taxes and contributed to state revenue through export taxes. Furthermore, plantations were based on European principles of ownership, labor, and production of a commodity for export. Native shifting cultivation was viewed as the quintessential opposite of European plantation cultivation and therefore unimportant to protect or even encourage.

In 1913, the Company introduced legislation known as the *Ladang Ordinance*,⁹⁶ the primary purpose of which "was to restrict the destruction of forests by felling them for temporary cultivation only."⁹⁷ But the ordinance was aimed at controlling only native forms of shifting cultivation, not European shifting cultivation. In the ordinance, *ladang* cultivation was defined as "the successive occupation of different pieces of land in such a manner that any one piece is not cultivated for more than two consecutive years and is then abandoned." Realizing that this definition would include estate tobacco, the Company specifically provides in this ordinance "that the use of land for the cultivation of 'Wrapper Leaf' tobacco shall not be deemed to be '*ladang* cultivation.'"⁹⁸

The Company obviously recognized the similarities between the land use methods of tobacco plantations and of shifting cultivation and even recognized that tobacco estates would exhaust land as quickly as native shifting cultivation. Both methods required regular, cyclical clearing of forests, but the Company chose to target native shifting cultivators as the scapegoat of forest destruction. Tobacco plantations were fostered and protected since they created a significant source of revenue and were considered to be "undoubtedly the most scientific form of planting in the East" (Rutter 1922:251).

In Company ideology,⁹⁹ the destruction of forests for commercial agriculture was glorified, whereas the destruction of forest by natives for subsistence agriculture was vilified. In 1913, a memo on shifting cultivation stated: "The Forestry Department here,¹⁰⁰ as everywhere, rightly hate shifting cultivation and continuously storm about it, but they offer no suggestion for a remedy . . . other than one akin to murder."¹⁰¹ In 1914, another report stated the following in reference to native shifting cultivation:

> The practice of shifting cultivation . . . is the origin of the greatest annual loss to the timber supply. It is the greatest evil with which a Forest Officer has to contend, and the less civilized and developed the country is, the harder it be-

comes to keep the annual destruction within bounds. . . . The property is ruined by shifting cultivation, inasmuch as the land is almost invariably subjected to fire which extends beyond the area designed for cultivation, and effectively kills all seeds and seedlings which may be in its range. When cultivation is abandoned "lalang" or swordgrass appears and the land is practically valueless.[102]

But in Owen Rutter's[103] description of a European planter clearing the jungle, the planter and fire are depicted as heroes of progress. In Rutter's words:

In North Borneo new cessions are either under virgin jungle or secondary jungle and the preliminary work of clearing the land is usually given out to the native contractors who thoroughly understand it. There is only one sight more inspiring than a great jungle giant crashing to the ground, and that is a block of jungle burning when it has been felled and stacked. The day for the fire is a most momentous question, for a good clean burn will save the planter thousands and a bad one will leave the estate strewn with useless timber. A burn on a fine day is well worth waiting for. The coolies are in the highest spirits, whooping with glee as they see the long tongues of fire leaping up, crimson as tulips; soon the whole hill-side is ablaze, rising and falling, a sea of flame. The smoke curling heaven-high, veils the rising sun and makes it glow a rich dull red as in London on a foggy November morning. . . . When it is over . . . the planter surveys the scene and feels content, for all has gone according to plan; *he has tamed the untamable* (1922:246; emphasis added).

The notion that native shifting cultivation was destroying the territory's forests was not documented in any scientific or systematic fashion by the Company. And the district officers voiced disagreement over the extent of damage caused by shifting cultivation. In 1930, H. G. Keith, the conservator of forests who was charged with finding areas to be designated as forest reserves, undertook an exploratory trip across North Borneo from Sandakan to Keningau via the Kinabatangan River. The following was reported: "Mr. Keith found that . . . the stand of timber in the region traversed was very poor, and confirmed his opinion that the timber supplies of the Territory have been greatly overestimated. He regards the 'inexhaustible supplies of the interior' as non-existent owing to damage caused by shifting cultivation."[104] In response to this report Resident C. R. Smith, overseer of the Interior, wrote:

The Conservator of Forests states that 'considerable tracts of valuable forest are annually being destroyed.' . . . but no indication is given as to where these 'considerable tracts' are situated. Possibly these 'tracts' are situated on the East Coast, but it is difficult to visualize heavy destruction by the scanty population there. My experience is that very little damage is now being done to virgin forest by shifting cultivation in this country.[105]

Three years later, Keith was still convinced of the deleterious effects of swidden cultivation on the forests of North Borneo and expressed his frustration at the inability of colonial officers to enforce the *Ladang* Ordinance. Keith wrote in a report: "It is obvious . . . that the *Ladang* Ordinance is almost inoperative and certainly the provisions of the Ordinance are disregarded in most districts. . . . As matters stand at present the Forest Department is emasculated of practically all powers to conserve and protect the forest of this Territory."[106]

The discrepancy between Keith's account of destruction of the forest at the hands of the natives and Smith's account demonstrates the disagreement within Company administration. District officers and the conservator of the forest saw their mandates in sharp contrast. The conservator of the forest was most concerned with the state of the forest, whereas the district officers came to the defense of the local people. Moreover, the conservator of the forest was no longer concerned with revenue production from timber (as had been the earlier role of the Forestry Department) but now was solely responsible for the management of timber reserves for forest protection.[107] Trained in the ethic of preserving forest for the permanent supply of timber, not "merely as area of forest set aside until the timber it contains can be conveniently used prior to giving up the land for other purposes,"[108] Keith waged a constant battle over the protection of forests.

It was not until after World War II, however, that the effects of native shifting cultivation in North Borneo were examined in any systematic manner. In 1948, the Committee on Shifting Cultivation determined that "25,000 natives practice shifting cultivation and from air photos it was estimated that not more than 0.315% of the colony was under shifting cultivation. It was agreed that the primary forest destroyed was relatively small."[109]

Unfortunately, it is not possible to obtain adequate figures on the extent of shifting cultivation during the height of the boom in land grants for tobacco estates in the late 1880s. But by comparing the amount of land estimated to be under shifting cultivation in 1948 with that alienated for tobacco plantations by 1889, one can gain a sense of the scale of forest clearance. According to the Forestry Department figure for 1948, native shifting cultivation was responsible for the clearing of 0.315 percent of the territory, or 40,320 acres of forest out of a total acreage of 12,800,000 in North Borneo. By mid-1889, 555,080 acres of land, 4.4 percent of the territory, was alienated for tobacco estates alone (see table 1.3). Clearly, there is no comparison between the extent of forest cleared for native agriculture and that cleared for European tobacco plantation agriculture, even without considering the impact of rubber, coffee, and tea plantations or the different periods of time.

But empirical evidence was not necessary to validate continued growth of the European plantation system since colonial ideology was so firmly entrenched that few colonialists doubted that the plantation system was inherently more scientific than native cultivation practices, that economic rationality was a far superior logic than other forms of production, and that there was an inherent moral weakness and ecological ignorance that kept indigenous people from advancing (Neumann 1998; Rajan 1998). Colonial notions of plantation agriculture as an intrinsically more scientific proposition than shifting cultivation can be traced directly to England, where increasing emphasis was placed on using science both to explore the geography and natural resources of the colonies and to direct the most rational methods of exploiting these resources (Worboys 1990:168). In particular, the main work of the British Department of Scientific and Technical Research in the nineteenth century was research in natural products and tropical agriculture (Worboys 1990). It has been shown that elsewhere in South and Southeast Asia one of the dominant myths about shifting cultivation, held by both colonial and postcolonial states, is that it is destructive and wasteful of forests (Pouchepadaas 1995; Dove 1983; Bryant 1997; Jewitt 1995; Chandran 1998). Implicit in the state's criticism of shifting cultivation is the contention that other uses of the forest, for either timber or plantation cultivation, are less wasteful (Rajan 1998; Dove 1983). Furthermore, other uses of the land and forest are more desirable than shifting cultivation because they yield more revenue for the state and are touted as being more "scientific" in their systematic and ordered control over natural resources (Rajan 1998). Often these claims are made despite the fact that there is no empirical evidence that shifting cultivation is any more wasteful or destructive of forest than other potential uses of the land (Dove 1983). Writing on the same trends in colonial Tanzania, Roderick Neumann comments that "these arguments—derived from the European-African, scientific-traditional, efficient-wasteful—obfuscated the fundamental question of *who would*

TABLE 1.3. Distribution of Land Alienated for Tobacco Cultivation in North Borneo, Mid-1889

Province		Number of areas alienated	Total acreage alienated	Location
Alcock		2	14,969	Banggi Island
		3	23,170	Benkoka River
		4	38,844	Marudu Bay
	subtotal		76,983	
Dewhurst		7	79,000	Sugut River
Martin		4	80,000	Labuk River
		3	20,000	Lokan River
		1	15,000	Tungud River
		1	8,000	Lamag/Segama River
	subtotal		123,000	
Myburgh		2	34,000	Sandakan Bay
		2	19,878	Segaliud River
		1	14,451	Suanlamba River
		17	152,000	Kinabatangan River
		1	10,000	Segama River
		1	3,768	Sepagaya River
	subtotal		234,097	
Mayne		3	33,000	Segama River
		4	9,000	Darvel Bay
	subtotal		42,000	
TOTAL		56	555,080	

SOURCE: "Memorandum in Tobacco Planting" (Government of British North Borneo, 1890:178–81). Also cited in John and Jackson 1973:94.

control access to and benefits from natural resources" (Neumann 1998:116; emphasis in original).

In this brief history of North Borneo can be seen occasional struggles between the upper echelon or "commanding heights"[110] of the Company, usually represented by the governors, and the district officers who worked more closely with the native population and were responsible for executing state directives. The governors, who had to report to the court of directors in London, felt directly responsible to the shareholders. As a result, they often focused their attention on the production of revenue. The district officers at times objected to the governors' actions when they felt that native rights or livelihoods were being threatened or when they faced strong native resistance to the Company's policies. For the most part, the governors' policies aimed at creating a capitalist-driven enterprise in the territory overruled the protests raised by the district officers. Such divergent and contradictory colonial views on the subject population are not uncommon throughout South and Southeast Asia, and therefore one should not be surprised by these apparent contradictions. Sarah Jewitt (1995), for example, in her analysis of British forestry policies and practices in India also draws attention to the conflicts between the normalizing, dominatory aspects of British rule and the paternalistic desire to protect the native population. In contrast, Richard Grove (1995) argues that in colonial India entirely contradictory motivations and ideologies survived together; colonial officers were motivated by both economic goals and a more complex desire to re-create a Utopian paradise in the tropical colonies. These nuanced understandings of variations within the colonial state show that even when power is not uniformly or completely exercised, it still can have the capacity to control people. In the final analysis, it is undeniable that the Company in North Borneo was privileging Western use of the land over the native systems, even when both systems had similar impacts on forest resources. Although the different viewpoints found within Company administration toward natives and their rights may have tempered the impact of the colonial state-making project on the native people and the landscape, ultimately the general trend was toward tightening state control over local people and whittling away at their customary land rights and access to natural resources.

Forms of capitalism spread all around the globe during this period of colonialism (Grove 1997:179). During the early stages of state building in North Borneo, the Company's recognition of native leaders such as chiefs and headmen came from a need to rule the territory indirectly (and with minimal expense), rather than from a commitment to recognize native legal systems and social structures. Adopting local social institutions served as a way to increase Company control across the territory. Yet as the Company became more involved in the economic and agricultural development of the state, native customary law became an obstacle to Company rule. As a result, the Company attempted to move away from recognition of native customary law toward fully replacing native legal systems with colonial statutory law. This pattern of diminished recognition of native customary laws and increased emphasis on Western legal and economic principles was found throughout British and other European colonies. Grove states this most succinctly, arguing, "Over the period of 1670–1950, very approximately, a pattern of ecological power relations emerged in which the expanding European states acquired a global reach over natural resources in terms of consumption, and then too, in terms of political and economic control" (1997:183).[111] From the colonial viewpoint, law, order, and scientific knowledge were considered key to the production of sound and progressive colonial policy within the paradigm of capitalism and the expansion of the British empire (Bonneuil 2000:259).

Colonial rule in North Borneo differed from other British colonial enterprises in the scant attention it paid to conservation, soil erosion, climate change, and many of the other environmental concerns that are documented in colonial India and South Africa (Grove 1995, 1997; Sivaramakrishnan 2000; Neumann 1998). Perhaps this occurred because the drive for conservation and environmental concerns emanated not from the colonial center in England but, rather, from specific colonial administrators in specific locations. It is not surprising that the Company, as a chartered enterprise dependent on revenues, was less concerned with the environmentalist discourse than were colonial states supported by the British central government.

The rise of the modern state in North Borneo transformed the relationship between natives and Company administrators into a lopsided union. The Company's discourses of rational law, scientific agriculture, and commercialization were used to legitimize colonial power and resulted in pushing native people and their customary laws into an increasingly peripheral position in relationship to the centralizing state. During this period, only glimpses of local reaction to colonial rule are found. The next chapter explores local agency from 1950 to the mid-1990s via recent data showing that, despite the general trend toward subversion of local interests through the imposition of Western law, occasionally new forms of Western law were also used as a mechanism by which society mobilized the ideology of the colonizers to protect native lands and to resist Company domination. By negotiating with the state and creatively appropriating their legal institutions, certain communities were able to use the new land laws to their advantage, in ways perhaps unanticipated by Company officials.

TWO

REDEFINING NATIVE CUSTOMARY LAW IN GOVUTON

Struggles over Property Rights between
Native Peoples and Colonial Rulers

[The village] is situated on the slopes of hills about 1500–2000 feet high with steep hills cut into ridges by numerous streams coming down, there is very little jungle, the slopes mostly being covered with turf kept short by numerous kerbau [water buffalo], cattle, goats, and pigs. The houses large and small numbering at least 200 face each other on the slopes and are surrounded by pinang [betel nut], coconuts, and other trees and altogether the place has the appearance of an old prosperous homestead. The ground has every appearance of being very rich. — PERSONAL DIARY OF W. R. DUNLOP

THIS DESCRIPTION OF THE VILLAGE I WILL CALL GOVUTON IS AS ACCURATE at the end of the twentieth century as it was one hundred years ago in 1897 when the British colonial administrator William Dunlop depicted the village in his diary (see fig. 1). Although many of the landscape features Dunlop described are still the same, in the past century enormous social transformations have occurred that have changed customary practices of resources use and ownership.

The distance from Kota Kinabalu, the capital of Sabah located on the western seacoast, to Govuton is only ninety kilometers, but takes nearly two and a half hours to reach by car. The road climbs from sea level to approximately four thousand feet by way of extensive switchbacks. During the rainy season, the road is often temporarily closed because landslides wash it down the

FIG. 1. Sketch of Mount Kinabalu from study site, February 16, 1897. Source: Personal diary of W. R. Dunlop in Sabah Archives.

steep mountain slopes. Along the trip only rare glimpses may be caught of the dramatic Mount Kinabalu, which dominates the landscape from the village of Govuton. Ever since 1851, when Sir Hugh Low was the first European to ascend it, Mount Kinabalu has held the fascination of tourists and scientists alike. And its enormous diversity of endemic plants has made Mount Kinabalu a magnet for botanists. At the same time that the mountain has been so inundated by foreigners, the village of Govuton, fewer than two miles away in a valley at the mountain's foot, has been largely overlooked. Govuton is at present a moderate-size village, with a population of roughly two thousand. It is divided into nine hamlets, or small clusters of homes, often based on extended kinship ties. The majority of the villagers belong to the Dusunic-speaking linguistic group and refer to their ethnicity as Dusun.[1]

When I first arrived in Sabah, my research sponsor told me to contact Angaw in Govuton. He had experience working for researchers on the mountain and could help me. I asked Angaw if he could introduce me to village leaders and suggest some field assistants. Quickly he ticked off on his fingers the scientists he had assisted: several botanists, a hydrologist, a geologist, and an ornithologist. He also worked as a guide for trekkers who wanted to ascend Mount Kinabalu. What did I want to study? he asked. The people in the village, I responded, leaving him dumbstruck. What was interesting about the people compared to the mountain? I explained that I wanted to work with farmers to understand their land use systems and the changes in these systems over time. Later he took me on a walk to his family's swidden field where his stooped-over, sixty-year-old father was working. As the old man set up an intricate system of rattan and bamboo devices to scare the voracious songbirds from his rice, we talked about the agricultural cycle and village life. Angaw warned me against romanticizing the life of farmers. It was all hard work and little payoff. According to Angaw, things were better in the village now that people could find jobs at Kinabalu Park. Anyone who could make enough money stopped farming or hired other people to work their land. This gradual shift away from total dependence on an agrarian economy has led contemporary agriculturists to deny that they are farmers, saying, in comparison to earlier times, "I just play with a little land." Apparently the larger, often Chinese-owned, commercial ventures that employed several wage laborers and yielded large harvests had become the measure of a true farmer.

During my months in Govuton, I discovered Angaw's observation that no one wanted to farm anymore was both correct and incorrect. It was true that most families had one or more people, usually the men and young adults, who worked in the park or in the district center. The cash they brought back to the family was a crucial supplement to the food from the gardens and forest and was used to pay for school for the younger children. At the same time, nearly every household had several people, usually young mothers and the elder men and women, who stayed home to garden, hunt, and collect resources from the forest. Families were often dismissive of the resources that such people contributed to the household economy since they had such little monetary value. But most families could not survive on wage labor alone; they were dependent on the subsistence foods they cultivated and the jungle produce they collected from the wild. These products would keep food on the table and provide extra income from selling surplus in regional markets. Although the younger generation of the village increasingly looked to the labor market outside of the agricultural sector for jobs, the underlying support of the village remained in the domesticated and wild resources that the families depended on for survival. Throughout this gradual social change in Govuton, property relations were, and still are, continuously redefined to meet the new economic needs of the village. In only forty years this village has gone from a completely agricultural-based village to one that is partially intertwined with the regional economy, while to some extent still dependent on agriculture. And it was only forty-five years ago that the jungle track that connected this village to the city of Kota Kinabalu was made into a passable road. This very change in the economy of the village is what makes present-day property relations so complex and so interesting to study.

The contemporary economic base in Govuton, and indeed the region, is a complex, composite agrarian economy—families mix subsistence swidden agriculture with commercial cultivation of temperate vegetable crops.[2] Additionally, as mentioned above, most extended families have at least one wage earner. Most of the fertile, arable land in the village is used for agriculture, but this land does not produce enough food and income for people. Therefore, many families also own wet rice fields and fruit orchards in distant villages, and it is not unusual to have part of the extended family, such as the grandparents, living in a field hut in a faraway rice field or fruit orchard.

This chapter begins by drawing on material from colonial archives, regional archives, and present-day oral histories to illustrate the political, economic, and social processes that led to the formation of particular property regimes in Govuton. It then presents ethnographic data on contemporary land use practices, property relations, and land disputes within the village. The goal of this analysis is to examine the impact of colonial codification of native customary laws on present-day society. Although many of the current land disputes may be understood as a legacy of the multiple legal systems implemented under colonial rule, it is also important to consider how land disputes are articulated in response to the values and social meanings attached to land and resource accumulation and how these issues are shaped by changes in the economic value of land, agriculture, and other resources, as well as changes in the nature of the state. As this study demonstrates, present-day land disputes result not only from legal pluralism but also from the continuously mobile nature of property relations, which have been redesigned to meet changes in the agrarian economy and political relations.

It was not until the late 1950s that the colonial policy of land settlement reached Govuton. In response to the anticipated land settlement, a group of local leaders mobilized to protect their communally owned village lands from colonial appropriation. Rather than request private title to lands that each family could rightfully claim under the colonial Land Laws of 1953, local leaders in Govuton turned to a little-used section of the land laws under which communal titles could be issued to villages, for "lands held for the common use and benefit of natives." Such communal titles were referred to in the land laws as "native reserves." The land Govuton's leaders wanted to protect in the native reserve included areas used for subsistence and commercial agriculture, as well as forested areas to which villagers traditionally had access for hunting and gathering of resources. Used by villagers for centuries, these lands and forests were both materially important in daily life and culturally significant in village folklore and ritual life.

Both archival data and oral histories shed light on the course of events in the formation of the native reserve in Govuton, often providing images that diverge in their accounts of the agency, or the motivating force, behind its establishment. Reports and letters produced by colonial administrators[3] emphasize the paternalistic need to protect natives from foreign land speculators. Letters from leaders in Govuton, as well as oral histories, express the desire to secure local access and traditional rights to lands in the face of potential state appropriation of village land, which would eventually open the door to land speculators. These accounts show how various actors employed colonial law in different ways to achieve the same goal—control over the land.

VIEWS FROM GOVUTON: PROTECTING TRADITIONAL LANDS

The impetus to form the native reserve in Govuton emerged as a result of local discontent with state polices that appeared to be aimed at state appropriation of village-owned agricultural and forest lands. In 1957, the director of agriculture expressed an interest in the highlands surrounding Govuton. A road connecting Govuton to the coast was near completion, and it was hoped that temperate fruits and vegetables could be grown commercially in the cool climate. At the request of the director of agriculture, the Lands and Survey Department began to survey the area. This was the first step required before land could be alienated to individuals for commercial, agricultural development. The arrival of the surveyors in Govuton signified that the state considered the land to be "state land." To the villagers in Govuton this meant that outsiders would soon follow, staking claims to what the state perceived as state land and what local people perceived as village land. Since native lands were still subject to compulsory acquisition by the state for plantation agriculture and other state projects, they had every reason to be concerned (Institute of Development Studies 1991:84).

Local leaders initially tried to resist the state's efforts to survey the land, claiming that the area in question fell within the village's "'reserve' for ratan

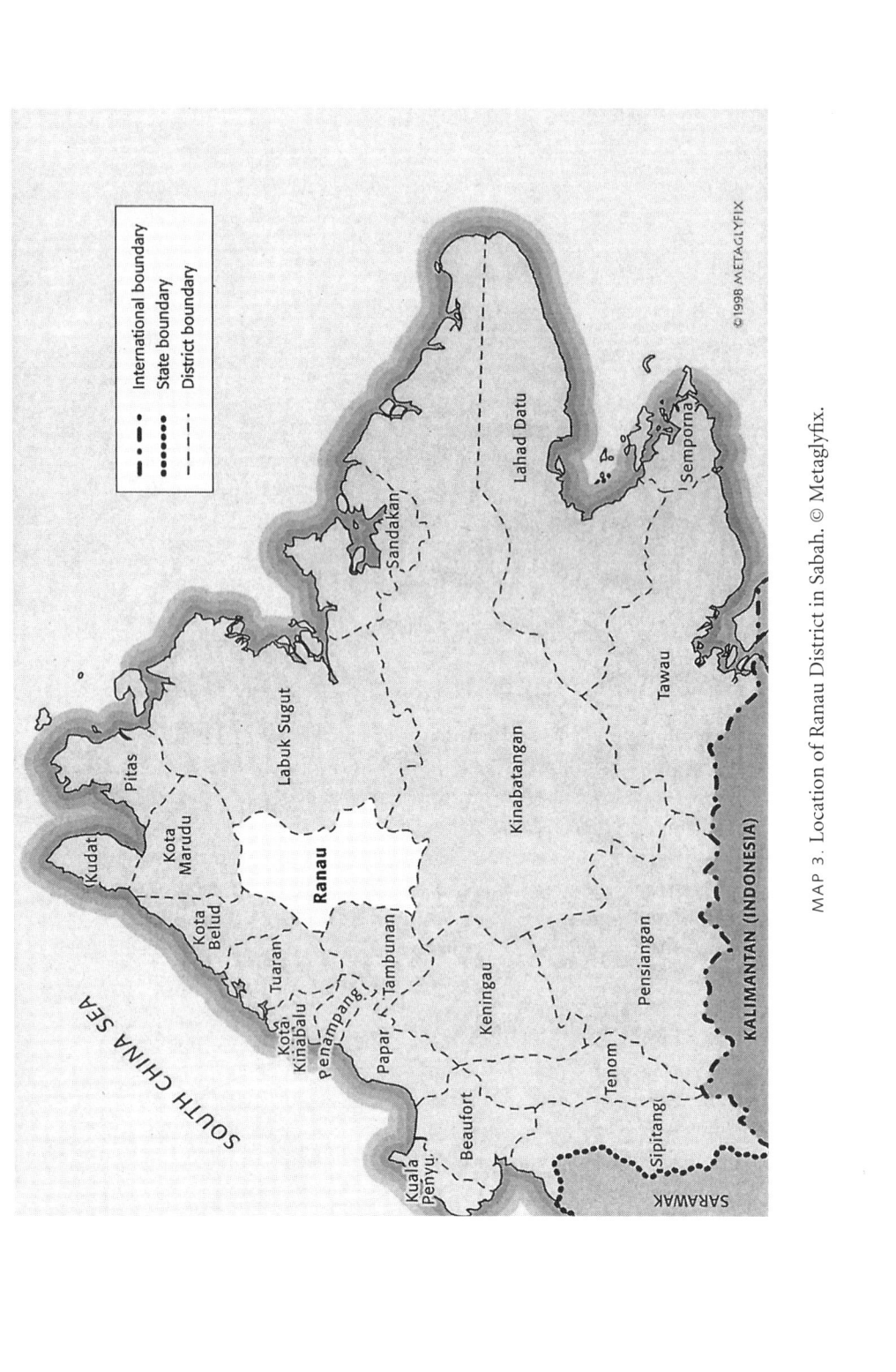

MAP 3. Location of Ranau District in Sabah. © Metaglyfix.

[*sic*] and roof-making leaves."[4] Thus, local leaders invoked notions of native customary rights of access, based on a tradition of using forest resources, in order to claim this area. Such rights of access were acknowledged in the Land Laws of 1953, which recognized that villages should be allowed access to timber reserved for subsistence use. But initial efforts to draw attention to native rights to the land were unsuccessful. In April 1958, the resident of the West Coast asked the conservator of forests to find "an alternative source of domestic timber and housing material for the village,"[5] indicating that the colonial administrator had no intention of allowing the villagers to claim the area in question on the basis of on native customary rights.

While some villagers were trying to gain legitimacy for the village's communal access to land within the statutory laws, others were trying to take advantage of the colonial project of land settlement by filing applications for native titles (individual, private ownership) to the land in question. Villagers did not speak with one voice nor act as a unified body in their attempts to seek state recognition of traditional rights of access to village land. These internal struggles over property rights within Govuton demonstrate how local people strategically used varying practices to gain access to land, asserting different interpretations of local property relations and state laws. Some asserted the primacy of their customary rights; others tried to use the new colonial land laws.

The primary advocate of community ownership of village land was a Govuton leader, Native Chief Gisil.[6] Native Chief Gisil found an ally within the colonial administration with the arrival of John Dusing as district officer for Ranau (see map 3). In 1961, Dusing recommended that the forested area around Govuton be declared a native reserve, thereby officially initiating the process of state recognition of village ownership of the land.[7] Although neither archival data nor oral histories state why Dusing supported the native reserve, there is some evidence to suggest that it was because he was the first district officer in Ranau who was a Dusun (the largest ethnic minority in Sabah and the ethnicity of the villagers in Govuton) and was sympathetic to native land matters. When Sabah achieved independence, the first native chief minister, Donald Stephens, appointed Dusing secretary of state. Tun Mustapha (the head of state) refused to support the appointment, claiming that Dusing would favor Dusun people in the distribution of government projects (Yahya Bin Mohamad 1990). Regardless of the reason the state supported the proposal for the native reserve, it was through political networks between the native chief from Govuton and the district officer from Ranau that the voices of leaders interested in village ownership of the land were privileged over other, dissenting, local voices. On November 1, 1966, Native Chief Gisil and the *orang tua* (headman) in Govuton officially applied to the government for the gazetting of 3,120 acres of land surrounding Govuton as a native reserve. Although the official signing of the gazette by the chief minister did not occur until 1983, some of the older men in Govuton remember helping the state surveyors to "plant stones" (*tenom batu,* meaning to set boundary markers) for the native reserve in 1968.[8] In the eyes of Govuton's residents, the native reserve and village ownership of the land and forests were recognized by the state by the late 1960s. The state, however, did not see it this way.

VIEWS FROM THE STATE: NATIVES AS UNSOPHISTICATED "WIGHTS"

A dominant discourse surrounding native land rights and land use systems emerged during the period when Sabah was ruled by the North Borneo Chartered Company and continued during Crown rule, as indicated in the colonial documents produced during this period. In one strand of this discourse, colonial administrators emphasized the perceived inability of natives to manage their lands in a rapidly changing market economy.[9] Evidence of this concern is found in the restrictions on natives from selling their native titles to nonnatives without governmental sanction. The notion behind this restriction was that natives did not understand commercial land transactions, and if they were not "protected from their own improvidence," they would sell all their land to foreign speculators and be left with no land of their own to cultivate.[10]

Debates within the colonial administration over the possibility that natives would sell all their lands to nonnatives peaked in the late 1950s. On one side were colonial officers who believed that the "North Borneo native is a poor unsophisticated wight,"[11] who is easy meat for a non-native land shark."[12] These officers felt that it was their paternalistic duty to protect natives "against the cunningness of the sophisticated non-natives, who carrot-wise, dangle treasury notes or trade goods before their noses."[13] Even in Peninsular Malaya official paternalism resulted in policies aimed at protecting the *orang asli* (lit. "the original people") from the "unseemly commercialization" of their life (Harper 1997:9). Commercialization of resources, apparently, was attractive only in the hands of Europeans. Yet other officers felt that the idea that natives were naïve regarding the commercial value of land was pure fiction. According to one colonial official:

The average North Borneo native is just as cute a land shark as any nonnative. Every native knows the value of a scruffy bit of land . . . to which he has done nothing for years and years, but which suddenly appreciated in value because of the proximity to urban . . . development or because it is served by a new road.[14]

Clearly, colonial administrators held contradictory images of the ability of natives to manage their land without colonial intervention. Records in the Ranau district office from the mid-1950s show that this debate was resolved in a way that represented concessions to both views: if natives wished to sell their lands to nonnatives, they could do so with government sanction, but they would be charged a substantial premium for the transfer of their native titles. Colonial officers in Ranau hoped that some natives would be deterred by the premiums that would lower the profits realized from the sale of their lands.[15] Importantly, in terms of state strategies of rule, if natives did choose to sell their lands, state profits would be high. Thus, state protection was offered to natives, yet they could choose to forfeit that protection for a price.

This debate undoubtedly influenced colonial administrators' decisions regarding the formation of the native reserve in Govuton. Although the impetus to form the native reserve came from leaders within Govuton, the final authority to gazette the area as a native reserve had to come from colonial authorities. Colonial land policies were dominated by a preoccupation with settling native claims only when such claims could be reduced to individual, private property. In other areas, native reserves had been abolished as land was opened up for cultivation (see chapter 1). Why then did the colonial state support the native reserve in Govuton, a situation in which village communal property was protected and no tax revenue was derived by the state? One way to make sense of the state's support is by examining the decision within the context of administrative debate over protecting natives and their lands from nonnative land speculators. In other words, colonial officers supported local communal rights in order to "protect" natives from losing their lands, despite the state's broader economic agendas. Viewed more critically, however, even this form of protection also had the effect of intensifying state control over the native population.[16] Local traditional land rights became contingent on formal sanction by and registration with the colonial government. Thus, local customary rights, which previously were derived largely from local practices, could gain legitimacy only through state legal institutions.[17] Although some villagers in Govuton may have celebrated their securing of communal title to large areas of their customary lands, time would show that they were assigned only limited rights, based in colonial laws. The Company constructed native customary law as unchanging and singular, removing the dynamic quality that characterizes native law and taking away the control local leaders had over adjudicating breeches of law. Ultimately, the formation of the native reserve isolated the natives in Govuton from broader economic changes associated with the commercialization of land that the state and nonnatives enjoyed throughout North Borneo, continuing the colonial trend of keeping natives in a marginal position in relation to the ruling elite. Although natives were "protected" in order to justify certain forms of colonial property law, the rhetoric of "protection" elides the important function of these laws in empowering the state.

The colonial laws concerning the native reserve were implemented by means of political and social networks drawn between local society and state agents.[18] Without pressure from the local population, it is unlikely that the state would have sanctioned the formation of the native reserve in Govuton. This case of Govuton emphasizes the notion that the relationship between state authority and local people is not always based on state domination and local resistance (see Nugent 1994). At the local level, conscious decision making and planning resulted in local attempts to negotiate with state agents to influence state practices. One of the goals of this study is to shed light on the political importance of local actions of autonomy, even when they take place within the limits of a predefined state power (contra Mitchell 1990).

CONTEMPORARY PROPERTY RELATIONS AND LAND DISPUTES IN THE NATIVE RESERVE

According to the Gazette Notification for the native reserve, the headmen[19] of Govuton and native chiefs of the district were appointed as the "trustees" of the reserve.[20] The Gazette Notification reads as follows: "(1) The Reserve is for the sole use of the native at Kampung [village] Govuton for the construction of dwelling houses and other ancillary buildings; (2) The residents of the Kampung [village] may be permitted to practice traditional Kampung [village] industries, rearing of fowl, domestic animals and do cash crop farming within the Reserve." Additionally, no individual may sell land within the native reserve since it is considered village communal property, not individual private property. These rules form the extent of the statutory laws about land use in Govuton and are a colonial representation of how native communal tenure should be codified into statutory law. Like other aspects of the colonial project, this synoptic reordering of property arrangements was an effort to make complex local society legible and manageable for centralized rule (see Scott 1998:33–45). The written colonial law delineating land use within the native reserve does not capture the complexity of local social relationships surrounding property rights in Govuton since in everyday practice statutory laws are overlaid with customary laws (*adat*), creating competing sources of legitimacy for property claims within the native reserve. This disjuncture between the government's panoptic visions and the local complexities of property relations led to conflicts in the interpretation of native rights to land and resources in the native reserve. Table 2.1, which summarizes the differences between statutory laws and local customary law governing land use within the native reserve, shows that state categories are far simpler that the native categories and practices.

Even though the Gazette Notification for the native reserve does not specify how the land in the reserve is used, the villagers divided the land into two local categories: village land (*tanah kampong*) and forest reserve (*hutan simpan*) (see map 4). "Village land" is the area within the native reserve where people may build houses, make vegetable and swidden gardens, graze their livestock, plant fruit trees, and build fish ponds (see fig. 2). The "forest reserve" surrounds the village. According to village *adat,* people may collect forest resources and wood for personal consumption in the forest reserve; they may also use it for hunting and gathering (see fig. 3). But even these local categories (village land and forest reserve) do not capture the complexity of daily practices or the de facto property relations formed through action. The discussion now examines the de facto practices of land use and property relations in Govuton and the ways in which contests over resource use play out in terms of divergent images of community[21] and divergent interpretations of rights of access.

Farmers in Govuton combine swidden rice agriculture with intensive cultivation of temperate vegetables for cash crops. As in many other communities in Malaysian and Indonesian Borneo, an "indigenous labor theory of value" forms the core of property relations (Li 1996).[22] Thus, a pioneer who clears the land from primary forest has permanent usufruct rights to that land. Although land in Govuton has been farmed for multiple generations and the original clearer of the forest has long since died, the notion that the first person to clear the forest can claim usufruct rights to the land is still embedded in local discourse surrounding property relations. This notion, how-

TABLE 2.1. Land Classification and Land Use in Govuton's Native Reserve

State land classification	Approved uses under statutory law	Village land classification	Approved uses under customary law
Native reserve	house construction making commercial gardens grazing of livestock practicing traditional industries	*tanah kampong* (village land)	house construction making small home gardens planting fruit trees making fish ponds grazing livestock making swidden gardens
		hutan simpan (forest reserve)	cutting trees for household construction and firewood hunting collecting wild vegetables

ever, is intertwined with principles of inheritance, as the usufruct rights conferred on the first person to clear the forest are passed from parents to children for generations. When asked how they came to have access to a specific plot of land, most villagers in Govuton said that they had inherited the land from their *nenek moyang* (D: ancestors), who first cleared it.

Primary usufruct rights in Govuton also include the right to sell the use rights to another person, if cash is needed. But the rights are limited in two ways: (1) it is expected that kin and neighbors needing a place to farm may borrow any land that is left fallow; and (2) useful products growing naturally on fallow land (such as bamboo [*Gigantochlae* spp.] and wild vegetables) as well as abandoned or naturalized crops (such as taro [*Caladium* spp.] and bananas [*Musa* spp.] that propagate naturally as fallow fields return to secondary growth) may be harvested by anyone needing them for consumption. These property relations correspond to Tania Li's findings in Sulawesi (1996), where rights of access to land delineate the boundaries of a "community," loosely defined in terms of kinship, proximity, and need.

Community access to fallow land in Govuton is elaborated through a "moral economy of peasants," in which reciprocity and exchange form the foundation of social relationships.[23] Central to this moral economy as expressed in Govuton is the notion that every member of the community

Hutan simpan: Forests

Tanah kampong: Houses and home gardens

Tanah kampong: Swidden fields

Terraced, commercial vegetable gardens

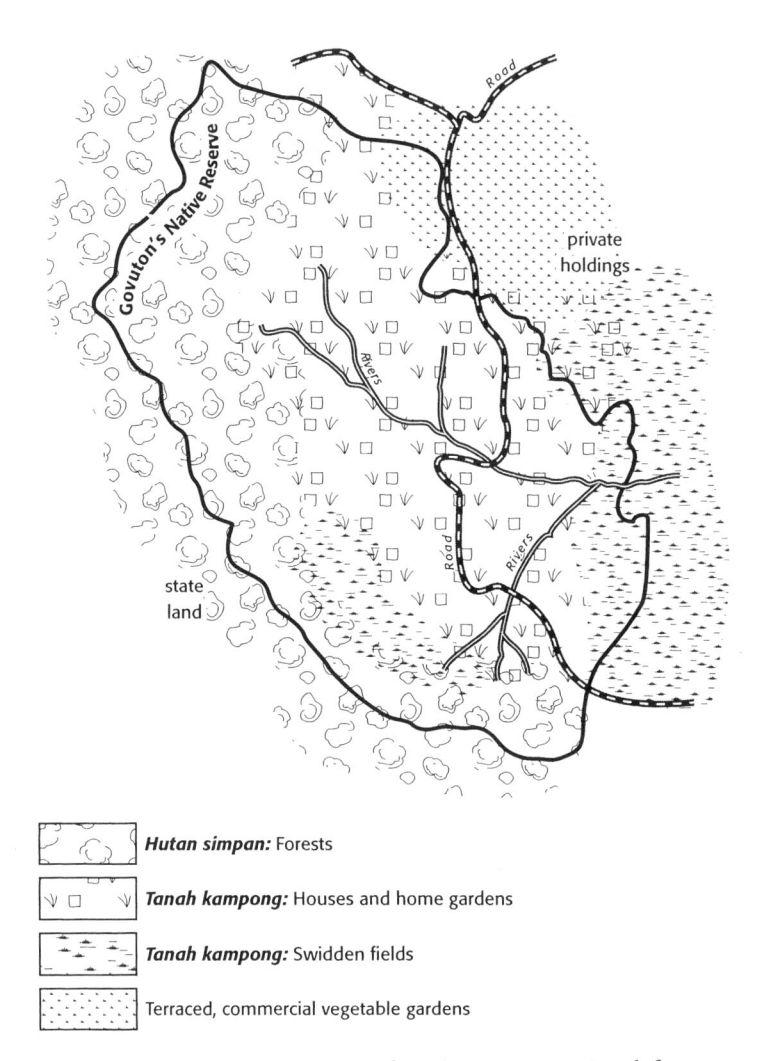

MAP 4. Land use in Govuton's native reserve. © Metaglyfix.

should have access to sufficient land and resources to meet basic subsistence needs. Such a notion of shared community access to agricultural land in the native reserve was possible in the past because of the agricultural cycle of a swidden field. Long fallow periods meant that land was available for community use when the family with primary use rights was not cultivating it. The use of fallow land by other people is culturally elaborated as a

FIG. 2. *Tanah kampong* in Govuton. Gardens closest to the houses are for vegetable cultivation. © 1996 by Michael J. Doolittle.

valuable service in Govuton since the secondary forest is kept back, and the owner is spared the hard labor of reopening the land in the future when he or she returns to it. Rather than emphasize the important ecological functions of regeneration for the swidden-fallow cycle, as do many other ethnic groups in Malaysia and Indonesia (see Dove 1983), villagers in Govuton place more significance on the value of keeping regeneration in check.[24]

These community rights of access to fallow village land are not well-articulated rights in present-day social life and currently are being subsumed as a result of two converging economic trends. First, as some villagers turn to wage labor instead of farming, their family's land lies fallow for extended periods of time. Second, an increasing emphasis on intensive, commercial vegetable agriculture means that some land is under constant cultivation.

FIG. 3. *Hutan simpan* in Govuton. Forested area is in the background and agriculture and houses are in foreground (*tanah kampong*). Swidden fields are on the steep hillside to the left. © 1996 by Michael J. Doolittle.

Land is thus removed from the swidden-fallow cycle and is no longer available to kin and other villagers in need. Consequently, although there may be more fallow land than in the past, if a farmer decides to use it for permanent agriculture, he or she effectively privatizes and encloses it, making it inaccessible to other villagers for an indefinite period. When a farmer uses previously fallowed land for permanent agriculture, he or she changes the terms by which land is accessible to community and kin; the land is removed from the village production system to generate income for an individual. The shift from reliance on swidden agriculture to intensive, permanent agriculture has thus rendered the property relations surrounding the community use of fallow land problematic.

In other places in Indonesian Borneo, research has suggested that notions of ethnic or community identity can come together in powerful ways to support an "ethic of access" that tempers the inequitable accumulation of resources that can arise as a result of commercial intensification (Peluso 1996). In Indonesian Borneo, this ethic of access is most prominent with crops that have social and ritual meaning, such as the long-living durian trees, which have complex intergenerational inheritance patterns and imbue the landscape with a social history of the community. Thus, kinship ties and community investment in the landscape link kin and villagers together in shared ownership of the commercially valuable durian trees.[25] Conversely, Nancy Peluso shows that crops such as rubber have different social meaning, and neither individuals nor communities form emotional attachments to rubber crops. Thus, land cultivated with rubber lacks an ethic of access and as a result is considered private, individual property.

A similar, although less clear, trend illustrating varying social meanings attached to crop type can be seen in Govuton. The notion of community access to fallowed swidden land can be seen as an ethic of access. Kinship and community ties and reciprocal relationships of exchange dictate that kin and neighbors in need should have access to fallow land. But at present, the more powerful emphasis is on the commercial cultivation of vegetables, overriding the ethic of access. In areas where people cultivate plots of land for the commercial production of vegetables there is an absence of locally agreed rules about how much land a single family can cultivate on a permanent basis. Wealthier families hire laborers to help them keep as much of their lands under cultivation as possible. In addition, sharecropping arrangements are arising, in which a family still allows neighbors or kin to use their land, but the primary owner demands a portion of the harvest or the profit (usually one-third) in return for the use of the land. In these instances, the community rights of access to fallow lands, or a local ethic of access, are overridden by the growing commercial production of crops, in which intensive commercial vegetable cultivation is gradually replacing swidden cultivation.

Under this current cultivation strategy of commercial vegetable crops, individual ambitions of wealth and resource accumulation are being emphasized over the needs of kin and neighbors. Consequently, the changing property relations are disrupting other social institutions. Various village members depict this trend differently. Some villagers draw on national discourses of development and modernity to validate their hard work and initiative to participate in agricultural development. One of the village native chiefs, for instance, believes that it is important for the village to do something more with its community forest reserves than "just letting trees grow." He has developed a master plan that would divide the village into different zones for vegetable cultivation, animal husbandry, and a restaurant and hostel for tourists visiting Kinabalu Park. In discussion with regional political and economic leaders, he has heard that a Japanese company has expressed interest in establishing tea, apple, mulberry, and mushroom agricultural schemes in Govuton. He believes that these developments would be good for the economy of the village. Part of his plan would include rezoning of land within the native reserve. He hopes that individuals could gain more secure title to their land, placing Govuton on a par with other villages in the region where people have individual title to land.[26]

Other villagers draw on local discourses that validate indigenous technical knowledge, innovation, and farming skills that allow one farmer to be more successful than others. Gupak, for instance, is known by everyone in the village as the most successful commercial vegetable agriculturalist; he is also one of the older farmers. Always eager to innovate in his garden, he experimented with growing coffee in the 1940s but found that it was too labor intensive. In 1946, he was the first person in Govuton to plant commercial vegetable crops, drawing on the resources of the Department of Agriculture. He says he now makes a profit of about M$6000 a year from his vegetables alone. With an understanding that farming is a long-term endeavor, he refused an offer of M$60,000 from an entrepreneur interested in purchasing his land. "I can make more than that from the land in ten years," he told me.[27]

Finally, other villagers see the trend toward resource accumulation as a disintegration of the cultural values that emphasize village equity in access to resources over individual accumulation. For instance, an anonymous letter dated June 1993 was sent to the district officer complaining about one man's accumulation of land within Govuton:

> The people of [Govuton] say with sadness and ask for sympathy from the District Officer since we have suffered abuse from Intang. He thinks he is rich and therefore can do whatever he wants. Those who have suffered under Intang need to work together to solve the problem that they are facing. We believe that if this issue is not defended by us our village will become the property of one person. Already several houses have been destroyed by him so he can make a garden.... Nearly everyone, from the young children to old people are involved in Intang's work as he buys our land either through sweet talk or force.... We are less loved than dogs by Intang who extinguishes us as he wishes. (Translated from Malaysian)

While this letter may be overly dramatic, it clearly indicates the depth of local antipathy towards Intang, who has consolidated ownership of a large amount of village land for extensive commercial cultivation of vegetables. Some of the mechanisms Intang has used to consolidate ownership of property are examined below.

New cultivation systems necessitate changes in village property relations (Appell 1985, 1987). Because there have been few formal discussions about the distribution of rights under this trend toward commercial and intensive agriculture, the same plot of land can be claimed by different parties, each relying on various strategic discourses to substantiate claims. For instance, a person may claim the right to cultivate fallow land through notions of communal rights of access. Yet with the new emphasis on commercial vegetable production, another person may claim the right to exclude community access on the basis of his or her primary rights of access derived from inheritance principles. Conflicting ways to legitimize claims on land become particularly problematic when a person begins to cultivate permanent crops on land previously left fallow by another person, thereby indefinitely removing the land from community access.

Many people in Govuton do not anticipate a future as agriculturists. They are counting on profits from intensive vegetable production to educate their children and to launch them in nonagrarian careers. Enclosing land in the native reserve for permanent, commercial vegetable agriculture is one of the ways by which profits can be realized. But, as the following land dispute demonstrates, an ability to appropriate fallow village land for individual, permanent use depends, at least in part, on integration into the broader legal, administrative, and economic systems outside Govuton.

Intang was one of the wealthier and more influential men in Govuton in 1996. He has thirteen children and a healthy belly, signs of a prosperous life. He has several gardens that are cultivated by day laborers and owns a gas cylinder business (cooking gas) and a small village shop. Despite all these enterprises, Intang has plenty of time to sit on his porch and talk with people passing by, a luxury few in Govuton can afford. His home is one of the few that has a cement foundation and sawed planks for walls. For many years, he worked for the district officer. During this time, he formed social networks with state officials in the district office, links that allowed him to act as a broker of state-derived power at the local level. For instance, Intang had unusual success in obtaining native title to land that he owned in villages outside Govuton. When I inquired with other villagers about land matters, I was often told that I should seek out Intang. After many months in the village, I learned that Intang's land expertise was viewed locally with some hostility since he has not necessarily shared his good fortune with his neighbors and, in fact, has used his skills in land acquisition to take resources away from neighbors. Like Intang, many people in Govuton owned land in neighboring villages and had filed applications for native title for these lands. Yet, unlike Intang, most of them had waited for more than twenty-five years, and still are waiting, for their titles from the state. Without connections to individuals in the Lands and Survey Department, connections that Intang had, applications for native title take decades to be processed. According to Intang, he received his titles quickly because he has close, intimate friends (*teman rapat*) in the Lands and Survey Department who put his applications on the fast track.[28]

Owning title to land held outside Govuton has far-reaching effects. In order to secure a bank loan, a person must provide a title to land as collateral. Thus, Intang has been able to borrow money from the bank to launch his business enterprises, although most other people in Govuton are unable to do so. When people in Govuton need money, unable to turn to a bank, they turn to Intang. As a moneylender Intang provides a valuable service, yet at the same time he is often disliked and distrusted. Many people feel that he demands too high interest payments on his loans and that he is taking advantage of less fortunate villagers. In short, Intang oversteps culturally acceptable boundaries of exchange and reciprocity by profiting from loaning money to villagers, yet he also provides a necessary service in a growing cash economy.

Intang's accumulation of wealth *outside* Govuton has facilitated his accumulation of village land *within* the native reserve. He owns a large, permanent vegetable garden on village land in the native reserve, and he sells the products from this garden in Kota Belud, a market center. This piece of land is unusually valuable for the commercial production of vegetables because it is located near the road and near a source of water for irrigation. Furthermore, it is one of the flattest pieces of land in this hilly region and, therefore, is less work to cultivate (see figs. 4 and 5). Intang bought the use rights to this particular plot from another villager, Momin, who claimed that, although his father had not cultivated the land for years, he had inherited the land from him. Thus, in order to gain access to this land, Intang strategically used the discourse of inheritance as the legitimate locus of ownership. Intang then maintained his ownership through permanent cultiva-

FIG. 4. Villagers prepare swidden fields on the steep hillsides in Govuton. © 1996 by Michael J. Doolittle.

tion, which further legitimated his claims through a labor theory of ownership. But by planting permanent crops, Intang has effectively removed the land from community access, creating local tensions.

Momin's right to sell the land to Intang was questioned by other residents in Govuton. Momin no longer lives in Govuton. Villagers argue that since his father had essentially abandoned his land, leaving it uncultivated for decades, it had become available for communal access. Indeed, another family, headed by Kemburong, had built a house on a small portion of this land. When Intang bought use rights from Momin, he evicted Kemburong from the house she had lived in for more than ten years.

Kemburong felt that she had primary use rights, at least to the area where her house was situated. She used the discourse of the rights of community access to abandoned land within the native reserve, on the basis of need, to legitimate her claim. Intang argued that he had purchased primary rights from the person who claimed to have inherited primary use rights. When the dispute went to the native court at the district level, it was ruled that, by abandoning the land and moving out of the village, Momin's father (and subsequently Momin himself) had relinquished his rights. The broader community then had access to the land, and Kemburong had the right to build

FIG. 5. Intang's commercial vegetable garden. Flat land, a raised irrigation pipe, and an abandoned house are in the foreground. © 1996 by Michael J. Doolittle.

a house there. The native court reasoned that abandoned village land had reverted to community land, and, therefore, Momin no longer retained the primary use rights nor did he have the right to sell rights to the land. The native court thus supported the customary law that allowed villagers in need to claim use rights to abandoned land within the native reserve.

Despite this ruling in the native court, Kemburong abandoned her house and Intang enclosed the land with a fence and began cultivating vegetables. Local gossip suggested that Intang had offered Kemburong money to move off the valuable piece of land after the court ruling. Kemburong herself denied this, but simply stated that she "felt unhappy" (*merasa sangat tidak senang*) about the land after the court battle and wanted to move.[29] This case demonstrates how cultural notions of access to property are adapted to meet new conditions and, in turn, structure daily land use practices (cf. Li 1996:509). By cultivating the land with permanent crops, installing an irrigation system, and building a fence, Intang strengthened his future claims to the land. Yet Kemburong's dilapidated house on one corner of Intang's garden provides a constant reminder that Intang acquired the land through contest and negotiation. Intang's ability to appropriate the land, even though the native court ruled against him, highlights the notion that his externally derived wealth and power provided him with leverage in local disputes. Intang's power allowed him not only to override the court ruling through his actions but also to alter potentially the future trajectory of changes in property relations in the native reserve.

This dispute shows that land rights provided by rules and traditions are not guaranteed but, instead, serve as points of leverage in ongoing negotiations (Li 1996). Although the court attempted to enforce the rules associated with customary law, neither the court nor other villagers were able to compel Intang to leave the land.[30] Instead, Intang successfully wielded his power and through his actions altered the ways in which customary rights of access to property are negotiated. Furthermore, villagers did not resort to social ostracism since many were dependent upon Intang for loans and work. Thus, negotiations over land rights include references to power and wealth that are not necessarily encompassed in the rules and traditions of customary law, but are powerful enough to change rules of access to land. In this particular dispute, Intang's individual ambition to provide his children with finances to pursue livelihoods outside Govuton overpowered notions of community access to fallow land. It is too early to tell whether this trend will continue. Perhaps other villagers will try to follow Intang's initiative and secure permanent rights to fallow land in the native reserve through the practice of permanent vegetable production.

The trend in Govuton toward individual accumulation of land, which is overriding older practices of community access to village land, must be viewed in the broader, regional context. Govuton's native reserve stands out in marked contrast to areas governed by other forms of native property rights in contemporary Sabah. Many native claims to lands elsewhere were recognized in colonial statutory law through the use of native titles. Today, farmers who have native titles may sell or rent their land without significant interference from the government (unlike during the more restrictive period prior to 1950). They can also secure bank loans in order to buy additional lands or improve current lands, using their native titles as collateral. Conversely, natives within Govuton's native reserve are restricted by the colonial codification of native customary laws that limits rights to land within the native reserve to use rights only. People in Govuton feel hampered by this restriction; in today's political economy, where access to cash is equally as important as access to land, the inability to sell or lease land or to secure bank loans is a significant impediment to individual rights and economic mobility. In order for people to advance in contemporary Sabah, money is necessary for schools, transportation, medicine, and other material goods, expenses that were less important in the 1950s when access to good agricultural land and forest resources were the primary factors that determined a family's quality of life.

Many people in Govuton express frustration with the form of local property rights that governs the native reserve. Their concerns center on the fact that usufruct rights to land in the native reserve are too limiting, particularly when compared with the rights of natives elsewhere in Sabah. For instance, some poor villagers complain that if they need money, they can receive only a small sum from community members for the sale of their use rights to land; land without a defensible title has very little commercial value. If a villager in Govuton wishes to sell use rights to a plot of land, he or she can usually obtain roughly M$500.[31] A similar plot of land held under native title outside the native reserve is worth between M$2,500 and M$3,000 because the title has value as collateral and is transferable without restrictions.

Other villagers complained that cultivating land in the native reserve is more work and more costly than cultivating land owned under native title, because goats, pigs, cows, and water buffalo all graze freely in the native reserve; to keep livestock out of their gardens farmers must build fences. Under native title, the situation is reversed; people must keep their livestock tethered or fenced on their own land. Individual rights take precedence over community rights outside the native reserve, whereas inside the native reserve the opposite is true.

In this context, the actions and discursive strategies of people such as Intang make sense, as they are competing with farmers outside the native reserve who have private property. The formation of the native reserve produced a static colonial interpretation of native life and native property relations during a particular political and economic period when village ownership of the land, reciprocity, and barter were more valuable than individual title to land. While leaders in Govuton in the 1950s saw the native reserve as a way to assert local autonomy and protect traditional lands, villagers today have less autonomy over land matters than do other natives in Sabah who own land under native title. The regional political-economic context has changed, making the native reserve less appealing to some villagers, particularly those who desire to grow commercial vegetable crops.

Conversely, other villagers find protection in and benefit from the native reserve, particularly when they have access to the forest reserve. Table

2.1 represents some of the ways in which villagers utilize the forest reserve on a daily basis.[32] Interestingly, there does not appear to be any direct relationship between wage income and use of the forest. For instance, Lumbow's wages are similar to those of Selimboi, Gitom, and Lehimboi (roughly M$1,200 per month), yet his family relies on forest resources much less than the other families do. In a three-month period, Lumbow's household only rarely spent time collecting forest resources. In contrast, groups of women from the households of Selimboi, Gitom, and Lehimboi spent roughly one-third of their working time collecting forest resources. Cultural values may be as important as subsistence needs in determining use of the forest reserve. For instance, according to Selimboi, "Sometimes you just prefer the taste of wild *lemiding* [D: forest ferns] instead of eggplant." And during special festival times, the older villagers enjoy roasted songbirds as an accompaniment to their *tapai* (rice wine) drinking. The fact that all the village land is not privately owned means that people in Govuton can enjoy wild foods to which they might not otherwise have access. For other villagers, such as Gamid, whose average monthly income is only M$201,[33] the forest reserve provides vital subsistence foods. He and his family rely heavily on access to the forest reserve in order to survive. Out of a three-month period, members of Gamid's household spent a significant amount of their working time in the forest gathering resources. They sold none of the resources, but rather used them for household consumption (see table 2.2).

In contrast to Intang, Gamid has five children, all of whom are quite thin. He and his wife are gone everyday from sunrise to sunset, working in the garden and then later in the forest collecting firewood and wild taro to feed to their pig and chickens. Gamid's house is one of the few in Govuton that is made entirely with traditional forest resources. The walls and floors are made of bamboo and tree bark, the roof of palm leaves. And their only source of cooking fuel is firewood. While most homes in Govuton are constructed with some products from the forest, the majority also have some features made from materials bought from outside the village, such as tin roofs and sawed planks. And while most have a hearth for cooking, they also have gas stoves to supplement the hearth. Whereas Intang's gardens are on flat land near the road, Gamid's are a half hour away by foot and are located on an incredibly steep slope, where erosion control is one of his primary concerns. Since the land does not produce enough food for the family, and Gamid has no wage labor, his wife makes a small income from selling yeast cakes used to make rice wine. A look at the wide range of ways in which people use the land and forest resources shows that property rights and access to

TABLE 2.2. Household Income and Dependence on Garden Produce and Forest Resources in Govuton

Name of head of household and household size	Average monthly income	Percentage of income from sale of nontimber forest products and produce from garden	Percentage of days spent gathering in nontimber forest products over 3–month period	Types of resources collected
Lehimboi 9	M$1,392	none	35	firewood, fish, squirrels, wild fruits, wild vegetables, fodder for pigs
Gitom 14	M$1,164*	garden:14 forest: none	34	firewood, fish, frogs, monkeys, birds, snake, armadillo, wild fruits, wild vegetables, fodder for pigs
Lumbow 18	M$1,078*	garden: 75 forest: none	4	fish, wild vegetables
Selimboi 15	M$1,062*	garden: 6 forest: none	30	firewood, fish, wild fruits, wild vegetables, fodder for pigs
Siking 4	M$1,025*	garden: 30 forest: none	10	firewood, fish, wild vegetables
Masin 10	M$878*	garden: 6 forest: none	41	firewood, fish, wild fruits, wild vegetables, fodder for pigs
Gamid 5	M$201*	garden: 69 forest: none	89	firewood, fish, wild fruits, wild vegetables, fodder for pigs

*This figure combines both wage labor and income from the sale of garden produce and forest products in markets.

resources within the native reserve vary tremendously, depending on both material and cultural needs.

Many factors influence the transition from community rights of access to land and resources within the native reserve to the individualization of rights to land within the reserve. Some villagers, such as Intang (described above), respond to material and political incentives for individualization. Others have material or cultural reasons for maintaining community access to land and natural resources. The colonial codification of native customary law does not adequately capture the complexities of the contemporary resource use regimes in Govuton, and as the village becomes increasingly stratified internally, villagers find it more difficult to reach consensus regarding rights of access to resources. In the face of continuously mobile social relations, the future of rights to land and resources in Govuton is by no means predictable. The current trend toward the individualization of land may continue as certain individuals gain power and wealth, increasing village stratification. Or villagers may once again mobilize to change the current statutory laws and reach a new agreement regarding the particularities of community ownership of the land and natural resources within the native reserve. This would slow village stratification, and individuals seeking substantial profits from natural resources would have to look elsewhere. What is certain is that the transformation of property relations will continue to reflect local and regional struggles over power, wealth, cultural meaning, and community identity. And these struggles will reveal the fractures within a community that is economically stratified and diverse in members' desires for change (cf. Ortner 1995).

Different state agencies, with diverse mandates, also present varying representations of community in their efforts to legitimize their control over land and resources. Of particular interest for Govuton is how the Forestry Department depicts farmers in order to contest village common ownership to the forested land within Govuton's native reserve.

The Forestry Department has a counterclaim on part of the land in the native reserve. Measuring 3,120 acres, the reserve was recognized locally in the late 1960s. Yet it was not officially gazetted until 1983 under the approval of the chief minister. In the same year, the Similiu Forest Reserve[34] was also approved by the chief minister as a protection forest under the authority of the Forestry Department. The Similiu Forest Reserve incorporates most of the forested land with Govuton's native reserve. In fact, there was an overlap of approximately 1,500 acres between the village's native reserve and the government's forest reserve (see map 5). As a protection forest, this means that laws strictly forbid any use of the forest resources. These laws are in direct conflict with the laws surrounding the use of resources within the native reserve.

These types of conflicting claims on land in Sabah are not unusual. They occur as a side-effect of the bureaucratic nature of the land alienation process. One forest ranger described the process as follows: the Forestry Department determines from aerial photographs areas of "good" forest cover (areas with extensive crown coverage). The area is then marked as a forest reserve on a map, giving it legitimacy through the science of mapmaking. The Forestry Department often fails to check with the Lands and Survey Department for any preexisting claims to the land. Instead, the proposal for a forest reserve goes directly to the chief minister for approval. According to one senior official in the Forestry Department, this process was particularly prevalent in the early 1980s (the time during which the Similiu Forest Reserve was gazetted), because the Forest Department was struggling to fulfill the mandate of the National Forest Enactment, which required that each state in the Malaysian Federation protect 30 percent of its forests. During this period there was a heightened sense of urgency in the Forestry Department to demonstrate its commitment to forest protection. As a result, the democratic, but lengthy, process of notifying the Lands and Survey Department in order to cross-check for preexisting claims was subverted in the interest of expediency.[35]

These conflicting claims to the forest land in Govuton have not been officially resolved. Forest Department officials, guided by an image of rural communities and shifting cultivators carried over from the colonial period, legitimize their claims to manage and protect the forest. Many Forestry Department officials argue that they must keep the Govuton villagers out of the forest reserve because they are "primitive" shifting cultivators who will destroy the forest, without thought for the future. As evidenced in the earlier description of local land use strategies, this claim has no basis. Villagers in fact have a deep respect for the importance of their forest resources. Furthermore, since the Forestry Department lacks the money and staff to police the Similiu Forest Reserve, Govuton villagers (who have legitimate claims on the forest resources) have unrestricted access to the forest. To date, however, they have not cleared the forests (even as the Forestry Department continues to suggest it will); rather, they hunt in it and collect forest resources for food and house construction. For the most part,

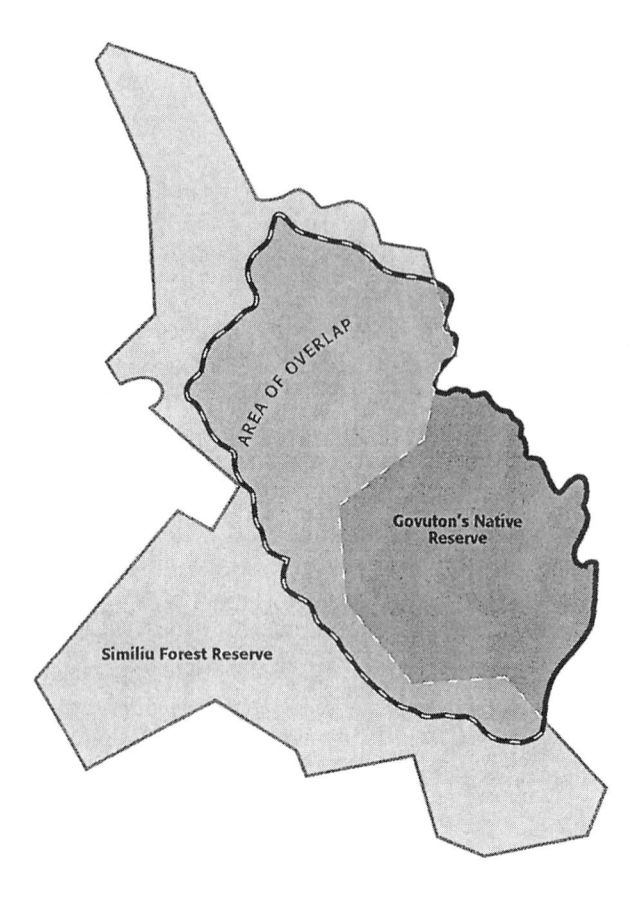

MAP 5. Overlapping boundaries between Govuton's native reserve and Similiu Forest Reserve. © Metaglyfix.

the villagers in Govuton use and manage the forest in the reserve in a conservative manner.

If the Forestry Department ever succeeds in prohibiting local use of the forest in its efforts to "protect" it, not surprising would be an increase in intensive and destructive agriculture on the *tanah kampong* (or village land within the native reserve) in order to compensate for villagers' loss of access to valuable resources in the *hutan simpan*. Certainly the experience of the burning of Bukit Hempuen suggests that local reactions to state actions can be unexpected. Yet officials of the Forestry Department rarely take such a broad view toward their actions; usually they fail to realize that their decisions will produce reactions in the local population that may undermine the Forestry Department's goals of resource protection.

The preceding case studies and analysis of property relations in Govuton from the 1950s to the present illustrate several points relating to the nature of both state-society relations and property relations. First, while states may attempt to systematize and organize the world according to principles that simplify local property relations (Scott 1998), local responses may pose obstacles or present alternatives that allow for creative and new forms of state control and local autonomy (Agrawal and Gibson 1999a, 1999b). These interactions between state and society take place from asymmetrical positions of power. Thus, while villagers in Govuton initially resisted state appropriation of village land in the 1950s, they acted within the new legal structures of colonial rule. In the end, a process of negotiation allowed for local control over community land, yet the realm of negotiation was restricted by the parameters of statutory law. State sanctioning of village community land as a native reserve stands out as an unusual practice in colonial law in Sabah. Elsewhere in Sabah, colonial administrators knowingly overlooked complex patterns of local property relations in their efforts to settle quickly native claims to land. In Govuton, local leaders who refused to allow their communally owned village lands to be appropriated by the state influenced colonial administrators.

Second, any state intervention in local property relations, no matter how partial or incomplete, consolidates state power over society. The native reserve emerged as an innovative form of state rule, created in response to local negotiation with state agents over property claims, and thus represents a moment when the state retreated in its ambition of providing each person with individual title to land. Yet, at the same time, the colonial state asserted control over native lands by providing Govuton with a community-held title that was based on colonial imaginings of how native customary laws should be codified in a singular, static way, not in a plural, multiple, and diverse way as customary institutions are known to be. In doing so, the colonial state took away from local leaders the ability to change their customary law to meet changes that they might encounter in the future. Therefore, the native reserve intensified state control, since recognition of native customary rights to land in statutory law was contingent on government sanction. Although local people were able to alter the direction of state control over people and land, ultimately the broader trend toward rural incorporation into the state's project of land settlement continued.

Third, while colonial control was redefined through the formation of the native reserve, so were local property relations transformed. In the past, an ethic of access contributed to the notions of community use of fallow land within the native reserve. Today, however, this ethic is increasingly eroded by individualized ownership of community land through the practice of permanent cultivation of commercial vegetables. The gradual enclosure of community land is motivated, in part, by farmers striving to profit from agriculture so that their children can be educated and find employment outside of the agricultural sector. But these individual goals are not compatible with an ethic of community access to fallow land. As a result, contests over access to land in Govuton are articulated in terms of competing representations of community and divergent images of rights of access. Notions of an ethic of access and rights to fallow land within the native reserve are placed in opposition to the principles associated with inheritance and the rights to transfer or sell inherited land. Thus, the traditions associated with customary land rights in Govuton do not guarantee access to land, but instead serve as points of leverage in ongoing negotiations (cf. Li 1996). Furthermore, cultural notions of access to property are adapted to meet the growing market economy and in turn structure daily land use practices.[36] Individual access to land is taking precedence over community access and is transforming property relations within the native reserve, despite its communal status in the land laws. Moreover, in struggles over access, negotiating points not only are based on internal village social relations but also rely on wealth and power that arise from external relationships. In their contests over access to land at the local level, the most powerful people in Govuton, such as Intang, rely on power derived from outside the community.

Fourth, by focusing on the temporal variations in local perceptions of the native reserve, the case of Govuton demonstrates that legal definitions of customary land tenure may be empowering in one time and place, yet disempowering in another. The formation of the native reserve countered colonial appropriation of local lands in the late 1950s and strengthened local claims of access to traditional lands. Moreover, this move allowed the community of Govuton to claim collectively more land than they would have been able to claim individually. Under colonial land laws, natives could claim access only to land that they could prove they had cultivated continuously for at least three years. But by drawing on the colonial concept of a native reserve, the village of Govuton was able to secure community access to land that the village used not only for cultivation but also for hunting and gathering forest resources. However, some villagers in Govuton feel that the native reserve is disempowering in today's political economy. Unable to gain access to credit or to sell their land for a significant profit, they express their frustration at not having a permanent and transferable title to the land they use. For these villagers, their ability to be socially mobile in a growing market economy is entirely limited by their inability to sell land. Other villagers, however, rely on the native reserve's forest resources for subsistence needs and cultural values, and they feel fewer pressures to convert their land to cash. Individual ownership of all land within the native reserve would make these uses of resources problematic.

In Govuton, local leaders were able to use the colonial legal system to protect a large area of native traditional lands from alienation to outsiders, and in the 1950s and 1960s local leaders were able to co-opt the colonial organizing symbols and legal practices to their advantage. However, social relations and property relations are always in flux. Although the formation of the native reserve may have frozen a particular vision of "native customary law" in the colonial legal system, it did not end local-level conflicts over cultural identity and power or the ways in which these conflicts are used as negotiating points in struggles over access to land. The transformation of property relations in Govuton continues today as these struggles are played out in daily practices that effectively overturn the statutory laws regarding the native reserve and that reflect other struggles within the social and historical contexts in which they are embedded.[37]

Finally, these conclusions have significance for advocates of reinvigorating native customary law and community control over natural resources. Conservation groups in Sabah have argued that the legal entity of the native reserve may be a useful tool to promote both community control over natural resources and conservation.[38] And advocates all over Southeast Asia are proposing to strengthen native customary law (Lynch and Talbott 1995; Moniaga 1993) and develop community-based conservation plans. Yet as this analysis shows, the notion of a native reserve relies on a static rendition of native customary law and on images of villagers in Sabah as homogeneous and timeless in their cultural identity and their natural resource management regimes. This constitution of community and native customary law does not adequately represent local concerns and has even become the source of contemporary conflicts over natural resource use. As the case study of Govuton illustrates, individuals within a community can have drastically varying notions about appropriate resource use, and one individual's connection to external forms of power and authority can be used to suppress alternative discourses and practices regarding resource use and management. External actors or institutions that attempt to form community-based conservation projects, or in any way alter a community's resource use patterns, must seek to understand the nuances of community identity, the potential conflicts over resource use between various sectors of the community, which local voices are heard and which are suppressed, and the local history of changes in property.

THREE

RESOURCES, IDEOLOGIES, AND NATIONALISM

The Politics of Development in Postcolonial Sabah

THE EXERCISE OF RURAL DEVELOPMENT IN SABAH, WHICH DETERMINES ACcess to and claims over resources, can be seen as a mechanism of state rule that justifies centralized control over local people and their lands.[1] An analysis of political patronage systems and rural development programs in Sabah reveals that elements of state policies and practices combine to result in the exercise of power over people and natural resources, a pattern that James Ferguson (1994) identifies as pervasive in development programs. Development practices do not necessarily raise the standard of living, as they are expected to, but do facilitate the expansion and entrenchment of the ruling, national ideology at the local level. In the context of Malaysia, expansion of state power imposes the ideology of Malayization and Islamization on all citizens, under the guise that these characteristics are "necessary" and "normal" components of a modern state. As a result, development plays a large role in the postcolonial state's claim to legitimacy; it is a central strategy for building a modern nation in which narrower concepts of national identity are integrated into local life (Majid Cooke 1999, 2002). Core concepts of national identity are presented as part of the development process as "normal" state activities; they are supposedly in the "national interest" and impervious to politics.[2] However, through emphasis on Islam and Malaysian nationalism, postcolonial rule in Malaysia is reshaping local identity, and through emphasis on modernization and economic growth, the state gains control over its citizens and their modes of production. Such narrow views of who constitute governable citizens are rarely above politics. The tensions between the exercise of power and the ultimate achieving of control over people and their resources are revealed in the following analysis.

Discussions of land laws and property rights, which were the primary focus of colonial interventions, have all but disappeared from state-sponsored discourses in contemporary Malaysia. Yet present-day development projects still clearly influence resource use through their endorsement of certain types of agriculture, uses of forest resources, types of property regimes, and "modern" actions and appearances considered desirable for the rural population. Development projects are an arena in which to explore the nature of state rule and state-society relations in contemporary Malaysia, just as land settlement is in the colonial period. Comparison of the two highlights similarities between forms of state rule in the two periods. That is not to suggest that the imperatives of the colonial and postcolonial states are the same; in fact, dramatic differences exist between the goals of the two states. Under Chartered Company rule, the primary goal of the state was to produce a profit through the extractive mining of natural resources. Since Independence, the goal of the postcolonial state has been to develop Malaysia into a modern, industrialized nation and to foster nationalism. Yet *despite* the conspicuous differences in the goals of the state in the colonial and postcolonial periods, the way in which state rule is accomplished is remarkably similar. Although the precise activities have changed, the institutional structures that allow the ruling elite, whether British or Malay, to insert state control into the livelihoods of marginal people remain the same. In both periods the production of knowledge about rural people and their resource use strategies has served to consolidate state power, and in both periods the policies resulting from the production of knowledge about the target population (rural subsistence agriculturalists) have limited local control over resources. But just as the colonial rule over native people and their land was fragile and contingent on specific peoples and their actions and on specific localities, postcolonial development practices have had only partial success in shaping a population of "modern," compliant nationalists out of Sabah's rural agriculturalists. What stands out is that the legacy of colonial rule consists of far more than a market-based economy. The most profound and pernicious legacy is the association of ethnicity or "nativeness" with political identity and power (cf. Mamdani 2001).

THE IDEOLOGICAL CONTEXT OF WAWASAN 2020 AND GERAKAN DESA WAWASAN

Wawasan 2020, or Vision 2020, is the master development plan for all of Malaysia conceived by its prime minister, Mahathir Mohamad. The primary stated goal of Wawasan 2020 is to make Malaysia a fully industrialized country with a standard of living similar to that of European nations by the year 2020 (Dentan et al. 1997:89). Thus, Wawasan 2020 is driven by an ideological commitment to fast-paced economic growth based on commercialization and industrialization. Mahathir has called for an annual economic growth rate of 7 percent for the thirty-year period, which started in 1990 (Jayasankaran and Heibert 1997:19).

The rural development initiative within the master plan of Wawasan 2020 is called Gerakan Desa Wawasan (Village Movement toward Vision,[3] henceforth GDW). Its goal is to transform rural agriculture from subsistence to commercial, "productive," "orderly" agriculture, emphasizing improved harvests, increased markets, and a growing reliance on new technologies (*Berita Harian* 1996:14). Under GDW, village structure must conform to "modern activities and industries" (ibid.) and rural people must learn "highly disciplined work habits" so that they can become involved in the global marketplace (ibid., 2, 9).

The literature on GDW follows a blueprint of what modern rural development initiatives should look like. The authors employ all the appropriate terms used in the formulation of the contemporary development problematic: human resources are emphasized over technological solutions, bottom-up versus top-down problem identification is stressed, and, citing Robert Chambers, planners are warned not to overexploit natural resources through "growth mania" (*Berita Harian* 1996:1, 10–11).

As is evident in the detailed ethnographies of agricultural social organization in Malaysian and Indonesian Borneo, rural agriculture in the region is already "orderly," "productive," and "disciplined" and has been connected to the global marketplace for centuries (see, e.g., Appell 1965; Dove 1983, 1986a, 1993b, 1994, 1999; Harrison 1971; Hefner 1990; Li 1999b; Padoch and Peluso 1996; Peluso 1983; and Tsing 1993). What, then, is the need for rural development?

In his book on the larger social processes that influence development initiatives, James Ferguson suggests that such blueprints for development identify a dominant problematic through which the underdeveloped regions of the world are identified. This problematic presupposes a central, unquestioned value or worldview that, in turn, shapes the nature of development interventions. But he argues that development initiatives are more than programs that define rural poverty and then aim to alleviate it through technical interventions; they are also ideological screens for other, concealed intentions—mere rhetoric (Ferguson 1994:xiii, 17):

> By making the intentional blue-print for "development" so highly visible, a "development" project can end up performing extremely sensitive political operations involving the entrenchment and expansion of institutional state power almost invisibly, under the cover of a neutral, technical mission to which no one can object. The "instrument-effect" then is two-fold: alongside the institutional effect of expanding bureaucratic state power is the conceptual or ideological effect of depoliticizing both poverty and the state. (1994:256).

Ferguson explicitly argues that the "instrument-effect" of development is unintended by the planners and results in powerful forms of "anonymous" control—"authorless strategies" (1994:20). He centers his exploration of the development industry on the "intelligibility of a series of events and transformations, not in the intentions guiding the actions of one or more animating subjects" (1994:18). This move to deflect analysis away from the intentions of the "state" is analytically sound—it is tortuously difficult to locate intention within state agencies and then draw broader conclusions about state policies. But in their critique of Ferguson's "radical critique of development," Sivaramakrishnan and Agrawal (2003:30 *n*101) argue that, since

> state agencies and officials are political creatures, one must be careful before seeing the entrenchment of state power and the extension of the capacity of state agencies as an unintended effect of development. Indeed, state actors interested in development, because they are political animals, may view development quite self-consciously as an instrument to extend state capacity.

Importantly, although Ferguson demonstrates that political issues are not raised in the development documents, he fails to demonstrate the "depoliticizing" effects of development discourse (Li 1999a). How can development both erase politics and pursue the very task of expanding bureaucratic power (Skaria 2000)? Tania Li (1999a) also questions this and correctly points out that Ferguson's study reveals that development officers in Lesotho were quite clear about the role that development could play in strengthening the reach of state power. And even the villagers in Ferguson's study seemed to realize that the development programs' technical initiatives might regulate their lives in unacceptable ways, and so they "feigned compliance, ignored them or sabotaged them accordingly" (Li 1999a:296).

In Malaysia, state bureaucrats at times *are aware* of the ways in which development initiatives can be used to extend state power. For some members of the Malaysian government, development is *intended* to strengthen the Malay-Muslim[4] elite as much as to raise the standard of living for the disenfranchised. Evidence of this is seen in the literature on GDW that not only outlines the government's policy on industrialization and economic growth but also includes references to the government's ideological commitment to Malayization and Islamization. A related point is that development programs in Sabah have the potential to create a politically charged arena in which relations of power and rule are worked out and reassessed, rather than to depoliticize the countryside, as Ferguson suggests. Li's recent work in Indonesia on resettlement programs (1999a) also highlights the powerful political nature of state development projects that use resettlement and "gifts" of modern social services as a way to take away from villagers the freedom to choose the configuration of their village and the types of agricultural practices that they prefer.

Mahathir's Wawasan 2020 goal calling for the development of a "Malaysian race working in full and equal partnership" (Jayasankaran and Heibert 1997:19) implies the subsuming of ethnic identity within a national, Malaysian identity or "race." Citizens are urged to be Malaysian first and Indian, Dusun, Iban, Murut, Penan, or Semai (to name only a few of the many ethnic groups in Malaysia) second. The government led by the United Malay National Organization (UMNO) continues to seek political legitimacy by stressing the importance of a Malaysian identity and a national unity—a trend that intensified after the 1969 race riots that shook Peninsular Malaysia[5] (Case 1995:73). Wawasan 2020 continues the processes of Malayization of all Malaysian ethnic minorities into a unified class of Malaysian citizens under the guise that these values are part of a "normal" or "natural" developmental path to modernization.

Furthermore, development in Malaysia has an Islamic coloring (Dentan et al. 1997:92) that is reiterated throughout the GDW literature, which repeatedly calls for "spiritual awareness" and for "spiritually uniting people with Allah" (*Berita Harian* 1996:3). Khoo Boo Teik, in his intellectual biography of Mahathir, points out that the

> *Mid-Term Review of the Fourth Malaysia Plan, 1981–1985* explicitly suggested that the "universality of Islamic values and the message of modernization it contains" did not conflict with "the value system of the other faiths" and the "sharing of these common values will further strengthen the bonds among Malaysians." ... The values listed in the *Mid-Term Review of the Fourth Malaysia Plan* were exactly the kinds of values Mahathir thought were needed to raise productivity at home, increase competitiveness abroad, and ensure political stability always. Among them were "better discipline, more self-reliance and striving for excellence" which, together with "thriftiness" and "a more rational and scientific approach in overcoming problems" were "values which are progressive and consistent with the needs of a modernizing and industrializing plural society." (Khoo 1995:181; as quoted in Ong 1999:227)[6]

While generalizations about Islam are treacherous to undertake, Michael Watts (2003:7) has pointed out that one powerful aspect of Islamic revival, particularly in Malaysia, are the strategic and political tactics that are employed to sway opinion in the voting booth and to build a parallel civil society. One should not be surprised, therefore, to learn that the Kemas organization, a political arm of UMNO, with an agenda to encourage the conversion of people to both Islam and UMNO, is instrumental in rural development initiatives (Crouch 1992:29; Shamsul 1986).[7] Kemas is an acronym for Kemajuan Masyarakat, or Community Progress (or Development). But Kemas also has a richer meaning that is central to the logic of development in Malaysia; the Malaysian meaning of the word *kemas* is "orderly, well kept" (as in a house). Thus the term has an interesting double meaning, emphasizing the value of "ordering" the social world to achieve progress. The political agenda of Kemas is depoliticized through its agents' role in development, which includes teaching adult education classes in cooking, sewing, nutrition, and hygiene.[8] Under Kemas's authority, programs were initiated in more than 75 percent (482) of the 642 villages throughout Malaysia that were included in GDW between 1991 and 1996. In the remaining 160 villages, programs were under the authority of institutions more traditionally associated with rural development, such as the Institute of Land Development and the Institute of Regional Development (*Berita Harian* 1996:4). Just as the rationale for British control through colonial rule was the need to build a stable economy and durable law and order over indigenous people, the postcolonial rationale for rule is to modernize (civilize) and make rural agriculturalists more efficient and disciplined through the principles of Islam.

FEDERAL AND STATE POLITICS: FRAGMENTED VISIONS OF MALAYSIAN IDENTITY

The development initiative of Wawasan 2020 must be situated within Malaysia's past development efforts, the most prominent of which has been the New Economic Plan (NEP), launched in 1971. A main objective of the NEP was to "accelerat[e] the process of restructuring Malaysian society to correct economic imbalance, so as to reduce and eventually eliminate the identification of race or ethnicity with economic function."[9] "Restructuring Malay society" translated into policies that would facilitate the expansion of the Malay educated middle class, which would in turn create a Malay entrepreneurial and shareholding class, and thereby correct the dominance of this sector by the Chinese and, to a lesser extent, the Indians. The implementation of the NEP involved measures that strongly favored Malays over non-Malays. Thus the NEP ushered in a new period in Malaysian politics in which the *bumiputra* (lit. "sons of the soil") were given preference over non-*bumiputra* (e.g., the Chinese and Indians). Governmental agencies were expanded to help Malays go into business, and preference was given to Malays in the distribution of manufacturing licenses, government contracts, and concessions to land (Crouch 1996:26). It was not uncommon for state and federal representatives from UMNO to "compete" for government contracts, and UMNO politicians had special access to land grants from the government (Crouch 1996:39). This blurring of state and UMNO business interests resulted in the increasing dominance of UMNO in the Malaysian economy and gave rise to what is called, in the Malaysian context, "money politics," which primarily benefits the Malay *bumiputra* community (Shamsul 1989:8). The same phenomenon of "consciously employ[ing] the ideology of the New Economic Policy to ... create a group of rich Muslim businessmen who would then ... underwrite political leaders, factions and parties" has also been observed in Sarawak and results in a vicious cycle of "timber politics," where business, politics, and ethnicity are tied together to exploit the timber resources in a powerful constellation of mutual interests (Kaur 1998:138).[10]

The *bumiputra* community in Peninsular Malaysia and that in East Malaysia (Sabah and Sarawak) have very different views of the *bumiputra* policy, based on the cultural and economic differences between the two regions. Malay-Muslims dominate the *bumiputra* community in Peninsular Malaysia (with the exception of the small and marginalized group of non-Muslims, the Orang Asli). Conversely, in East Malaysia, the majority of the *bumiputra* community is non-Muslim. Furthermore, the majority of the Malays in Peninsular Malaysia were peasants at the time of independence from Britain, but the *bumiputra* of East Malaysia are highly heterogeneous, some urbanized, some peasants, and many, like the marginalized Orang Asli of the Peninsula, are shifting cultivators and hunter-gatherers (Shamsul 1998:31). As a result, the *bumiputra* community in East Malaysia does not feel that the agenda of the federal *bumiputra* community reflects the interests of all *bumiputra*. The policy of privileging the *bumiputra*, or indigenous people, over the non-*bumiputra* has reversed colonial hierarchies, but as Mahmood Mamdani (2001) has shown in Africa, nothing has changed from the colonial era. "Nativeness" or indigeneity is still the ultimate test for determining rights and entitlements.

In more recent years, the *bumiputra* policy has been challenged on several fronts within Malaysia. In Sabah, the most significant challenge has occurred as a result of the political movements of non-Muslim *bumiputra* who feel that Christianity and native animist religions are not accorded equal status with Islam (Shamsul 1998:25). The Kadazans, the ethnic majority in Sabah, have begun to resent the Malay-Muslim domination over Sabahans and the apparent treatment of Kadazans as second-class citizens (Wah 1992). As one Kadazan leader said,

> The Kadazans consider themselves the true natives of Sabah and claim that they are the definitive people ... [yet] in reality, the Kadazans have found themselves to be subordinated to the Malays and discriminated against in favour of Muslim natives who also claim to be Malays by virtue of their religion.[11] (Kitingan 1984:236–37; as cited in Wah 1992:245)

This political conflict over the national identity of *bumiputra* sparked the rise of "Kadazan nationalism" and the formation of the Parti Bersatu Sabah (PBS), or United Sabah Party,[12] a Kadazan-controlled party that ruled Sabah for nearly a decade between 1985 and 1994. The period in which the following case study of rural development is situated is the era in which UMNO managed to "win back" Sabah politically from PBS control. Yet, despite UMNO rule in Sabah, the fire of Kadazan nationalism was still burning, and PBS was able to win a large number of parliamentary seats in the 1995 elections (Shamsul 1998:32).

A QUESTION OF INTENTIONALITY:
HIDDEN MEANINGS BEHIND RURAL DEVELOPMENT

Some political leaders in Malaysia may be ideologically committed to the notion that the principles of a Malay-Muslim nation and poverty alleviation in fact are linked as normal and universal values, just as many colonial officers truly believed in the ideologies put forward under colonialism. And certainly this ideological belief is given center stage in the state discourse on development, which emphasizes that modernity in Malaysia must be achieved without sacrificing Islamic values (Khoo 1995; Mauzy and Milne 1986:90). Yet, on another level, some officials seem to recognize that development plans are inherently political and that the attention paid to the perceived "natural" link between development and the moral code of Islam is an ideological screen, obfuscating a political agenda of Malay-Muslim dominance over other ethnic and religious groups. Viewed from this perspective, the underlying or implied intention of linking development to Islamic conversion becomes the expansion of state bureaucratic power.

An interview with a federal official in the Ministry of Rural Development, whom I call Datuk Yakub, indirectly sheds light on the question of whether state officials are aware that development programs have multiple outcomes, not all of which are related to poverty alleviation. Discussing the causes of and solutions to rural poverty, Datuk Yakub said that such problems in Sabah were complex. "Sometimes," he said, "the lack of electricity in interior villages should not be considered a problem. The people do not really need it and in fact the lack of electricity has tourism potential."[13] Although tourism in Sabah is on the rise, the number of people willing to visit rural villages and experience the local lifestyle, without running water and electricity, is extremely small. In interviews with local people, I found no one who could see the "tourism potential" of villages with no electricity. Datuk Yakub turned the government's failure to bring electricity to its citizens (a failure of development) into a potential success under a different strategy—tourism development. Rather than focus on the local experience of poverty, Datuk Yakub saw the success and failure of development in terms of broader issues of state economic growth, especially for the political and economic elites, who might benefit from increased tourism.

Intellectual leaders in Sabah more openly acknowledge the connection between the expansion of federal power and development initiatives. One Sabahan scholar told me, "Kemas and the ministry of rural development use development as an entry point into local villages for politicians. It is all about using development to get votes." Many Malaysians thus see that the material rewards of development, no matter how feeble they might be, are gifts the state provides in return for voter loyalty. Foucault's conceptualization of power and governmentality can help explain the role of securing votes through development promises as a technology of rule. Although some of the state's policies for obtaining votes are far more coercive, such as providing illegal immigrants with working papers and a Malaysian identity card in exchange for votes (Chua 1995), rural development projects are presented as serving the "national interest" and therefore are not coerced but are contingent on local compliance. Although villagers always have the "power to" vote against the Malay-Muslim politicians, so does the minister of rural development have the "power to" withdraw governmental support. And, in fact, the UMNO party did just that in 1995 in Govuton when villagers supported the PBS in the elections. In 1996, no funds for development projects were forthcoming for villagers in Govuton.

THE ARRIVAL OF "MODERNITY": GERAKAN DESA WAWASAN IN TEMPULONG

Early in April 1996, the head of the regional UMNO office, Datuk Sukarti, arrived in the rural village of Tempulong accompanied by a dozen women wearing colorful, silk *baju kurung* (long Muslim blouses and skirts) and *kerudung* (loose Muslim head coverings). These women lived in the district center of Ranau, about twelve kilometers from Tempulong. Since the majority of Tempulong residents follow the religion of the Borneo Evangelical Mission (Sidang Injil Borneo),[14] and make their living as farmers, these women in their Muslim dress stood out as exotic and cosmopolitan (see figs. 6 and 7). These Muslim women belonged to Kemas, the arm of UMNO concerned with converting people to Islam and promoting loyalty to Malay nationalism. To the villagers in Tempulong, these women might have appeared as foreign as the Company officers did in the nineteenth century. This point was brought home when one Muslim woman who saw a cow in the road began to run, shrieking, "Put him in his stable!" A woman from Tempulong looked at me and said, "Where does she think we have a stable?" This incident further promoted a discussion about some of the villagers who had left to go work in Peninsular Malaysia. When they returned, I was told, their accents had changed and they pretended to forget local place-names.[15] Both rural Malaysians and the ruling Malay-Muslims thus struggle with ethnic histories as they find their place in the hierarchy topped by Malay-Muslim *bumiputra*.

Datuk Sukarti and the Kemas group had come to Tempulong at the invitation of Sindeh, the chairman of the Authority for Village Development and Protection (Jawatankuasa Kemajuan dan Keselamatan Kampung, or JKKK).[16] In his capacity as chairman, Sindeh was often seen pacing the village with a legal pad in hand, ready to take notes on local concerns and issues that he felt should be brought to the attention of regional politicians.

Local gossip accused Sindeh of using his political appointment for personal aggrandizement and material gain. In local-level politics, the chairman of the JKKK is a political appointment, and therefore individuals associated with the UMNO party control the office of the JKKK. Government aid is directly channeled to the village as a whole, or to the very poor, through the chairman of the JKKK. In reality, the chairman often appropriates a healthy amount of this money for personal use (for a discussion of this trend elsewhere in Malaysia, see Crouch 1992:28; Shamsul 1989; Scott 1985:220–31). For instance, Sindeh received money from UMNO, which he was supposed to allocate to four families, living below the poverty level, for home improvement.[17] He used two of these four allotments for improvements to his own home, including building a new office for himself. Therefore, he benefited not only materially from Datuk Sukarti's visit to Tempulong but also symbolically, since his association with a regional UMNO official and his access to development funds would increase his prestige and authority locally. Simultaneously, Sindeh's material gains rewarded and reinforced his support to the UMNO party. This demonstration of political strength was important to Sindeh since the headman in Tempulong, Gani, was constantly challenging his local authority.

Datuk Sukarti, the regional head of UMNO, launched GDW in Tempulong with an inspirational speech. He described another village, supported by GDW, deep in the interior of Sabah:

> People in the village were encouraged to clean up their litter and to plant ornamental flowers around their houses. The goal was to beautify the village. The Kemas group taught women how to cook spicy, flavorful food. When the men came home from the fields, they would find the children quietly doing their schoolwork. The smell of blossoming flowers would mix with the smell of good food. The beautiful and calming images would pacify any domestic problems. Even if the wives had no sugar for the coffee, the husbands would not be mad because the home was so beautiful. In this village everyone was

FIG. 6. Women from Kemas greet the federal minister of rural development during his visit to Tempulong. © 1996 by Michael J. Doolittle.

so inspired that they would meet at dawn before going to the fields and sing the national anthem.[18]

With the help of money from GDW, he concluded, Tempulong could be as beautiful, peaceful, and modern as the village he had just described.

Datuk Sukarti's speech suggested that Tempulong was unlike that modern village, and, in fact, one of the early initiatives of the GDW in Tempulong—the removal of cow manure from the roadside—supports this view.[19] By emphasizing the aesthetic nature of village life and prioritizing beautiful, well-kept landscaping,[20] Datuk Sukarti, and by extension the state's development initiative, deflected attention from political realities such as severe shortages in Tempulong of both arable land and wage labor and insecure property rights to existing agricultural lands. By focusing on more neutral, technical, or, in this case, aesthetic problems, one may more easily overlook more complex social and political problems. The notion that a basic restructuring of regional political-economic inequities might be warranted was never raised.[21] Village beautification is, in fact, a dominant theme in the

FIG. 7. Local women from Tempulong, who were not represented by Kemas, out gathering forest products on the very day of the federal minister's visit. © 1996 by Michael J. Doolittle.

GDW programs throughout Malaysia. State and federal competitions are held for the prize of "cleanest, most beautiful and progressive" village. According to the women from the village that won the award in 1997, "There had been very little progress here ... [so we] decided that it was time we mobilized a *gotong royong* [cooperative work group] and cleaned things up" (Visvanathan 1997). This national award emphasized the notion that villages must first and foremost be clean and orderly, and then the rewards of modernity will fall into place. How cleanliness, orderliness, and discipline are part of a natural progression toward the goals of Wawasan 2020—that is, achieving a standard of living similar to that in Europe—is never questioned.

Villagers in Tempulong were confused by Datuk Sukarti's talk. They imagined that he had described a very modern and, therefore, desirable way of life, and they assumed that this was the way that the rest of the world lived. The lure of modernity was clear. Yet, it was incomprehensible to these villagers that any group of adults would gather to sing the national anthem before work. "Who would feed the children and get them ready for school?" asked Rumihin, a young mother. Another woman queried, "Are they making fun of us?" One wonders what the government officials think of rural people when the article about the village that won the prize for the "cleanest, most beautiful and most progressive" village refers to the population as "simple but exceedingly warm-hearted and hospitable" (Visvanathan 1997). A sample of national headlines indicates that the government perceives that the rural population is in need of a strong (and, of course, modern) hand to help it change its "culture and attitude" to be more progressive: "Government Agencies Play Vital Role in Changing Values" (Mokhtar 1994); "Start Adopting Modern Technology, PM Advises Farmers" (*New Straits Times* 1996b); "Toward a Better Life for Villagers" (Idrus 1998); "Rural Dwellers Must Adopt Competitive Attitude" (*Bernama Daily Malaysian News* 2000); and "Changing the Mindset of Rural Populations" (*New Straits Times* 2003a). All of these headlines suggest that rural villagers somehow have an inappropriate "mindset" and that governmental intervention is necessary to correct this problem.

Conflicting Forms of Local Authority

Approximately thirty people, about 25 percent of the adult village population in Tempulong, attended Datuk Sukarti's speech. At least one of those, Rineh, was paid to be there. Rineh is the sister-in-law of Sindeh (the chairman of the JKKK) and is a single mother with five children. Unable to plant a swidden field without help from an adult male, she tries to find casual wage labor nearly every day in order to earn cash. On this particular day, she was scheduled to work for M$10 cleaning out debris from the Montokuon River. Since this work was funded by UMNO, Sindeh was responsible for paying her (and others) for a day of work. Rineh told me that she needed the M$10 but that Sindeh wanted her at the meeting, so they agreed she would be paid anyway. Apparently, Sindeh was willing to pay people to attend the meeting in order to create the illusion that he had village support of his leadership. Sindeh did have reason to worry that people might not show up, for in the past the headman of Tempulong, Gani, had been accused of encouraging villagers not to attend village meetings that were sponsored by either Sindeh or UMNO.[22]

By inviting Datuk Sukarti and GDW, Sindeh was creating an opening for the "Malayization" and "Islamization" (through the involvement of Kemas and UMNO) of Tempulong. Notably absent from the meeting were Gani, the headman, and Tarajun, the former chairman of the JKKK. For various reasons, both of these men objected to the presence of Datuk Sukarti and the GDW project. Gani—an elderly man who staunchly believed in the importance of traditional *adat* (customs) and the value of their historically proven land use strategies—saw no need for rural development. Gani was not only the headman of Tempulong but also the *bobohizan* (D: priest) for the traditional animist religion. He objected to the increasing power of the Muslims in Sabah, as it diminished his influence over village matters. As headman and *bobohizan*, it was his responsibility to resolve village disputes in accordance with local customary practices, or *adat*. But the tenets of both the Muslim religion and the Borneo Evangelical Mission often conflicted with the principles of local *adat*. The more villagers turned to the Muslim and Christian faiths and their religious leaders for advice, the less they followed Gani's leadership.

Tarajun, who served as the chairman of the JKKK in Tempulong when the PBS (Parti Bersatu Sabah), the Kadazan-led opposition party to UMNO, governed Sabah, objected to GDW for different reasons. A manager at the Winekek Copper Mine, Tarajun was careful and studied in his comments about politics and development. He felt that Sindeh was deeply involved in "money politics"[23] and was not a scrupulous leader. Tarajun refused to attend the meeting because he did not want to "be involved with political people" (*campur tangan dengan orang politik*). "There is a time for campaigning and a time for development," he said, "but you should not mix the two. It only confuses people."[24] Although Tarajun is no longer the JKKK chairman, he still holds significant influence in the village. By not attending the meeting, he sent a clear message to the rest of Tempulong that he disagreed with Sindeh's political motives.

What most concerned Tarajun was Malay domination over Sabah's ethnic minorities. In the eyes of many Sabahans, an allegiance to UMNO represents a betrayal of Kadazan (or Dusun) ethnic identity, since UMNO stresses a unified vision of Malaysia through the ideology of "one language, one culture, and one religion" (*satu bahasa, satu kebudayaan, dan satu agama;*[25] see Wah 1992:230). Belief that loyalty to UMNO represents a betrayal of local ethnic identity is evident elsewhere in Sabah's rural villages. For example, in a neighboring village, the chairman of the JKKK, Masiri, stepped down from his position when PBS lost the state elections in 1994. By refusing to accept his position of chairman under the UMNO government, Masiri, in effect, refused to form an alliance with that government. The price of this action was the loss of government subsidies for his village and of a salary for himself. He commented that this was a dark time (*zaman gelap*) in Sabah, when politics and religion were too closely tied. Fiercely proud of his Kadazan/Dusun identity and his leader (the ex-chief minister and head of PBS, Datuk Pairin Kitingan), he felt PBS would eventually regain power in Sabah. Until that time, Masiri counseled villagers to refuse money and development projects from UMNO politicians.[26]

Building Shrines to Modernity

In April and May, some Tempulong residents began to work together to fulfil the goals of GDW and prepare their village for the arrival of the federal minister of rural development in June. Several times each week, cooperative work groups, or *gotong royong*, gathered to clean up the litter and cow manure in the village and plant ornamental flowers around the houses (the supplies were paid for by UMNO, but the labor was not reimbursed). The state sees these cooperative work groups as the hallmark of citizens' capacity to engage in collective voluntary labor to make the village a better place (Li 1999a). Of course, cooperative labor is hardly a new sign of modernity, as swidden farmers in Malaysia have worked collectively and voluntarily for centuries to clear neighboring plots of land quickly during the dry season. Most people in Tempulong did not engage willingly in the work for GDW. Some, notably those loyal to Gani, who rejected these plans for modernizing Tempulong, refused to show up for any of the work. Others complained that there was too much work to be done in their swiddens and vegetables gardens to waste time planting flowers. In the end, Sindeh's extended family and the young adults in the village, who did not have to worry about feeding their own children, completed most of the work.

The most noticeable part of the project was the construction of a cement sign welcoming people to the village of Tempulong, beneath which was an inspirational slogan made out of river rocks painted white: "*Yakin kami boleh kami*" ("If we believe [in ourselves] we can [achieve our goals]"). Such slogans are common in the recent history of postcolonial Malaysia. Amri Baharuddin Shamsul (1989:6) points out that the government introduced a series of "sloganeering and change-awareness campaigns" in the 1970s in what was considered an essential "preconditioning process to achieve modernization."

Next to the village meeting house (*balai raya*), a small rock fountain was erected. There is a certain irony in these shrines to modern development. Women must carry water and food into the *balai raya* every day for the kindergarten school lunch, since there is no running water or cooking facilities there. Yet it is through building these small monuments that the state and its funds for development are made concretely visible not only to the villagers but also to outsiders passing through. The signs symbolically assert that Tempulong villagers are no longer "backward"; they now have the capacity to reorder their environment along predetermined notions of cleanliness and modernity, under the generous guidance of UMNO. The welcoming signpost, fountain, and white river rocks that can be seen in many rural villages in Sabah have become ubiquitous symbols of GDW and state authority. These short-term results of the development process have been referred to as development "cover crop" (Shamsul 1989:5)—objectives that do little to change the long-term quality of life.

THE THEATER OF DEVELOPMENT: FEDERAL VISITORS

At the end of June, the federal minister of rural development came to tour the village of Tempulong and inspect its progress as part of GDW. Muslim women from the Kemas group spent the entire day preparing food and decorations for the celebration. After the food was ready, they prepared to greet the federal minister of rural development, as well as Datuk Sukarti and other regional officials. The dignitaries rolled into Tempulong in a fleet of Toyota four-wheel-drive vehicles. They all filed into the *balai raya*, followed by the women from Kemas, who greeted the federal minister and then during his speech joined the audience, "acting" as the local population. Through this performance, the unsavory characteristics of Tempulong that Datuk Sukarti had indirectly referred to months earlier in his speech were sanitized by the extra-local Muslim women, who prepared the *balai raya* and then represented the "local" people for the federal minister. The entire event appeared as a staged act, in which the officials and supporters of the federal government played out both state and local roles, for the benefit of Tempulong villagers. The "play" not only asserted the legitimacy of the state officials in their capacity as national leaders but also modeled for the local population how modern Malaysian citizens should appear and how local people should relate to their leaders. In Indonesia, similar instances have occurred of the state's use of an already "modern" group of citizens to provide guidance for those who do not yet understand the state discourses. Tania Li (1999a) found that, rather than try to settle true nomads, resettlement officials look for potential program recipients who are sufficiently isolated or primitive to meet the program criteria, but who are not especially difficult cases. This way the state is more likely to succeed, and the nomads, the actual targets of resettlement, see other resettled people as role models and as examples of modernization (Li 1999a).

The speeches made inside the *balai raya* were unimportant to the villagers in Tempulong. Many listened to the speeches from outside the *balai raya*; others simply stayed at home. Perhaps they recognized the inherently theatrical nature of the federal minister's speech, or perhaps they knew that they would have little say in the future course of events. This delocalizing of the celebration of GDW, which is supposedly devoted to a "new" paradigm of development that strives for "bottom-up development" and the "active engagement of local people in the planning process" of development (*Berita Harian* 1996:2), may seem to some to be an external sign of the failure of state-sponsored development. To the contrary, the speeches succeeded in expanding state power at the local level by making blatantly clear the association between UMNO, Islam, and development funds and by modeling for the villagers how modern Malaysian citizens should appear.

Sitting on the hillside listening to the speeches going on inside the *balai raya*, two older women from the village laughed at the costumes and officious attitudes of the Kemas women. Later, about ten of the younger, unmarried men and women from the village put on a "traditional" dance performance for the visitors. A group of village elders criticized this supposed local participation in the celebration of GDW, since the youths performed Iban dances and not the traditional dances of Tempulong. Iban dances represent the quintessential Borneo native and thus represent local life as "indigenous" or "traditional" to federal officials, demonstrating that the national hierarchies of local versus state, and indigenous versus modern, have been internalized at the local level. The contradictory responses of mockery and contempt by some residents and the dancers' desire to represent the "native" or traditional culture of their village illustrate the ambiguity of the local view of development and modernity. As Li (1999a:296) points out, engagements at this level between state and society often result in "reflections on the pomposity of a speech, the tedium of a spectacle, or stupidity of a plan," all of which were present in Tempulong.

Although the activities surrounding the visit of the federal minister were theatrical entertainment to some people in Tempulong, they also had a darker side. One young woman said to me with utter disdain in her voice: "There are more Muslims from Ranau here today than people from Tempulong. I don't think much of what is happening. It seems as if the *Semenanjung* (Peninsula) is taking over Tempulong and making it their village. They're telling us what things should be done, but no one is asking us what we need or want."[27] Underlying this statement is a deep local animosity toward the federal government (which is located on the Peninsula), its commitment to Malay-Muslim domination, and its apparent efforts to take over the Sabah state government.[28]

WHO BENEFITS FROM GERAKAN DESA WAWASAN?

The events unfolding during GDW in Tempulong dramatically illustrate several points about the relationship between the state and society in Sabah. First, the state has presented rhetoric of a "new" paradigm of development that strives for "bottom-up development" and the "active engagement of local people in the planning process" of development (*Berita Harian* 1996:2), poverty alleviation, and the empowerment of local people, but development projects in Malaysia are clearly an attempt to ensure loyalty to the UMNO-led government. This has wide-ranging implications. It shows that the liberal development rhetoric emphasizing "people first" is susceptible to incorporation or co-optation by the state for political purposes. Most notably, this occurs through the allocation of government development funds to villages that have demonstrated electoral support for the UMNO representatives. Embedded in support for the UMNO-led government is the acceptance of a government ideologically committed to Malay-Muslim domination. Thus, this development program fosters a narrower concept of "national identity" and political participation.[29] Second, by focusing on the aesthetics of village life, GDW places a specific value on appearance. The political realities of poverty are swept away by development that fails to change significantly the standard of living for rural people or to recognize political-economic inequities that underlie land insecurity and poverty. Questions of political and economic reform go ignored. However, since poverty alleviation is not the only goal of development initiatives, the "failure" of programs to raise the standard of living is not necessarily a concern of development planners in Malaysia. Instead, emphasis is placed on the use of development initiatives to build up a modern citizenry that supports the state's ideological platform.

Villagers in Tempulong did not unconditionally welcome GDW. Many questioned and even rejected the value of the program and the level of federal involvement in local issues. Furthermore, that only a small percentage of villagers willingly helped Sindeh prepare Tempulong for the federal minister's visit suggests that many were not convinced that their participation in the project would result in material benefits either for the village as a whole or for themselves individually. Recognizing the political message behind the rhetoric of rural development, Tempulong residents, as a result of GDW, did not fully embrace the UMNO ideology, the Islamic religion, or Malaysian nationalism. In fact, in some instances, the project even fueled anti-federalist (or anti-Malay *bumiputra*) sentiments. Just as land laws in colonial Malaysia were unambiguous on paper while the actual settlement was open to negotiation, development has not unilaterally imposed the image of modernity and Malaysian nationalism on the population. Such state development practices do provide room for local people and state agents to engage, maneuver, and compromise (Li 1999a:297–300) and thus offer a forum for all groups to assert their power relations.

Even those in Tempulong who appeared willing to accept the government's political agenda had ulterior motives. Kimin, a village elder, told me that he had taken UMNO money (bribes) to vote for the UMNO-supported political candidate in the last election. But, he said, "Deep in my heart I will always be a PBS supporter. When I go to vote on election day, who knows which way I vote?"[30] Although villagers were aware that the dispersal of development funds was contingent on support for UMNO political parties, they not only were sceptical of the value of the funds but also knew how to manipulate the political machinery.[31]

Although GDW did not fully succeed in promoting the state's discursive agenda, legitimizing the state, and delegitimizing the status quo, it did extend partial bureaucratic reach to the village level. The federal minister ended his visit with the promise of federal housing funds for several families in Tempulong. By procuring these development funds, Sindeh strengthened his political base. Importantly, UMNO leaders did secure his loyalty; with Sindeh in charge of dispensing development funds locally, a position that he had abused in the past for his personal gain, they made sure that the UMNO-led government's political agenda would be promoted. The very process of such a development project creates the space for what Li calls the "complex cultural work at the interface between development projects and those they target" (1999a:296).

At the federal level, the push for modernization through GDW remains strong into the twenty-first century, despite—or perhaps even because of— the model's lack of success. Newspaper articles from the years 2000–2003 repeatedly quoted these statistics: only 462 villages (15 percent) of those involved in GDW have shown "vast improvement"; 1,066 (35 percent) have shown "moderate improvement," and the remaining 1,461 (48 percent) have shown "no improvement" (*Bernama Daily Malaysian News* 2000; *New Straits Times* 2001; *Bernama Daily Malaysian News* 2003a; *New Straits Times* 2003a). The articles did not suggest that the model for development was flawed. Instead, rural people were consistently pointed out as the obstacles to success. The rural development minister, Azmi, pointed out that rural people are "not self-reliant" and that they "lack a competitive spirit," characteristics that will "eventually destroy the community" (*Bernama Daily Malaysian News* 2000). In order to make GDW more successful, the government planned a new set of service-oriented programs "aimed at changing the mindset of villagers" (*New Straits Times* 2003a). Implicit here is the notion that the government is doing all that it can to modernize and improve rural peoples' lives but that rural people lack the initiative to follow through with government programs. Mahathir blatantly articulated this view: "The older generation must be able to change their attitude and be more receptive to changes and new ideas. It would be very difficult if they refuse to adapt to new changes and in fact it would easier if they refused to work [as subsistence farmers]" (*New Straits Times* 1996b). The implied criticism is that the older generation is stuck, perpetuating a traditional lifestyle that holds the younger generation from achieving modernization. This is not surprising, according to James Ferguson (1994); failures in development strategies are generally interpreted as evidence that more resources and more effort are needed to overcome backwardness. Even two of Sabah's leading economists from the Institute for Indigenous Economic Progress seem to believe at least partially that marginal people are responsible for their place in the national hierarchy. Writing on the causes of poverty in Sabah, they uncritically state that one theory of poverty argues that "poverty results from some limitations, maladjustments, and shortcomings of individuals" and that the "attitudes of the community could be one of the main contributions to poverty." They also argue that "the poor often display clear symptoms of dependence, helplessness, [and] prejudice and have an unscientific attitude towards life" (Tangau and Tanakinjal 2000:216). Such ideas, presented uncritically by contemporary thinkers in Sabah, strikingly resemble the colonial rationale for rule. In the logic of state rule, longer and more focused state interventions into local livelihood strategies are needed to bring order to the "primitive chaos."

One can begin to see the political consequences of development projects through the preceding examination of the discursive practices of the projects' principle advocates and recipients. This analysis has shown that a discourse of Malay-Muslim domination is embedded within the discourse of rural development and economic growth, that development initiatives in Malaysia are used as a tool for the expansion of state bureaucratic power, and that in the Malaysian context, development projects are at times *knowingly* constructed as ideological screens for the entrenchment of the ruling UMNO-led government and the promotion of Malay-Muslim dominance. Furthermore, the political nature of development is widely recognized in the state bureaucracy and in local society. Gerakan Desa Wawasan's imperfect expansion of UMNO control in Sabah is the result of the ongoing tension between the exercise of power and achievement of control.[32] Perhaps the heavy-handedness of the UMNO politicians in their categorizing of rural people makes their actions more transparent to marginal people who have experienced generations of this type of "normalizing" and domineering governance.

Considerable continuity, not a cleavage, exists between the colonial and the postcolonial periods in the forms of state authority and rule. Donald Moore (1999:655) makes a similar point in his study of the colonial period in Zimbabwe, saying, "poststructural theoretical fascination with discontinuity and rupture has elided the recognition of salient historical continuities in the disciplining of agriculture, the spatial ordering of rural settlements, and the operations of colonial and postcolonial governmentality." There are several implications of this continuity in rule for marginal people in Sabah and their use of natural resources. First, despite Independence, the postcolonial government, like the colonial government that preceded it, emphasizes resource commodification and commercialization that ultimately privileges elite concerns over local concerns and subsistence uses. Second, the postcolonial government continues to invent discourses that justify centralized rule while deflecting attention away from the quality of life and the poverty experienced by those who live on the margins and whose lives depend directly on natural resources. In the same way that the colonial state constructed images of native people, their customary laws, and their land use regimes as unproductive and backward in order to justify state control over land settlement, the postcolonial state constructs knowledge about the rural people in Sabah. This knowledge includes references to acceptable types of agriculture (e.g., commercial, "productive," "orderly" agriculture that produces improved harvests, increased markets, and a growing reliance on new technologies [*Berita Harian* 1996:14]) and to how rural people must look and act in order to be more modern (e.g., exhibiting "highly disciplined work habits" and a commitment to Malay-Muslim values). When rural people in Sabah are constructed as failing to meet these standards, a need for state intervention is created. Moreover, despite significant differences between the colonial and postcolonial state projects in terms of the desired outcome (revenue production versus industrialization and modernity), the effect of those projects on rural people and their natural resources is the same.

Third, while overlooking legal, political, and economic structures that influence the ways in which rural people use resources, both the colonial and postcolonial states blame rural people, who live in close proximity to the forest, for resource degradation. And most important, both the colonial and postcolonial states make it difficult for marginal people to define their own interests in their own terms. Thus, many present-day development programs—like the British interventions over rural society that preceded them—are more about controlling resources and people than about significantly changing the standard of living for the subjects of development.

FOUR

LAND DISPUTES IN TEMPULONG

Colonial Land Laws, Customary Practices,
and the Postcolonial State, 1950–1996

THE TRIP FROM GOVUTON TO TEMPULONG IS ONLY TWENTY MILES, BUT it is marked by dramatic changes in landscape and climate. Many mornings of the year, especially during the rainy season, Govuton is shrouded in clouds and mist, but as one drops from more than 4,000 feet to 1,800 feet above sea level the climatic change is striking. By the time one arrives in Tempulong, the average midday temperature is ten degrees centigrade warmer than in Govuton (Kitayama 1992). The landscape also changes dramatically, from lower montane forest surrounding Govuton to lowland tropical rain forest in Tempulong (Kitayama 1992). The unusual tree ferns that characterize the steep upper slopes of Govuton are replaced with towering dipterocarps by the time one arrives in Tempulong. Lianas loop down from the forest canopy into the undergrowth, creating a characteristic image of a tropical rain forest. The hot, steamy forest surrounding Tempulong contrasts sharply with the cooler, damp forest in Govuton. Choruses of cicadas and birds can be heard, and in fruit season the smell of ripe tarap (*Artocarpus* spp.) perfumes the air.

Most outsiders who pass through Tempulong are on their way to visit one of the substations of Kinabalu Park, which is adjacent to the village. Most notice neither the clustering of forty or so houses surrounded by home gardens nor the children playing alongside the road. The fact that cows napping on the warm tarmac often block the road is more of a nuisance to the average tourist than it is evidence that people live nearby. But people have lived right next to the park boundaries since it was established in 1964, and prior to that the forests within the park were part of the natural resources that villagers from Tempulong used and managed on a daily basis.

Today, hunting and gathering of forest resources within the park are illegal; the local traditions of resource use are now criminalized. Most villagers do not dare break this law since the fine is high—M$1,000 per offense (approximately US$400), equivalent to nearly two months' salary (see table 4.1)—and plenty of park rangers monitor the areas closest to village access. But conflicts between the park and villagers are also minimized because the park offers employment, which is hard to find in Tempulong (32 percent of the household heads were employed in the park in 1996, and another one-quarter of the villagers work there in temporary jobs),[1] and, perhaps most importantly, villagers have access to other forest areas that provide them with subsistence resources.

A COMPOSITE AGRARIAN SYSTEM: MULTIPLE LAND USE STRATEGIES AND PROPERTY REGIMES

In the mid-1990s, Tempulong had four types of agricultural land use systems: home gardens, swiddens, vegetable gardens, and fruit orchards.[2] As one passes through the village, carefully avoiding sleeping livestock, one can see houses clustered on either side. Houses are built on quarter-acre "house lots" (*lot perumahan*), which are gazetted in statutory law as village land, not private land. The headman assigns each lot to a single family, and each family has the usufruct rights to the land to build a home and to plant small gardens around it. These home gardens usually consist of useful trees (such as *pinang*, or betel nut palm [*Areca catechu*]) and medicinal and ornamental plants. Although the villagers improve these lots, they do not have the right to sell them to outsiders or to other villagers. According to both customary village practice and statutory law, if a family leaves, then the lot reverts back to the village, and the headman can reassign it, perhaps to a newly married couple who wish to establish their own household separate from their parents.[3]

Past the house lots is a mosaic landscape of forests and gardens. The forest (D: *himba'an*) lies within the park, on the private property of the villagers, and in the areas known as Nababak and Tarasan. The dense green forest vegetation is periodically broken by yellow, brown, and light green patches of clearings for gardens and by secondary forest regeneration on fallow agricultural land (D: *tumulok*). There are numerous footpaths lead-

TABLE 4.1. Household Income and Dependence on Garden Produce and Forest Resources in Tempulong

Name of head of household and household size		Average monthly income	Percentage of income from sale of nontimber forest products and produce from garden	Percentage of days spent gathering in nontimber forest products over 3-month period	Types of resources collected
Sani	13	M$657	garden: 3 forest: none	58	firewood, fish, wild fruits, wild vegetables,
Rineh	6	M$583	garden: 9 forest: 18	67	firewood, fish, wild fruits, wild vegetables, vines for basketry
Rumihin	6	M$958	garden: 14 forest: 8	57	firewood, deer, squirrels, fish, wild fruits, wild vegetables
Juriam	5	M$976	garden: 17 forest: none	30	firewood, deer, squirrels, fish, wild fruits, wild vegetables, fodder for pigs
Juliah	6	M$846	garden: 2 forest: 1	71	firewood, fish, bats, squirrels, snakes, armadillos, birds, wild fruits, wild vegetables, vines for basketry

*This figure represents income from wage labor as well as from sale of garden produce and forest products.

ing from the center of the village to the gardens and the forest. Within this forest-field mosaic there are three other types of agricultural areas.

Most families have a swidden field (D: *tagad*) planted in dry rice, cassava, corn, and other vegetables for household use. Some villagers also have vegetable gardens (D: *gopu*) in which they specialize in commercial produce that they can sell to the park restaurant and to buyers in Ranau. These vegetables are mostly leafy greens and green beans; the temperate vegetables such as cabbage and tomatoes that are grown in Govuton do not thrive in the heat and humidity of Tempulong. This type of vegetable garden is relatively new to Tempulong; only in the past few years have farmers experimented with new vegetable crops. These crops require a significant investment of time, labor, and chemical inputs, yet are considered temporary crops, with several harvests a year.[4] Since both swidden fields and vegetable gardens yield what are considered short-term, temporary crops, they are often planted on land to which villagers do not have secure title; if access to the land is lost, then long-term cash crops are still secure.

Finally, there has been a growing interest in planting orchards (*kebun buah-buahan*). With an increasing number of tourists coming to the area and with better communication with the coast, durians (*Durio zibethinus*), tarap (*Artocarpus* spp.), rambutans (*Nephelium* spp.), and other fruit trees have grown in value. One local schoolteacher, who planted fruit trees fifteen years ago, is now able to make M$8,000 (approximately US$3,200) a year from his orchard.[5] Many villagers hope that orchards will provide them with more cash income than they can earn from their swidden and vegetable gardens. Farmers usually plant permanent, long-term crops like fruit trees on land to which they have private and secure title.

Usually a family tries to diversify plantings and, therefore, has swidden, fruit, and vegetable gardens. In this way it can lower the risk of investment in long-term, high-yielding cash crops such as durians with short-term subsistence and cash crops. A dual emphasis on food and cash crops functions as a subsistence safety net. When the market value of fruits or commercial vegetables declines, there are always rice and subsistence vegetables to carry the household through.[6] The amount of land a farmer plants in fruit trees, therefore, depends on several variables, including how much land is held under private title and how much access he or she has to other land for short-term subsistence and cash crops. Most people in Tempulong also hunt and gather forest resources, often on a daily basis. This composite forest-field-based economy forms the foundation of the agricultural cycle and property relationships.[7]

Two areas of forest figure prominently in daily agricultural life in Tempulong and are locally referred to as Nababak and Tarasan. Two absentee landowners hold private titles to the land in Nababak, totaling a 1,200–acre plot. Villagers use this area communally for collecting forest products and for making temporary gardens. Tarasan, a 260–acre plot owned by the state, is the source of a dispute between the state and the village that began early in the 1990s (see map 6). Table 4.2 summarizes the variations in how both

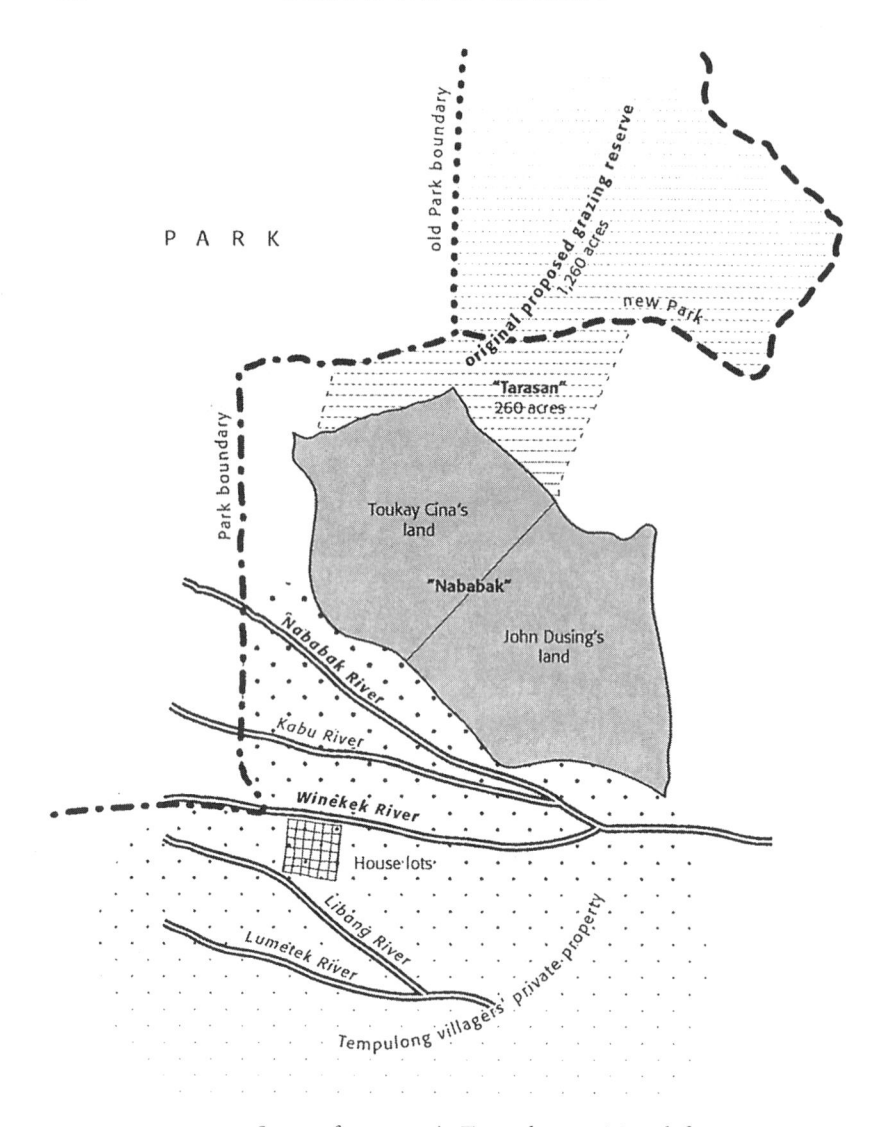

MAP 6. Status of property in Tempulong. © Metaglyfix.

Tarasan and Nababak are classified by the state and by the village and highlights the variations in land use sanctioned under each classification.

The property regimes that govern access to land and resources in Tempulong also vary from those in Govuton, and a study of these illustrates several interrelated points. First, multiple systems of property relations co-exist, drawing on both statutory law and customary practices. At times farm-

TABLE 4.2. Village and State Classifications of Landownership and Land Use in Tempulong

State land classification	Approved land use under statutory law	Village land classification	Approved land use under customary law
Private property Owned by Toukay Cina and John Dusing	discretion of owner	"Nababak" village customary practices allow villagers usufruct rights to the land and forest resources	making swidden gardens making vegetable gardens harvesting forest products hunting collecting of firewood planting fruit trees
State land	grazing reserve for several villages	"Tarasan" village customary practices allow villagers usufruct rights to the land and forest resources	making swidden gardens making vegetable gardens harvesting forest products hunting collecting of firewood planting fruit trees

ers invoke customary practices to contest statutory property laws, and at other times they invoke statutory property laws to contest customary practices. Second, a relationship exists between property regimes and land use systems, so that the composite agrarian economy is facilitated by the existence of multiple property regimes. For instance, farmers in Tempulong are able to plant fruit trees on their private property only because they can plant swidden gardens elsewhere on the land of the absentee landowners to which they have temporary access or usufruct rights.

And, third, similarities exist between Govuton and Tempulong in an "ethic of access"[8] to forest resources and fallow land, although several key differences between the two villages affect present-day property relations. During the implementation of colonial land settlement polices, the two villages had opposing experiences. In Tempulong, all native lands were settled during or soon after colonial rule. In Govuton, corporately held village land was recognized under the formation of the native reserve. More recently, differential development of cash crops has affected the expression of this ethic of access in the two villages. In the highlands around Govuton, temperate vegetables (short-term crops) are the primary cash crops; in the lowlands around Tempulong, tropical fruits (long-term crops) are grown commercially. Differences in the length of time needed to grow a cash crop

TABLE 4.3. Relationships among Crops, Land Tenure, and Use Rights to Borrowed Land in Tempulong and Govuton

Crop or resource	Land tenure	Payments
TEMPULONG		
short-term vegetables, minor cash crops	1. borrowed land (preferred for short-term crops)	1. no payment—"ethic of access" supports borrowing land
	2. personal land	2. no payment
annual swidden crops	1. borrowed land (preferred for short-term crops)	1. no payment—"ethic of access" supports borrowing land
	2. personal land	2. no payment
long-term fruit trees, major cash crops	1. borrowed land	1. no payment, but implies an attempt to counter-appropriate the land
	2. personal land, private property (preferred for long-term crops)	2. no payment
forest resources or naturalized crops	1. borrowed land	1. no payment—"ethic of access" supports harvesting these resources
	2. personal land	2. no payment
GOVUTON		
short-term vegetables, major cash crops	1. *tanah kampong*, borrowed use rights	1. 30 percent harvest (replacing an "ethic of access," which supported borrowing land in the past)
	2. *tanah kampong*, personal use rights	2. no payment

Crop or resource	Land tenure	Payments
annual swidden crops	1. *tanah kampong*, borrowed use rights	1. 30 percent harvest (replacing an "ethic of access," which supported borrowing land in the past)
	2. *tanah kampong*, personal use rights	2. no payment
forest resources or naturalized crops	1. *tanah kampong*, borrowed use rights	1. no payment—"ethic of access" supports harvesting these resources
	2. *tanah kampong*, personal use rights	2. no payment

in Tempulong and Govuton (fruits versus vegetables, respectively), influence the expression of property relations and the ethic of access to certain categories of land and natural resources (see table 4.3 for a comparison of crops, property rights, and payment for borrowing land in Govuton and Tempulong). Thus the landscape is more than the geography encompassing a village; the particularities of landscape and place also influence social action, local economy, and property regimes (Escobar 1998).

COLONIAL CONTACT IN TEMPULONG

As in Govuton, the Dusunic-speaking people who traditionally subsisted on swidden agriculture populate Tempulong. Unlike Govuton, Tempulong is a small town, with slightly more than four hundred people.[9] According to village oral histories, sometime after World War II the market center of Ranau began to experience a land shortage. Consequently, people from Ranau migrated to Tempulong, where the population density was low and there appeared to be plenty of forested land. As in Govuton, the customary practice was to allow pioneers (the first people to clear the forest) to become landowners and to invest owners with primary use rights to land and ownership of all the crops that they planted on the land.[10] Following local customary law, when people from other communities wanted to clear the forest and thereby claim primary use rights to the land within a specific village territory, the

TABLE 4.4. Headmen in Tempulong and Their Actions
in Regard to Village Territory

Name	Year	Action
Gunsalam	1960s	gave land to John Dusing and Toukay Cina
Sian	1970s and 1980s	began negotiations with state over access to "Tarasan"
Gani	1990s	took action to counter-appropriate state land in "Tarasan" by cultivating the land

permission of the headman had to be obtained first. In the early 1950s, when land was plentiful in Tempulong, the permission to clear land was easy to secure from the headman, Gunsalam. In fact, it is often suggested today by villagers who resent that there is not more land for the village to cultivate that Gunsalam was making a personal profit by giving outsiders land within the village territory in exchange for cash (see table 4.4).

A wave of migration to Tempulong occurred before the villagers were familiar with the colonial process of issuing private title to land. But newcomers to Tempulong were more connected to the colonial power structures and realized the value of individual, private title within colonial legal and economic systems. Of particular concern and importance in present-day land use practices and land disputes in Tempulong are the two large holdings that were authorized in the 1950s by Gunsalam in the area called Nababak. One of these holdings was given to John Dusing, the district officer in Ranau at the time. Gunsalam gave another plot to a Chinese merchant, locally known as "Toukay Cina," who intended to plant coffee and rubber. Radani, a grandmother who migrated from Ranau to Tempulong in the early 1950s in search of vacant land, explained to me that, at the time, villagers were hopeful that Toukay Cina would provide them with wage labor: "In 1951, I worked for Toukay sometimes. He paid me $M2 a day to plant coffee and rubber. At that time it was a lot of money. But after a few years his money ran out and he returned to the Philippines."[11]

Dusing and Toukay Cina's estates measure more than six hundred acres each and therefore represent a significant amount of the village territory; jointly they are referred to as Nababak since the Nababak River flows between the majority of the village land and these two plots (refer to map 6).

It is not possible to determine from oral histories or from regional archival data whether Gunsalam gave village land away out of personal greed (financial gain) or out of cultural norms that emphasize shared access to plentiful natural resources. Regardless, most of the villagers in Tempulong today consider the loss of more than twelve hundred acres of village territory as a great misfortune (*kemalangan*). Land is now scarce, and as the younger generations start families, they are unable to find sufficient land to farm.

The scarcity of unowned land in present-day Tempulong was brought into sharp relief by a young husband and wife who had recently acquired a small, long, thin plot, measuring fewer than two acres. They got this land through intensive study of landownership maps in the Lands and Survey Department in Ranau.[12] Boundaries of private property are marked on maps according to rough surveys made at the time of the application. Often the official boundaries are not established until decades after the land is applied for. Once official surveys are completed, the maps are redrawn. This young couple located a small splinter of land between the boundaries of two plots that became available when the survey lines were redrawn. Earlier survey maps had incorporated this strip into the adjacent properties. Unclaimed or unowned land in Tempulong is so scarce that this small piece was considered a great find.

By the end of the colonial period, most of the villagers in Tempulong had applied for native titles to the land for which they had use rights. By the late 1990s, all land within Tempulong's village boundaries was privately held (by both villagers and outsiders), and no vacant land was unclaimed. Unlike in Govuton, villagers in Tempulong did not negotiate with colonial agents over the implementation of colonial land laws. Instead, local oral histories suggest that they aided the colonial state agents in their project of land settlement. Whereas Govuton villagers rejected the possibility of individual private title to land in favor of a village title to the native reserve, villagers in Tempulong accepted private titles to their lands. Thus, in Govuton, villagers share access to village land for agriculture and establish use rights through cultivation. Furthermore, the substantial area of land in the *hutan simpan* (forest reserve) in Govuton allows villagers shared access to forest resources.

THE DURABILITY OF CUSTOMARY
PRACTICES: CONTESTING STATUTORY LAWS

Multiple social, economic, and political factors shape land use systems, property relations, and land disputes in the village of Tempulong. These factors include the intricacies of cultural practices surrounding resource management regimes and power struggles between local leaders over the best ways both to achieve the state's goals of modernization and to maintain village autonomy. Most important, contemporary property relations in Tempulong are articulated through cultural idioms associated with mutual exchange and reciprocity. These customary practices have been both expanded and constrained by the imposition of statutory law that emphasizes individual profit from resources rather than community reciprocity. The intermingling of customary law and statutory law provides farmers with competing sources of legitimacy in resource-related disputes and creates multiple strategies that can be mobilized by farmers to gain access to land. But as villagers take opposing sides as to whether customary practices or statutory law should prevail, disputes have arisen with increased frequency in Tempulong. The kinds of impasses that result from the inherent incompatibility of customary law and statutory law are evident in several property disputes, analyzed later in the chapter, which show how property relations are transformed over time and illustrate the nature of state-society relationships in Tempulong.

Although all individuals in Tempulong applied for private title to their land during (or soon after) the colonial period, local customary rules of access have endured to the present, overlaying the statutory laws associated with private property. Thus, statutory law and customary law are intermingled in locally specific and culturally acceptable patterns of property relations. For instance, as in Govuton, a landowner in Tempulong (a pioneer or inheritor) also has primary use rights to the land and all the crops that he or she plants. The colonial officials misinterpreted these primary use rights as private property rights during the land settlement process, yet even today, ownership to land under native title in Tempulong is limited in two ways by customary practices. Similar to the custom in Govuton, it is expected that kin and neighbors needing land to cultivate may borrow any fallow land, even if it is private property. And useful forest products growing naturally on fallow land, as well as abandoned or naturalized cultivated crops (e.g., taro [*Caladium* spp.] and bananas [*Musa* spp.], which propagate naturally as an abandoned field returns to secondary growth), may be harvested by anyone in the village who needs them. As in Govuton, this customary practice of community access to certain categories of land and resources can be conceptualized as an ethic of access rooted in cultural values.

In Tempulong, the ethic of access to fallow land and forest resources is culturally elaborated through two intertwined discourses. The first emphasizes societal norms and is similar to that found in Govuton. A "moral economy of the peasant," in which reciprocity and exchange form the foundation of social relationships is drawn on to justify community access to fallow land (cf. Scott 1976, esp. chap. 1). An important element of the moral economy, as also seen in Govuton, is the fact that it is place-specific, resource-specific, and period-specific. As such, the moral economy is undermined at particular moments when individuals feel that particular plots of land or specific resources (previously seen as communally owned) are removed from the broader production system in order for one person to make a profit. The second discourse, specific to Tempulong, emphasizes the "natural," nondomesticated state of resources. Individual people do not cultivate resources found in the forest, so no one person can claim ownership of these, nor can they attempt to exclude other members of the community from access. Community access to forest resources, even those growing on private property, is articulated through a local discourse denying that individual people may own plants that they do not cultivate. Wild growing forest products are referred to as *kepunya'an hutan,* or as belonging to the forest (lit. "the property of the forest"). Table 4.5 contrasts the justification of different customary practices under various local discourses (such as reciprocity and *kepunya'an hutan*). This perception of *kepunya'an hutan* is distinctive to Tempulong, even though Govuton is not far away geographically and culturally. Thus, it is important to keep in mind that one cannot make generalizations about agricultural-based societies in Sabah, but instead must consider that ecological, socioeconomic, and cultural variations influence the expression of social relations surrounding resources.

The following story about the formation of village boundaries in Tempulong, told to me by Suali, a village elder, highlights the moral economy of community access to forest resources and the value of exchange and reciprocity in forming acceptable, local norms of resource use.

> Many years ago the people in Tempulong shared a hunting area with the neighboring village of Bongkod. It was the custom (*adat*) of the two villages to share a campsite in the forest. When people from Tempulong were ready to return to their homes after hunting they would leave a supply of meat (D: *onsi*), vegetables (*sayur-sayuran*), and rice (D: *bagas*) for the next hunting group from Bongkod. People from Bongkod would do the same for Tempulong hunters. One day a hunting group from Tempulong stopped at the campsite. The storage bin (D: *lingkut*) was filled with deer meat (D: *onsi planduk*), monkey meat (D: *onsi monyet*), and plenty of vegetables and rice. As a trick or

TABLE 4.5. Land Use and Local Discourse in Tempulong

Land use sanctioned by customary law	Discourse used to justify action
making swidden gardens making vegetable gardens	"Moral economy": access to fallow land for temporary crops is part of system of exchange and reciprocity between kin and neighbors. These activities are not attempts to claim the land for permanent, personal use.
harvesting forest products hunting collecting firewood	*"Kepunya'an hutan"* (belonging to the forest): forest products are not owned by individuals but by the forest, and therefore the whole village has equal access to these resources, regardless of who owns the land. These activities are not attempts to claim the land for permanent, personal use.
planting fruit trees	Pioneer of the land: the first person to invest his or her labor in unowned land can claim that land for personal, permanent use. These activities are attempts to counter-appropriate land for permanent, personal use.

ruse (*tipu*), when the people from Tempulong left, they filled the bin not with food, but with feces (D: *ta'i*). When the Bongkod hunters later found the bin filled with feces they were furious. They put a curse (*sumpah*) on the village of Tempulong. They said that the boundary (*batas*) between the two villages was fixed, near the river called Naluwad, and that they would no longer share the hunting area. People from Tempulong could never cross over into Bongkod land. If they did, great misfortune (*kemalangan*) would fall on them. The curse also said that Tempulong villagers would never be prosperous and that no important headman would live to an old age.[13]

This story must be interpreted in the context of village boundaries, shared natural resources, and resource management. The theme of a moral economy of shared access to resources and the importance of reciprocity in forming social bonds is reiterated throughout. A shared hunting ground between two villages suggests that cultural norms associate the absence of boundaries with culturally appropriate resource management strategies; valuable social bonds are forged through shared access to forest resources. When cultural norms based on a moral economy of exchange and reciprocity are followed, the result will be good resource management.[14]

The story suggests that physical boundaries to resources also result in social boundaries between villages, which would undermine the traditional economic system of exchange and reciprocity that is found in many societies in Malaysia and Indonesia. Shared access to natural resources is symbolized not only by leaving a portion of the hunt but also by leaving cultivated foods, which represent sharing aspects of village life. Such food-oriented hospitality is embedded in local notions of exchange and generosity and demonstrates symmetrical social relations and kinship ties.[15] In contemporary village life in Tempulong, whenever a hunter kills an animal, a portion of it, no matter how small, is shared with all extended family members. This practice is culturally elaborated as sharing one's good fortune (*keuntungan*), and such generosity will be repaid when family members who in the past have benefited from one's good fortune return the favor. It is warned that a hunter who does not share his bounty will fall victim to a hunting accident. As in the story, when resources are not shared, misfortune is forecast. Social and economic relationships based on exchange are interwoven in the story through the shared responsibilities of resource management, mutual exchange of wild and cultivated resources, and responsibility for the welfare of kin and neighbors.

Parallels can also be draw between this story from Tempulong and the region-wide belief known as *kempunan,* according to which refusal to eat (or to touch) food that is offered in hospitality will cause one to be attacked by evil spirits, often in the form of snakes, centipedes, or scorpions. The story from Tempulong in which people are the victims of a curse, not for refusing food, but for failing to offer it in the first place, can be interpreted as the flip side of the belief of *kempunan*.[16]

By leaving feces instead of food in the cache, the villagers from Tempulong violated cultural norms of reciprocity; they acted in a greedy manner, taking resources but giving nothing of value in return. It is implied that the failure to share the bounty of natural resources violates indigenous norms for redistribution and reciprocity and, therefore, bears a cost.[17] At the end of the story, the punishment for Tempulong's greedy behavior is the dissolution of the shared hunting ground, essentially an enforcement of exclusive property regimes. The boundaries cut off both access to natural resources and social relations between the two villages. The story suggests that without these social bonds of reciprocity, Tempulong and its residents would be isolated and village leadership would be weak.

The indigenous discourses of a moral economy of community access to forest resources and redistribution of bounty are represented not only in stories but also in everyday practices in Tempulong. The notion that physical boundaries disrupt social relationships that are based on exchange and reciprocity is also seen in many of the contemporary resource-related disputes in Tempulong.

Village *adat* in Tempulong allows any person to stake out a campsite at the foot of a wild durian tree to await the fall of the fruit, no matter who owns the land on which the tree grows. Furthermore, if a second person joins in waiting for the durian harvest to fall, the first person is obligated to share the harvest equally. The community shares access to the natural resources of the forest, regardless of who owns the land. There is no evidence that villagers in Tempulong contest this notion of community access to wild durian trees on private property, and this customary tradition is still practiced today, despite the fact that all land is privately held. This practice is articulated through the discourse surrounding the wild (i.e., not cultivated) state of the naturally occurring durian trees, which are regarded as *kepunya'an hutan*, not as an individual's private property. Lenieh, an elderly woman in Tempulong, described the wait for the wild durian harvest:

> Even if a wild durian tree (D: *sukang* or *topolow*) is on your own land, you must guard it when the fruit begins to ripen. If you are not there, someone else can take the fruit. You must even sleep in a *sulap* (D: temporary shelter) under the tree. In one day 50–200 fruits will fall. The season lasts for 30 days, but each day the harvest diminishes. Everyone who sits under the tree can have a share of the harvest.[18]

However, the practice of community access to natural resources on private property is also being challenged though other methods of resource management in Tempulong, particularly as the commercial value of some forest resources emerge. The following example of a state-sponsored effort to conserve rare rafflesia plants (*Rafflesia* spp.) and local efforts to profit from rafflesia growing naturally on private property demonstrates the incompatibility of the cultural patterns of resource use with the ideologies embedded in private property and commercialization of natural resources.

In the early 1990s, Kinabalu Park began an initiative to protect the rare and endemic rafflesia plants that are found in and around its boundaries. As the largest flower in the world, the rafflesia is a natural tourist attraction. Researchers within the Sabah Parks Department established a "hotline" where tourists could call for the location of blooming rafflesia plants. A few villagers in Tempulong decided to take advantage of this interest. When one man set up a small booth on the roadside bordering his land and charged tourists M$5 to take pictures of a blooming flower, many people in Tempulong were angry with him. According to the cultural norms of community access to forest resources, it was inappropriate to make a personal profit from the rafflesia flower, even if it grew on one's own land. Such personal bounty would be based not in relations of exchange and reciprocity but in greed. Tension over this issue grew during the period of my fieldwork and culminated in the destruction of the farmer's rafflesia plant, in the middle of the night, by another villager. Parallels to the burning of Bukit Hempuen in response to state control of the lands that villagers believed they had rights to through customary law (described in the introduction of this book) are not difficult to draw. In both cases, anonymous individuals responded to what can be seen as a breach in the ethic of access or moral economy surrounding resources. The message sent, by the anonymous destruction of the resource, in both cases was this: if an individual attempts to remove valuable resources from the community's production system, then community members could also find a way to render the resources valueless. In the end, a single person would not be allowed to gain a profit, if that profit resulted in a loss of community resources.

Conflict between community access to forest resources and private ownership of land and the resources on the land is not new in the Ranau District; transition from customary rules governing access to resources to the imposed colonial laws associated with private property has been slow, even though the legal institutions have been in place for at least two generations. Local customary practices do not disappear just because a new statutory law replaces them. Instead, the two principles mingle together, creating locally acceptable patterns of resource use. When customary practices can temper the effects of private property, conflict is minimized or eliminated, as in the case of continued community access to wild durian trees. But when local individuals try to enforce their private rights, exclusive of community rights, conflicts arise, as in the case of the rafflesia plants.

A 1977 case from the Ranau native court demonstrates that conflict between the customary practices of shared access to forest resources and the exclusive rights associated with private property has existed for several decades[19] and illustrates the ways in which statutory laws and customary laws conflict. The court record tells us that Siking took Wasin to court for taking ten lengths (D: *galong*) of rattan from Siking's private property. The court ruled that the rattan was Siking's property because it was growing on his land. Wasin was fined M$25 per length of rattan, a total of M$250, not an insignificant amount to many farmers in Sabah.[20] Surprisingly, Siking refused to accept the money from Wasin, stating that he simply wanted the "advice" (*nasihat*) of the court on the matter and was content to know that Wasin had been taught the rules of private property. He warned Wasin, however, that if he took rattan from his land again, he would be expected to pay for both the current and the subsequent offenses.[21] By taking Wasin to court but then refusing to accept the fine, Siking drew on both the statutory laws associated with private property and the norms of customary practices. Implicit in his actions was a warning to Wasin and others that, now that they had been educated about the rules of private property, in the future Siking would expect that his rights associated with private property would be respected, regardless of customary practices.

In the rafflesia incident, customary practices were used to contest statutory laws. Conversely, in this case, statutory law was used to contest customary practices. Although statutory law prevailed in the native court ruling, Siking remained reluctant to enforce it, because the law conflicted with customary norms of reciprocal access to forest resources. As active local struggles over how and when to invoke customary law versus statutory law arise, these two contradictory cases demonstrate that one system seldom prevails over the other; rather, the various laws and institutions are used as mechanisms to create new opportunities to control natural resources.

As seen in the above discussion, the overlapping systems of customary practices of community access to fallow land and forest resources, on the one hand, and statutory laws associated with private property, on the other hand, are at times unchallenged and at times the source of disputes between villagers in Tempulong. Villagers invoke images of community access versus individual access in resource-related disputes within the village, based on the interests of the individuals involved. Variations also exist in the discourses and practices invoked to justify access to the largest piece of fallow land in Tempulong—Toukay Cina's and John Dusing's land in Nababak.

In 1963, Toukay Cina went bankrupt, abandoned his land without ever harvesting the coffee or rubber, and has not paid taxes since. Although Dusing's[22] taxes are paid, he has never used the land that he owns, so the villagers also consider him an absentee landowner. Every family in Tempulong has at some point used the land in Nababak for swidden gardens, and each justifies this practice by invoking the customary practice of community access to fallow land. As in Govuton, this use of someone else's fallow land is culturally elaborated as a valuable service; they are keeping the secondary growth back and saving the landowner the future labor of having to clear the land. Furthermore, the land in Nababak is a valuable source of forest resources. People go through the forested areas daily looking for wild vegetables, fruits, and rattan and hunting for meat, justifying this in terms of the tradition of shared community access to the resources belonging to the forest that cannot be privately owned. Land in Nababak is treated much like the *tanah kampong* (village land) and the *hutan simpan* (forest reserve) in the native reserve in Govuton, where all villagers have access to fallow land and to forest resources.

Other people, however, are taking bolder steps to use the land in Nababak—they have begun to plant fruit trees. These farmers, drawing on different images of customary rights to land than do those who plant only annual or short-term gardens, justify their actions by referring to customary practices that stress the investment of labor in the formation of property rights. In other words, the person who invests his or her labor in the land acquires it. Attempting to counter-appropriate Dusing's and Toukay Cina's land on a permanent basis, some of these farmers boldly state that, if the landowners ever come back to reclaim the land, they will drive them out, using their fruit trees as evidence of their rights to the land. Others, taking a less firm stand, say that they will demand compensation for the improvements they have made to the land and for the trees that they have planted there. Such claims are made through direct action and are articulated through the convergence of culturally acceptable practices such as claiming land through pioneering and using fruit trees as evidence of landownership. Although none of these ways to claim land are recognized by the current statutory laws, they represent ongoing attempts to use customary practices to contest statutory law and to claim land where land is scarce and where villagers have few alternatives.

The consequences of planting trees are different from those of planting temporary crops. Planting temporary crops and gathering forest resources are actions embedded in the moral economy associated with shared access to fallow land and forest resources. These actions are aimed not at establishing ownership but at using community resources that are abundant. Planting trees is a local strategy to claim ownership over the land.[23] Thus, the customary practice of planting permanent crops in Nababak is used to make claims of ownership against outsiders. In this case, customary practices are used to contest statutory law. Furthermore, planting permanent crops is an action that is aimed at altering ongoing property relations. This local practice of treating areas of state- or privately owned land as communally and/or privately held within the community has been demonstrated in other areas of Southeast Asia (Peluso 1992; Gauld 2000).

The state, however, will not recognize these customary rights asserted through daily practice. Gani, the headman of the village during my research, petitioned the district officer and the Land Office to release the land in Nababak to the village of Tempulong, based on the notion that the villagers have customary rights to land within their village boundaries that has been abandoned by the owner. According to customary law, when a landowner leaves the village, his or her land is redistributed to the remaining villagers who need it. According to the statutory law, villagers must apply to the state for ownership of vacant land. And according to the regional director of the Land Office in Ranau, the villagers in Tempulong will never obtain state-sanctioned ownership of the land in Nababak. Since Toukay Cina has failed to pay taxes for thirty years, the government will auction off his land to raise money; the highest bidder will become the new landowner. In the eyes of the state, Tempulong's past claims on the land as village property were revoked when Gunsalam signed the application for land on behalf of Toukay Cina in the 1950s. All notions of community access to land and forest resources are erased with the notion that the state has proprietary rights over all "waste land," including abandoned private property. Even though John Dusing has never used his land, all taxes are paid, so the state would never allow villagers to challenge his title.

IMAGES OF MODERNITY: NEGOTIATION AND RESISTANCE IN LAND DISPUTES BETWEEN TEMPULONG AND THE STATE

Local leaders from Govuton were able to negotiate with the colonial state over native customary rights to land by co-opting concerns that were central to colonial rule, that is, concerns with settling native rights to land, assigning statutory rights to native customary rights, and "protecting" natives from losing their land to land speculators. Using these colonial agendas to their advantage, local leaders from Govuton influenced the implementation of colonial law and facilitated the formation of the native reserve. This type of negotiation and accommodation between local leaders and the state government was by no means widespread in Sabah, but it illustrates one of the ways in which local society and state agents can work together in the production and implementation of state rule.

Since the early 1980s, leaders from Tempulong have tried—without resolution—to negotiate with the state for village ownership of an area known as Tarasan. In this struggle different views compete. In the realm of political discussions, land claims are articulated according to certain images of modernity. In the realm of practice and action, land claims are made through a reinvigoration of customary practices. At the time of my research, the chairman of the JKKK was the political negotiator, and the headman of the village acted directly through customary practice. The two were unable to act collaboratively to influence the state; instead, each strategically invoked contradictory images of modernity and tradition to legitimate local claims to the land.

The original request for the land in Tarasan came in 1982 from Lagas, the headman from Tempulong. In a letter to the district officer, he requested that 1,260 acres bordering Kinabalu Park be set aside for his village. He explained that Tempulong needed this land because a large area of the village's agricultural land was destroyed when the Winekek River flooded in the mid-1970s, covering the fields with toxic effluents from the Winekek Copper Mine.[24] By 1986, no action had been taken on Lagas's request, although the park boundaries were officially surveyed for the first time since its formation in 1964. On the basis of the new survey, the park boundaries were moved from the original pre-survey boundaries, and it was determined that 1,000 acres of the land in Tarasan officially fell within the park (see map 6). As a result, the amount of land left available for potential use by the villagers in Tempulong was reduced to 260 acres.

In 1995, the current chairman of the JKKK, Sindeh, began to pursue the issue with new vigor. Sindeh (whose connections with state politics and the rural development initiative were explored in chapter 3) attempted to co-opt the language and concerns of the state in his negotiations over the land in Tarasan. Specifically, he emphasized the need for a grazing reserve for the livestock owned by Tempulong's villagers. Although this strategy can be seen as politically savvy, Sindeh's efforts to establish a village grazing reserve were based not on the needs and realities of village life but on the concerns of state representatives who felt the presence of livestock in the middle of a village was evidence of a lack of modernity; free-ranging livestock represented a backward way of life. Sindeh located the village's claim to the land in Tarasan in the extra-local complaints that cows and water buffalo were wandering around the tourist area (*kawasan pelancong*) in Tempulong. In fact, the cows grazed around the house lots and the along road, but not in any officially designated "tourist area." The concerns of the state representatives did not reflect local concerns; none of the villagers in Tempulong expressed any interest in grazing their livestock in Tarasan. Rather, they complained that Tarasan was so far away that they would not be able to mind their animals.[25] And since only 39 percent of the villagers owned livestock, the majority would not benefit from a grazing reserve.

Although Sindeh lacked the support of the community, he continued to pursue this negotiating strategy with the state authorities in the district office. By invoking images of modernity, he cemented his ties with regional political officials but not with the majority of his neighbors.

Many villagers articulated resentment and disappointment over Sindeh's efforts to acquire the land in Tarasan as a community grazing reserve, instead of as agricultural land. Rumors circulated the village suggesting that Sindeh was benefiting personally by his negotiations, since he did not appear to be acting in the interest of the whole community. One man told me, "His words are sweeter than sugar."[26] According to a woman, "He is smart at writing letters, but after that he just plays around."[27]

In the end Sindeh's strategy was deemed a failure in the eyes of many villagers when the district officer decided that four other villages (in addition to Tempulong) should also have access to Tarasan as a grazing reserve. Several people complained that Sindeh must have had taken bribes from other village leaders allowing them to be included in the negotiations. Although Sindeh had partial success at co-opting the state's images of modernity to legitimate local claims on Tarasan (the village did obtain access to Tarasan as a grazing reserve), the majority of the villagers felt that there was nothing in it for them. They needed agricultural land, not a grazing reserve, and so they began to stake their claims to the land in Tarasan by planting gardens, thus contesting both Sindeh's and the state's decisions.

In 1995, the headman of Tempulong, Gani, organized four or five families to clear land in Tarasan and establish swidden gardens there and thereby establish claims through revival of the customary practice in which a pioneer can claim the primary use rights to land. Gani argued that the land should be considered village land (*tanah kampong*), to which all villagers may claim a portion of the area for agriculture. Although this mechanism for claiming land is not recognized by the state and was a direct act of resistance against the state's designation of Tarasan as a grazing reserve, the state did not interfere.

It is not surprising that Gani led the movement to stake claims to the land on the basis of customary practices. As headman, he was responsible for settling local disputes according to *adat* and was a stalwart defender of *adat*. Yet many villagers did not back his decisions that were based on *adat*. For instance, at a village meeting that had been called to resolve a dispute over how to punish young men who were wondering around the village after dark, allegedly looking for young women, Gani determined that according to *adat* the youths should each be fined M$5 and chicken. The money and food would be used in a village-wide feast that would serve to "cool" the village from the "heat" caused by the youth's bad behavior. Such fines and redistributive feasts that are demanded in payment for transgression of customary laws are referred to as *sogit* (D: "to cool"). According to the *Gambala* (Shepherd) of the Borneo Evangelical Mission, the villagers who have embraced the Borneo Evangelical Mission—the majority, who no longer follow the animist religions—"do not need to follow old *adat* in which offenses are cooled with a *sogit*. Only God can make a judgment based on forgiveness and redemption."[28] The village meeting ended in a fight, with Gani on one side insisting that the *sogit* was necessary and with supporters of the church on the other side arguing that only Gani and his friends would eat the feast, since the rest of the village did not follow the old *adat* and did not believe in the possibility of forgiveness through *sogit*.[29]

Gani's movement to claim the land in Tarasan by cultivating it drew on *adat*, which he was responsible for preserving and enforcing. Given the friction in the village over the contradictions between *adat* and the Borneo Evangelical Mission, it is not surprising that only a few families followed him; those who joined him in clearing the land in Tarasan considered themselves animists and were not members of the Borneo Evangelical Mission.

In struggles over access to resources, statements on land rights—whether based in a revival of tradition or national images of modernity—are themselves resources that individuals can draw on to legitimate claims to land (Li 1996:514). In the case of Tempulong, Sindeh's statements were backed by the power of the state, yet their effectiveness was undercut because they did not resonate with local concerns. Conversely, Gani's statements lacked the power associated with state support but produced more immediate results. These strategies delineate different ways of representing the community, one based on a traditional lifestyle and ethic of access to resources and the other on state-sponsored images of modernity. Furthermore, they represent different ways of responding to state policies: Sindeh negotiated with the state over access to the land, whereas Gani resisted the state's policies by planting a garden.

Throughout the struggles in Tempulong over the ways to gain access to Tarasan, local leaders tried to invoke images of community, tradition, and modernity to their advantage. Other state agents and elites, concerned with conservation in Tarasan, emphasized other images of community, modernity, and villagers' use of resources. Villagers were caught between state discourses of modernity and conservationists' images of appropriate community resource management.[30]

When farmers who needed agricultural land planted swidden crops in the area designated as a grazing reserve, park officials expressed dismay at the destruction of forest resources (see fig. 8). A park ranger recounted his conversation with Gani: "I warned the headman not to clear the land. In twenty years he will be sorry when there is no water for the village and no place to get wood for their houses."[31] Such concern over farmers who cut small areas of a forest with an ax to grow their crops is ironic when logging companies not far away use trucks and machinery to fell vast tracts of forest in an afternoon for governmental projects such as a golf course and dairy farm.

Park officials and other extra-local people involved in overseeing land management in Tarasan often mention the perceived benefits of community management of forest resources for conservation. Members of an international NGO working to promote conservation in Sabah frequently argue that Tempulong villagers should be taught to manage the land in Tarasan in a more sustainable way; instead of destroying the land for swidden cultivation, they should learn alternative land use practices such as agroforestry techniques.

Most important, extra-local elites, arguing for community-based forest management, ignore the complexities of local property arrangements and the relationship between property rights and land use systems in Tempulong. For instance, farmers use forested areas such as Tarasan for swidden gardens, rather than for fruit orchards, precisely because they *cannot* gain state-sanctioned ownership of the land, and they are not willing to risk the investment of a long-term cash crop on land that they do not own. Thus, historical circumstances and political and economic inequalities have made

FIG. 8. Land clearing in "Tarasan" viewed from within Kinabalu Park boundaries. © 1996 by Michael J. Doolittle.

it difficult for villagers to manage resources with a long-term time frame in mind. If they were permitted secure access to the land in Tarasan, it is likely that many villagers would be interested in agroforestry cultivation systems. Ironically, converting the forests in Tarasan to fruit orchards and other agroforestry land uses would be a useful strategy for developing a buffer zone between the park and more intensive land uses. The primary constraint to planting orchards in Tarasan is not the villagers but, rather, the state officials who are unwilling to facilitate village ownership of this land for permanent agriculture. An opportunity for more effective conservation of biodiversity and development of a local, sustainable fruit industry was lost because regional state agents lacked the ability to think creatively about resource management within the landscape as a whole (not just the village versus the park) and over a longer time frame. Such stances toward local peoples suggest that the community cannot manage natural resources independently of state controls, thereby privileging state "scientific" knowledge and justifying continued state control over resources (cf. Gauld 2000).

Government officials recognize that insecurity of tenure is an obstacle to conservation programs. A state representative working for the Sabah

Foundation's Environment and Conservation Service Department told me that their efforts to initiate community cultivation of rattan in state-owned forest reserves had been entirely unsuccessful because local people were reluctant to plant rattan when there was no guarantee that the Forestry Department would let them harvest it in the future. These people knew that neither the colonial state nor the postcolonial state has ever fully honored local use rights to forest resources.[32] Out of reluctance to address the political and economic institutional reforms that would be necessary to make changes possible, state representatives overlook both constraints on local people and possibilities for creative resource management alternatives. Such reforms would require ideological shifts away from blaming local people and their land use strategies for the loss of valuable natural resources and toward accepting that political, social, and economic inequalities are in fact more responsible for destructive uses of natural resources. Although local subsistence land use patterns are represented as degrading in the conservationists' image of community, even more degrading activities—such as copper strip-mining, commercial dairy farming, and forest clearing for golf courses and tourist hotels—occur in the region. A comparison of illustrations 8–11 suggests that forest conversion under indigenous land uses is far less intensive and extensive than the forest clearance resulting from state-sponsored projects. Yet, when attention is focused on the perceived backwardness and shortsighted behavior of villagers, attention and responsibility are deflected away from the state and the land use practices it sponsors. The rhetoric of community-based resource management invoked by conservationists associated with Tempulong both shifts the blame for resource degradation to local people and shifts the responsibility of changing resource practices onto their shoulders. The possibility that rural people and the forests to which they live in close proximity are impoverished by external factors (such as a shortage of land and insecure tenure) is obscured by this rhetoric (Dove 1993a). Emphasis on community-based conservation also shifts resources away from local strategies for livelihood and empowerment and toward resource management strategies that serve other institutional interests, such as conservation, tourism, and nationalistic images of a modern state (Brosius et al. 1998).

Property relations emanate from several connected arenas: local social relations and cultural values, customary practices associated with access to land, state legal institutions, interactions between local society and state agents, and even ecological factors. There are both similarities and differ-

FIG. 9. Golf course built on land removed from Kinabalu Park for tourism development near Kundasang. © 1996 by Michael J. Doolittle.

ences in the trajectory of transformation of property relations in Tempulong and Govuton, and the particularities of these transformations draw attention to several points relating to contemporary studies in state-society relations.

First, in terms of state-society relations, the attempts of the leaders in Tempulong to negotiate with state officials over access to the unowned land in Tarasan proved less successful than the negotiations between Govuton's leaders and the colonial state over the formation of the native reserve. Although the chairman of the JKKK in Tempulong was able to mobilize ideas of modernity (e.g., pastures, not villages, are the appropriate place for cows) in order to gain a foothold in the negotiations for village access to Tarasan, other village members did not support this move. These state images of modernity did not resonate with local needs and therefore were rejected at the local level when livestock owners refused to move their animals to Tarasan, when villagers opened the land for gardens, and when they circulated gossip about the chairman of the JKKK that questioned his motivations for negotiating. It seems that Sindeh's efforts to negotiate with the state were motivated less by a desire to alter the state's policies regarding land

FIG. 10. Dairy farm on land removed from the Kinabalu Park for economic development near Kundasang. © 1996 by Michael J. Doolittle.

than by one to garner regional political backing for his role as village political leader. Likewise Sindeh was motivated less by community goals of increased access to agricultural land than by personal goals of political advancement.

A second finding in Tempulong and Govuton is that statutory laws and customary practices intermingle in culturally acceptable patterns of property relations at the village level. Although statutory laws institutionalizing the legal concept of private property have been in place for several decades in Tempulong, their effect has been modified by customary practices. Customary practices do not simply vanish when statutory laws are set in place, in part because customary practices are so deeply embedded in local social institutions and relationships, such as the social institutions of reciprocity and exchange that form the core of village resource management strategies. When these social institutions remain unchallenged, statutory law and customary practices coexist with minimal conflicts, but when they are broken, the contradictory nature of the two systems is highlighted. When oppositions arise between the two systems, innovative expressions of rights to resources are seen. At times statutory laws and images of modernity are

FIG. 11. New hotel construction near Kundasang and across the road from the boundary of Kinabalu Park. © 1996 by Michael J. Doolittle.

used to contest customary practices; at other times customary practices are reinvigorated to contest statutory laws.

This notion that statutory laws and customary practices intermingle to form property relations is not new; it was most notably brought into academic discourse by Sally Falk Moore (1986b) in her work on customary law in Tanzania. But the contrast between Govuton and Tempulong on this point is interesting. In Tempulong the ethic of access supporting community access to fallow land and forest resources was more strongly articulated than in Govuton. At first glance this is surprising since property rights in Govuton are more strongly rooted in customary practices than those in Tempulong, where private property rights were implemented under colonial law. Thus, one might expect to see more strongly articulated and elaborated practices based on an ethic of access in Govuton than in Tempulong, rather than the reverse. One explanation for this anomaly is the link between landscape ecology and agrarian economy and the effects of this on property relations. In Govuton, the primary cash crops are temperate vegetables, short-term crops. Since the value of these crops is well known, when a villager requests to use a piece of fallow land in the native reserve, the person with primary use rights usually demands one-third of the harvest. In addition to seeing the use of fallow land as a valuable service simply because it keeps secondary forest growth back, Govuton villagers emphasize the economic benefits gained through short-term use of fallow land. In Govuton, the customary ethic of access has expanded to include the expectation of a sharecropping arrangement. By contrast, in Tempulong, where the primary cash crops are fruit trees, villagers do not request any payment for the use of fallow land, which is used for temporary crops that do not yield a high return and are generally for household use only; the ethic of access remains unchallenged. Furthermore, the ethic of access to fallow land is a critical component in the development of fruit orchards as cash crops. Subsistence crops are always the priority. But farmers will reserve their own private property (with permanent title) for fruit trees, if they have access to other fallow land for subsistence crops, even if access to this land is temporary and insecure (see table 4.1).

This relationship between short-term and long-term crops and property relations leads to a third finding. Although fruit trees are attractive cash crops, they are also a long-term investment since most tropical fruits take at least fifteen years to reach fruit-bearing maturity. Such long-term crops are usually planted on land to which farmers have secure and defensible title. Yet farmers in Tempulong are able to tie up their private property in newly planted fruit trees only because they have access to land in Nababak for short-term cash crops (vegetables) and swidden gardens for subsistence. Thus, the ecological aspects of crop productivity, the economic and subsistence needs of farmers, and the nature of property relations are interrelated. In addition, both temporal and spatial variations in ecology are important factors shaping property rights. The relationship between long-term cash crops, village access to land for swiddens, and secure title for the fruit lands demonstrates how a convergence of economic and ecological factors can shape property relations. If fruit trees were valuable cash crops in the native reserve in Govuton, a whole different set of social relations surrounding property would be seen than it is today. This point is extremely important for any development or agricultural extension project to consider. Once a new crop is introduced, the likelihood is high that it will affect a number of social relations in the village (cf. Schroeder 1993; Agarwal 1994b). Close attention must be paid to the ecological and economic characteristics of introduced crops since these are factors that are likely to alter ongoing property and power relations.

A final conclusion, while less clear but nonetheless evocative, is that terms like "community" and "tradition" are inherently fluid in their meaning and thus easy to manipulate in resource-related disputes. Gani, the headman in Tempulong, for instance, used the notion of "traditional community" to reinvigorate the ways in which villagers claimed access to state land and simultaneously to resist state policies aimed at designating Tarasan as a grazing reserve. In contrast, a park ranger used the same term to emphasize the primitive and destructive land use systems of local people. Sindeh used the idea that Tempulong was a "traditional community" to demonstrate a lack of modernity and to attract state development funds, whereas a state agent used the term to evoke images of a simpler, idyllic lifestyle that would attract tourists. These terms are not universally accepted concepts but instead are powerful discursive tools used in negotiations over access to resources. Discursive strategies mix with political negotiations and with daily actions in many ways to influence the complex expression of local property relations.

The historical and ethnographic analyses of this study suggest that land disputes in Sabah are a product of changes that were initiated by the British during colonialism and continued after Independence, modified in both periods by local agency that is deeply rooted in both enduring cultural values and instrumental goals aimed at changing the conditions of agricultural life. This research has shown that neither exploration of state practices nor study of practices of village life sufficiently explains the factors that influence the continuously mobile nature of property rights. Each view is partial and overlooks the ways in which one side is influenced by the actions of the other. These two fields of analysis must be brought together in order for there to be an understanding of how they mutually influence the shape of property relations. Furthermore, when the forms of rule employed by the colonial and postcolonial states are observed from the same analytical perspective, interesting continuities are revealed. Thus, the present makes sense when viewed in light of the past, and the past makes sense when viewed in light of the present.[33] My effort here has been simultaneously to denaturalize the colonial project as a unique moment in the history of state-society relationships in Sabah and to denaturalize the postcolonial project as a significant rupture with the colonial past.

CONCLUSION

IMAGINING NEW
ENVIRONMENTAL FUTURES

Alternative Strategies for Natural Resource Governance

WHILE THE PERIOD OF MY RESEARCH FOR THIS BOOK ENDED IN 1996, THE situation in Sabah in terms of native land rights, access to resources, and agricultural development remains much the same. There continues to be disagreement over which group of people have the right to call themselves "natives" and enjoy the benefits of native titles to land.[1] The state remains committed to aggressive agricultural development in the form of large-scale oil palm and rubber plantations, while emphasizing cash cropping for smallholders.[2] To meet these goals there are continued threats from the state that it will seize "idle land," and farmers fear that their fallow land may be taken from them, continuing farmers' century-long concern about their insecure property rights. And natives are still seen as uncooperative and the one barrier to agricultural development.[3] At the same time, observers also note that decades of logging without sufficient reforestation have left the state with a shortage of raw materials for wood-based industries.[4] And pressure from the government on smallholders to abandon shifting cultivation in favor of the production of cash crops has had unintended negative effects for rural agriculturalists and their land. One study in the Crocker Range of Sabah found that, when shifting cultivators were encouraged by the state to plant cash crops, land was put into continuous production, rather than allowed to rest for a fallow period, and there was a significant increase in herbicide and pesticide use. The results have been land degradation, slope instability, and soil infertility (Lim and Douglas 1998). After one reads the social history of resource access and use in the preceding pages, none of these current events will come as a surprise. The challenge in the twenty-first century remains to stop blaming local people for resource degradation and to find ways to achieve equitable access to natural resources and more sustainable land use practices.

One afternoon toward the end of my fieldwork, I went on a hike through the Similiu Forest Reserve with two regional forest officers, Salim and Rahim, and their "native guide," Ansaw. When looking for a conversational gambit, I inquired about the scientific names of the trees we were walking past; Salim and Rahim informed me that they really did not know them. As forest officers they were trained to recognize only the commercial trees that dominated the Sandakan District;[5] highland, noncommercial trees in the Ranau District were not familiar to them. As we walked along a ridge, Salim and Rahim explained why Ansaw's help was necessary—it had been eight years since they had visited the reserve (even though it is less than thirty kilometers from the Ranau headquarters), and they were afraid of becoming lost. I listened to the traffic from the road below us (although out of sight) and wondered how we could possibly become lost. Ansaw was as amused as I was. Later in the day, when Rahim and Salim fell farther and farther behind as a result of fatigue, Ansaw told me that he had never been to this particular reserve before either, nor was he from the area. His "nativeness" seemed to lie in the fact that he was better dressed for a hike and more competent in the forest. He wore tennis shoes and work clothes and carried a machete. The forest officers wore leather dress shoes and office clothes and carried sugar candies in their pockets. "Native" can thus mean trained in "traditional," forest-based skills as opposed to modern, office-based skills. Rahim and Salim, like many "modern" Malaysians, signal their distance from the nation's "primitive" or "backward" history through both their education and their lack of skills in the forest. They are not ashamed of their incompetence; rather, it is a source of pride that they have removed themselves so far from the forest lifestyle that it seems foreign to them.

As we continued on our walk, the forest officers stressed two points. First, although they did not know what species of trees grew in the area, they knew that this patch of forest had "one of the world's highest rates of biodiversity of plants." Many of these plants, they said, had local medicinal values. Therefore, the area would be invaluable for pharmaceutical research. They hoped that a M$3 million grant would come from the federal government for developing the forest reserve as a research site. Embedded in their rhetoric is the notion that local use of medical plants is noteworthy when their medicinal properties are recognized by the international pharmaceutical industry. Local (i.e., native) needs and uses of the forest do not make the Similiu Forest Reserve special and worthy of protection; only when local uses become global uses is an area assigned conservation value, as international and scientific (i.e., modern) potential raises its status. Ironically, although one needs to be a native to understand the forest, to know it well, to negotiate the landscape, and to recognize the trees and plants, native uses of the forest are not acknowledged by the forest officers as valuable in the modern world of conservation and commercialization of resources.[6] This contradictory rhetoric is used to push local people further to the political and economic peripheries as the elite in Malaysia endeavor to make the nation more "modern."

The second point that Salim and Rahim emphasized during our walk was that local hunters used the area heavily. They picked up a stray gun cartridge as evidence, and they claimed to smell recent cigarette smoke from an unseen hunter. The forest officers shook their heads at these illegal uses, claiming that they were incapable of keeping the "backward," local people out, powerless to stop the degradation of the forest. They described how they had tried to survey and mark the boundaries so that local people would know where village land ends and the state forest reserve begins, but they had been chased away by locals wielding *parangs* (machetes) before they could complete their work. In short, they lacked both the manpower to monitor the area and the force to ensure local compliance with the statutory laws.

As we walked along the worn hunting path, Salim periodically stopped and surveyed the area, looking for a spot on which to build a rest house for the forestry department. He explained that a retreat was needed for the forest officers, and they were hoping to find a site with a view of Mount Kinabalu and a natural spring to supply water. "The cool mountain climate is good for relaxation," Salim told me, and with excitement he recounted his plan to introduce rabbits into the forest reserve so that the forest officers could hunt while on retreat. How could such sport hunting be justified while local subsistence hunting was illegal? Were they unaware of the ecological consequences of introducing exotic rabbits into a tropical ecosystem?

This walk through the Similiu Forest Reserve brings into sharp contrast both the interconnectedness and ambiguity of the terms "native," "traditional," and "local." It seemed important to the forest officers that they appear nonnative or nonindigenous, set off as an educated class of modern Malaysians. Modern Malaysians, even forest officers, become lost in the forest; natives do not. Natives use medicinal plants on a daily basis; modern scientists research medicinal plants for international use and global commercialization. Natives degrade the forest by hunting wild animals for subsistence; modern Malaysians hunt rabbits for sport while on retreat in the mountains. Natives live in the forest; modern Malaysians go there for relaxation. Natives use the forests in unsustainable ways; modern Malaysians protect the resources for conservation and international research.

Paradoxical to this opposition of nativeness to modernity is the fact that the *bumiputra* population, literally the "sons of the soil," is the right-bearing group within the current postcolonial government in Malaysia. But, as previously mentioned, this right-bearing class does not include all of the "sons of the soil." Other natives have access to the privileges assigned to "sons of the soil" only if they are willing to forgo their traditional lifestyle and convert to Islam (Ong 1999). In this context the label "native" has helped a certain group of people advance in status. Although these privileged Muslim "sons of the soil" feel entitled to ownership and control of the land, they also desire to be distanced from working the land. And, not surprisingly, intimate local knowledge of the land and its resources is spurned. Why are practical, local (native) knowledge and ways of interacting with natural resources so scorned by scientists, politicians, and the elite? One reason, aptly explained by James Scott (1998:305), is the "simple reflex of high modernism, namely a contempt for history and past knowledge. As the scientist is always associated with the modern and the indigenous cultivator with the past that modernism will banish, the scientist feels that he or she has little to learn from that quarter."

This reflexive contempt for indigenous knowledge and ways of interacting with the natural world has even permeated some of the publications of the Institute of Development Studies (IDS) in Sabah, an organization that presumably would have some understanding of local social institutions and resource use practices. A 1992 IDS report on community forestry in Sabah uncritically stated, "The Forestry Department claims that shifting cultivation has been a contributing factor in the vast degradation of the state's forest reserves as a substantial volume of commercial timber is destroyed by such practices" (IDS 1992:9). How can this sustained critique of shifting cultivation continue in light of current land use statistics in Malaysia? Between 1975 and 1995, 2.8 million hectares of forests in Sabah were logged for commercial timber (Mannan and Awang 1997:2), and in 2000, nearly 1 million hectares were planted in oil palm plantations.[7] By way of comparison, agricultural statistics estimated that in 2000, 46,815 hectares were planted in rice (wet and dry). The moonscape of row after row of oil palm and areas of clear-cut forests does more harm to an ecosystem than any forest-field mosaic that a shifting cultivator can create with an ax, but the state rhetoric never brings this conflict into focus.

Every action of the state associated with land and natural resources, from the colonial to the postcolonial period, has whittled away at native customary rights in Sabah. In the current Land Acquisition Ordinance there are fourteen different enactments that provide for compulsory acquisition of native land by the government. Native lands may be acquired by the forest department, tourism bureau, energy authority, water authority, sports and cultural board, housing development, credit corporation, land development board, forest development board, rubber board, national parks, village development corporation, and the fishing authority. A pre-acquisition hearing is not required, so owners are deprived of their land with no fair explanation of why the land is being taken from them (IDS 1991:30). It is not surprising that many natives who have native title to the their land do not feel secure, given that their lands are not exempted from compulsory acquisition by the state for any number of large-scale projects (ibid., 85). Transparency, democracy, and accountability are completely lacking from these governmental policies.

Furthermore, sometimes "native" status is granted to corporations. This allows the state to register the land under "native title," thereby suggesting that corporations are preserving the status of native lands. This is one of the few instances in Sabah's land laws where native status appears to be beneficial. Such provision of native status is certainly a breech in the land laws that were designed to preserve native lands for the native people who live and work on those lands, not for corporations (IDS 1991:39). Corporations appear to be granted native status for the sole purpose of acquiring land registered as native holdings, even though these large-scale developments do not directly benefit the community. And whereas natives have waited decades for legal title to their land, private companies and government agencies obtain temporary occupation licenses and are able to evict natives quite easily (ibid., 96).

Policies that allow for the easy acquisition of native lands by government agencies or private companies have created a political environment where farmers who have lived and worked on the land for generations can be labeled overnight as squatters. For instance, in 2002, farmers from thirty remote villages in the Kota Marudu District were told that several private companies participating in the state forest plantation program (designed to ease pressure on the forest reserves) now owned the land that the farmers were working and for which they had applied for native titles (Sawatan 2002). The assemblyman who represented the region advised them, "I hope the villagers can be calm about it while we sort out this matter. Perhaps in the next three months we will see something come up." This type of policy and the laissez-faire official attitude that in postcolonial Malaysia emphasize large-scale development over subsistence use of land, just as in the colonial period, demonstrate that certain forms of state rule share similarities that are not contingent on the particularities of the state's ideological platform. In Malaysia, the invention and confirmation of knowledge—about the perceived inadequacies of native people to manage natural resources and the perceived ability of the state to manage resources for the greater good of all humanity (in the case of the colonial state) or for the greater good of Malaysian nationalism (in the case of the postcolonial state)—have emerged as one of the most basic forms of state power.

When viewed in the context of particular state practices and contemporary village life, colonial land management and postcolonial rural development are revealed to be mechanisms of the same political urge to achieve a particular vision of modernization. An examination of the histories of state rule and goals of modernization, such as the history explored in this book, allows one to trace the recurrence of ideas and imageries and to chart the tropes of discourse surrounding modernization and development across the nineteenth and twentieth centuries. Such a detailed social history demonstrates that rather than move along an inevitable trajectory, changes in the landscape and resource base (i.e., environmental changes) are the product of the decisions, actions, and behaviors of state agents and civil society and are often motivated by mutually exclusive goals. By revealing the patterns found in the rhetoric of modernization, it is hoped that more nuanced laws and policies surrounding natural resource management will be constructed. If policymakers and development planners attend to histories such as this one, any usage of rhetoric or logic that has been exposed as a mechanism to further the consolidation of power should be a flag for rethinking the policy or project at hand.

Despite the pervasive and pernicious nature of state interventions into rural agriculturalists' modes of production, property relations, and overall social organization, both colonial and postcolonial states' achievement of control has been notably uneven and fragmented. Thus, local villagers often have considerable power to negotiate and collaborate with state agents in order to alter the outcomes of state policies. And it is this very tension between the ruling state and an active civil society that underlies this analysis of property relations. This book has pursued two important analytic goals. First, it has combined in a single analytical field both the state and society in order to understand more completely why civil society makes certain choices about property relations and natural resource use. This parallel analysis of the historical and contemporary drivers of change in society and in the landscape should provide rich lessons for policymakers, who tend to view power, land use decisions, and property relations in ahistorical ways, as it simultaneously acknowledges the possibilities for human agency and recognizes the broader constraints placed on agency through the exercise of state power. Using property relations as a window onto broader issues of governmentality, this study has demonstrated that localized expressions of agency are never completely external to broader structures of state power.[8]

The second analytic goal of this book has been to focus on state-society interactions on negotiation and collaboration, rather than resistance. This has allowed one to see social actors working in subtle ways as historical agents (Ortner 1995). Through negotiation, local society presents obstacles to state policies that can result in new forms of both state control and local autonomy. The focus on collaboration and negotiation is important in the context of natural resource control in Sabah, because unlike in other localities in South and Southeast Asia (see Brosius 1997; Ramachandra Guha 1989; Peluso 1992), people in Sabah rarely act with open resistance to alter the conditions of their lives, nor do they solely rely on passive resistance to signal their discontent. Instead, many actively work within the confines of state rule to express their interests. To focus solely on the more overt ways of resisting state control would risk missing the critical forms of local agency that are found in villages such as Govuton and Tempulong and would overlook, or "sanitize" (using Ortner's term [1995]), the ambiguities regarding state-society relations found within these communities. The result would be that the importance of these political actions would be lost in the analysis. Most important, interpretation of negotiation and even collaboration as expressions of human agency allows for an accounting of the apparently contradictory ways in which society both resists and supports the existing system of power (Ortner 1995). Many villagers in Govuton and Tempulong simultaneously strive for autonomy in decision making over their land use and landownership and seek incorporation into the state as full citizens. These contradictory goals can be reconciled through local negotiations with state agents in which the outcomes are never predetermined or obvious.

Through discussions with state agents, villagers can voice their concerns over their current lifestyles, express their opinions about state interventions, and act as citizens who are able to influence the implementation of state policies that affect their lives.

The effects of both colonial and postcolonial interventions in resource use at the local level are shaped, and occasionally altered, by older, persistent practices of social relationships and property regimes. Private property law imposed by the colonial state and reinforced by the postcolonial state does not simply override or replace customary law but, rather, intermingles with it in a process of continual negotiation. Local-level property relations in both Tempulong and Govuton, influenced by deeply rooted cultural values that combine with current livelihood and power struggles, shape the ways in which property relations are transformed by historical factors and present-day circumstances.

These transformations do not follow a single evolutionary trajectory in which customary practices are incrementally replaced with statutory laws. Instead, in negotiations over property rights, farmers draw on various meanings of concepts such as "traditional" and "native customary law" in ways that strategically influence their access to natural resources. Both customary law and statutory law provide people with new opportunities and are intertwined in strategic ways. Selective and varying interpretations of statutory law, customary law, and traditional practices all influence land use and property relations in ways that are not always anticipated by state representatives. In attempts to justify access to land and natural resources, farmers turn alternatively to reinvigorated customary law and to statutory law, depending on which best serves their needs.

The narratives and case studies presented here illustrate linkages between historical factors, political-economic changes, cultural values, present-day land use strategies and changing property relations. All of the conflicts explored in this book emerged under two periods of state rule and resulted from state practices that promoted an ideal of appropriate natural resource use that did not take into consideration local livelihood needs, land use strategies, and cultural values associated with natural resources. With over a century of state practices that have resulted in ecological injustices and have eroded community and cultural identities, how is hope to be found for future resource management regimes in Malaysia? And how can the Malaysian state be expected to change its approaches to economic growth and environmental management when leaders such as President Bush of the United States see conservation as a "personal virtue" and the United States' energy industry is considered capable of regulating its own emissions on a voluntary basis (Watts 2002:1313)? Economic globalization, the latest version of European colonialism, is profoundly affecting natural resource use worldwide in ways that are similar to the localized effects of colonialism in North Borneo. The opportunity exists for policymakers to consider environmental histories like the one presented here as useful lessons on the consequences of the inequitable distribution of resources.

Poor conservation outcomes from decades of intrusive and at times coercive state control over natural resources (Peluso 1993; Neumann 1998; Saberwal 1997) have prompted policymakers and scholars to reconsider the role of communities in resource use and conservation (Agrawal and Gibson 2001). In the past decade, there has been an upsurge in community-based natural resource management projects that valorize community as the appropriate locus for conservation efforts. But such community-based approaches often assume that communities are homogeneous and stable and that the benefits they receive from conservation will create incentives for them to become good stewards of resources (Agrawal and Gibson 2001; Western and Wright 1994). In academic study and in conservation practice, communities instead reveal complex and often contradictory social processes as various groups or individuals struggle for power and control (Agrawal and Sivaramakrishnan 2000). Arun Agrawal and Clark Gibson argue that, if conservation at the community level is expected to succeed, then attention should be paid to the multiple actors with multiple interests within communities, the processes through which these actors interrelate, and the institutional arrangements that structure their interactions (2001:12–13).

This historical and contemporary examination of property relations and natural resource use in Govuton and Tempulong provides nuanced descriptions and analyses, such as those called for by Agrawal and Gibson (2001), by demonstrating that these two communities involve multiple factions, strategic interactions among community members, and layered alliances between the community and state and that they rarely share a single set of norms that constrain or facilitate action. Whether seeking political leverage, claiming access to unused land, or simply trying to make a living, individuals in Govuton and Tempulong are motivated by wide-ranging goals and aspirations. Equally important, no inherent "ethic of conservation" appears to exist in Govuton and Tempulong. Instead, there is a true appreciation of the value of land and natural resources, and of the benefits these resources could provide for people, and a fear of a future in which the loss of access to land and resources by government appropriation is a real possibility. In these communities, decisions about resource use are rarely, if ever, influenced by Western notions of a conservation ethic; rather, they are based on various strategies to gain control over resources. This drive for success in the power struggles over resources is not unique to Sabah; it is a desire shared by many resource-dependent societies (see Jackson and Chattopadhyay 2000).

Acknowledging the messiness and unpredictability of social relationships, including property relations, does not suggest that community-based natural resource management will always fail. Tania Li has suggested, "Conservation efforts that are consistent with market-related strategies of resources users are more likely to be effective than those that overlook them" (2001:175). In Tempulong, such a community-based natural resource management program might include land reform in which the state gives the lands of Tarasan and Nababak (land owned by absentee landowners and the state) to the village to manage as fruit orchards, providing a buffer zone between Kinabalu Park and the more intense management of swidden fields farther way from the park's boundaries. This type of land reform could prevent more intensive, albeit illegal, uses of the land and natural resources that local people are more likely to undertake when they lack land security. And in Govuton, a program that provided villagers with secure title to their agricultural lands might work as a component of a landscape-level management plan for the village land and the forested area within the native reserve. This, of course, would also be contingent on the Forestry Department's relinquishing its competing claims on the reserve. A starting place for a stable, landscape-level management plan in both Govuton and Tempulong might be state legalization of villagers' de facto practices through a democratic local process that is supported by state political institutions. Additionally, recognition of the value of biodiversity found in composite forest-field mosaics, particularly in contrast to intensive state development plans, is needed (Dove, Sajise, and Doolittle 2005. See figs. 8–11, chap. 4). And, finally, integration of the specific economic and ecological factors at play in each village must be incorporated into any interventions in the local agro-ecosystem.

Community-based natural resource management programs like the ones mentioned above are difficult to implement. And practitioners should expect obstacles to emerge and should be able to think creatively about how to redirect their work to achieve success when problems occur. For community-based natural resource management to work, many important and highly contentious issues need to be addressed, the first of which is the location of the boundary between state rule and social autonomy (Mitchell 1991). Again, Tania Li's insights on power and resource use in Sulawesi provide a valuable guide. Li suggests that such boundary making is not useful, since "however carefully they are crafted, conservation initiatives and institutional arrangements that assume or impose a separation between 'community' and 'market' or 'state' have no prospect. If they are designed on the assumption that rural people are fully implicated in economic and political processes of a powerful and sometime overwhelming nature, they could make a difference." She cautions, however, that the latter kind of initiative may not resemble what many people have come to imagine community-based natural resource management to look like. And, in many cases, such initiatives will increase rather than decrease state involvement in local affairs (Li 2001:175).

Many social scientists involved with the changing resource management regimes at the global and local levels have drawn attention to the increasing importance of the role of civil society in shaping changes in resource control and governance (Sonnenfeld and Mol 2002; Florini 2003). David Sonnenfeld and Arthur Mol point out that even when civil society initiatives are weak, as they are in many African countries, they can have profound repercussions when coupled with the changing global power relations on environmental issues (2002:1331). An example that Sonnenfeld and Mol (2002) and Michael Watts (2002) draw attention to are the increasingly violent conflicts occurring in oil-producing areas, such as the Niger Delta, between ethnic minorities and multinational oil companies. Worldwide, there is growing attention to and discomfort over the convergence of ecological degradation, human rights violations, and the inequitable external control of valuable resources found in deeply impoverished communities. Philip Stott and Sian Sullivan (2000) have identified human rights injustices, which can be wrought by inappropriate use and control of valuable resources, as one of the concerns at the heart of the growing field of political ecology.

What, then, might these new initiatives of community-based natural resource management look like? How can local cultural autonomy, economic security, and sustainable resource use be facilitated? A starting point would be to take Li's (2001) advice close to heart and not make a discreet and artificial boundary between state and society. In order to increase environmental management equity and efficiency and justice for local people, many environmentalists have argued for decentralization of natural resource management (Ribot 2002). But Li warns decentralization could be achieved not through withdrawal of the state but rather by building mutually supportive, democratic governance at both the central and local levels (Ribot 2002: 2; Li 2001). This requires a strong central government able to mandate minimum environmental standards that could enable a community to exercise autonomy in decision making about the particularities of resource management and use. Because this type of resource management is highly site-specific and difficult to transfer from place to place, policymakers may be reluctant to adopt the intensive and long-term view that this approach requires. However, only this kind of approach can meet the multiple desires and needs of society and the state. Social scientists have widely acknowledged that the search for an "environmental universalism is frustrated by local factors inherent in heterogeneous cultural frameworks" (Sonnenfeld and Mol 2002:1331; see also Peet and Watts 1996; Rocheleau, Thomas-Slayter, and Wangari 1996).

It is now time for governments and policymakers to acknowledge also the absence of any single best framework for managing natural resources. For this shift to occur, the dominant class of decision makers needs to shed the notion that resource management plans must emanate from nation-states. Furthermore, such a shift in policymaking requires a turning away from the neoliberal notions that the regulatory mechanisms of global capitalism must underlie all resource management plans. And, finally, a reorientation of policymaking requires a focus on place-based resource management and decision making based on local economies (Warner 2000:262). This type of shift in a world that functions on a neoliberal model of growth and change may be extremely difficult to achieve and will require leaders willing to take risks.

To date the potential benefits of decentralization remain unrealized at the village level (Ribot 2002). And in countries like Indonesia, where decentralization has occurred in de facto practices without any central oversight or planning from the government, the results have been dismal and have even resulted in violent interethnic conflicts (Peluso and Harwell 2001; Rhee 2003). An important component of decentralization that could bolster its success would be the strengthening of both community and national governance. One potentially useful model for democratic participation in natural resource management is the Aarhus Convention, which was signed in 1998 by thirty-five nations and the European Union and aims to provide the public and NGOs with "common tools and standards to monitor performance and engage in environmental decisions on issues ranging from nuclear power to infrastructure development" (Petkova and Veit 2000:1).

The Aarhus Convention does not argue for decentralization of authority regarding resource use and management, but instead builds three solid components or "pillars" of governance that give civil society a much more active role in decision making (Petkova and Veit 2000). The first pillar requires that governments and corporations disclose environmental information to the public. The second calls on the public and public interest groups to participate in environmental decision making. And the third affirms the right of the public and public interest groups to seek juridical remedy for noncompliance on the part of governments and corporations within the legal framework established in the first two pillars (Petkova and Veit 2000:1). Such transparency in governance assumes that a democratic government is in place and is willing to uphold these regulations, which is not always the case in developing nations. Nevertheless, it provides a starting point for civil and state engagement in decision making over the governance of natural resources.

It is possible to imagine a scenario where these principles are brought into play at the community level, where decentralization has a greater potential to work, since it would provide a mechanism to address the differing voices within a community by means of democratically elected leaders who are accountable to their constituents. Equally important is that there be a sufficient transfer of institutional capacity, technical knowledge, and regulatory authority from the state and other institutions to sustain any resource management regimes that are designed at the community level. This necessitates a close working relationship between society and state. It is unlikely that a frictionless and tightly coordinated relationship of this type will be seen in the near future. But a model based on decentralization, transparency, accountability, and access to judicial remedy has great potential for a future in which civil society, NGOs, and the state all prod one another along, forcing accommodation of one another's interests and better forms of environmental governance. Current changes in global concerns with environmental management, environmental and human rights, and corporate accountability and transparency are the result of a critical rise in the power of civil society to shape global issues. No matter how difficult it is to implement this type of local-state power sharing in governance, this approach will at least support a more equitable and just distribution of access to natural resources, decision making regarding resources, and profits associated with long-term resource management. After centuries of resource mismanagement in the hands of centralized state control, and decades of failed community-based natural resource management projects, this form of state-society alliance appears to be the only path to a just and equitable ecological and economic future. Such an alliance would require a radical paradigmatic shift; states would have to stop seeing communities as obstacles to resource management plans and begin viewing them as valuable partners. Such a shift in power sharing, along with creative forms of joint local-national resource governance, could facilitate a critical shift in governance that would finally break the pernicious cycle of blaming local people for resource degradation such as that seen in Malaysia. States then could truly represent local interests through participation and make individuals at all levels accountable for their resource use decisions, processes that to date have never occurred in Malaysia, or in many other countries around the globe. And as rural agriculturalists in Sabah continue their century-long struggle to gain access to land and enjoy small successes, they are also restructuring broader political and social injustices in Malaysian society.

GLOSSARY

Malaysian and Dusun Words, Phrases, and Abbreviations Used in Text

(*indicates Dusun words)

adat   traditions, customary laws and practices
bagas* rice
bahasa   language
Baik la tuan, jikalu Prentah kasi masok jail tidapa, kalu mati, tidapa juga   "Fine Sir, if the Government puts me in jail, never mind, if I die, also never mind"
baju kurung   long Muslim blouse and skirt for women
balai raya   village meeting house
batas   boundary
bising   noisy
bobohizan* priest
bodoh   stupid
bukit   hill
bumiputra   literally "sons of the soil"; natives
campur tangan dengan orang politik   to be involved with (lit. to "mix hands with") political people
galong* a length of rattan
Gambala   Shepherd, leader of the Borneo Evangelical Mission
Gerakan Desa Wawasan (GDW)   Village Movement Toward Vision, a rural development plan
gopu* a permanent garden; same plot or land returned to year after year
gotong royong   cooperative work groups
himba'an* forest
hukuman   trial or penalty
hutan simpan   forest reserve
Jawatankuasa, Kemajuan dan Keselamatan Kampung (JKKK)   Village Authority for Development and Safety

jalan   road or path
kampong or kampung   village
kawasan pelancong   tourist area
kebun   garden, usually small
kebun buah-buahan   fruit orchard
kemalangan   great misfortune
Kemas   acronym for *Kemajuan Masyarakat,* or Community Progress (or Development); an arm of the United Malaysian National Organization (UMNO) concerned with conversion to Islam; literally, *kemas* means to be orderly, as in a well-kept house.
kempunan   calamity, misfortune, owing to not having satisfied an urgent desire to eat something particular; or to refuse to eat
kepunya'an hutan   literally "the property of the forest"; belonging to the forest
kerudung   loose Muslim head covering
keuntungan   good luck, fortune
ladang   swidden cultivation
lapar uang   greedy; literally, money hungry
lemiding*   forest ferns
lingkong*   a vine (*Lygodium* sp.) used as a substitute for rattan in basketry
lingkut*   storage bin made out of tree bark
lot perumahan   house lot
merasa sangat tidak senang   to feel badly, not happy
nasihat   advice
nenek moyang*   ancestors
NEP   New Economic Policy

onsi*   meat
onsi monyet*   monkey meat
onsi planduk*   mouse deer meat
orang asli   "the original people"
orang putih   white person or people
orang tua   headman
pajak   to lease
parang   machete
Parti Bersatu Sabah (PBS)   United Sabah Party; the Sabah-based opposition party led by Datuk Pairin Kitingan from 1985 to 1994
pinang   betel nut palm, *Areca catechu*
rentis   boundaries; cleared path through forest
Sahaya potong rentis lagi tuan   "I have been clearing more boundaries, Sir"
sambar or sumbar   a deer, *Cervis unicolor*
satu bahasa, satu kebudayaan, dan satu agama   one language, one culture, and one religion
sayur-sayuran   vegetables
Semenanjung   peninsula, refers to Peninsular Malaysia
Sidang Injil Borneo   Borneo Evangelical Mission
sogit*   a redistributive fine and feast used to "cool" a village from the "heat" caused by an offense or transgression; literally "to cool"
sukang*   a type of wild durian
sulap*   a temporary shelter or garden hut
sumpah   curse
tagad*   swidden garden
ta'i*   feces
tanah kampong   village land

tapai   rice wine
teman rapat   close, intimate friends
tidak benar   untrue, untrustworthy
tipu   a trick or ruse
topolow* a type of wild durian
tumulok* secondary forest
UMNO   United Malay National Organization, the dominant party in the federal government; it is ideologically committed to Malay-Muslim domination
UNKO   United National Kadazan Organization, founded by Donald Stephens
Wawasan 2020   Vision 2020; a national development plan
Yakin kami boleh kami   "If we believe [in ourselves] we can [achieve our goals]"
zaman gelap   dark era or period
zaman orang putih   era or period of the British (lit. "the white people")

NOTES

INTRODUCTION

1. Mount Kinabalu is the highest peak in Southeast Asia and supports a rich and unique botanical community (see Beaman and Beaman 1990; Davis, Heywood, and Hamilton 1995). It is also one of the primary tourist destinations in Sabah, Malaysia. In 1995, there were more than 146,000 visitors to Kinabalu Park.

2. In a 1984 unpublished report, "Bukit Hempuen and Its Botanical Significance," Dr. John Beaman (a prominent botanist who has made the study of the botany of Mount Kinabalu part of his life's work) wrote about the many rare and endemic species found on Bukit Hempuen. He believes that this report may have been a significant part of the motivation to include Bukit Hempuen in Kinabalu Park (Dr. John Beaman, personal communication, March 8, 1997). This theory was confirmed by a park warden in an interview on July 19, 1996.

3. *Jalan* is the Malay word for "path" or "road."

4. The Malay word *sumbar,* or *sambar,* refers to a large deer (*Cervis unicolor*).

5. "The Royal Society of North Borneo Expedition Committee, September 1962, Report to the H. E. Governor of North Borneo on the proposed National Park of Kinabalu," draft of an unpublished manuscript, pages unnumbered.

6. Spurr (1993) devotes his book to twelve rhetorical modes, which he suggests should not be considered as definitive. Surveillance, aestheticization, classification, debasement, affirmation, naturalization, eroticization, and appropriation appear and reappear throughout the texts on the colonial experience. Spurr groups both the modes I refer to above together under the broad rubric of "appropriation." I dis-

cuss more completely the details of this discourse in the context of North Borneo Chartered Company rule in chapter 1.

7. One final example of how pervasive this rhetoric was can be found in the comments made by Lord Granville, secretary of state for foreign affairs. Referring to North Borneo, he said: "The experience of three years shows that the peaceful and intelligent development of the great natural resources of the country is steadily increasing, and there is every reason to believe that a sound and liberal system of administration will be established by the Company, which will spread the benefits of civilisation among the native population and open up a new and important field to British trade and enterprise, and to the commerce of all nations" (as cited in West 1897:337).

8. This notion of linking property rights to the economic principles of a market economy and the formation of legal institutions to protect property rights can be traced back to John Locke ([1690] 1963).

9. For a study of how contemporary representatives of the Indonesian state employ a similar rhetoric toward the end of increasing the power and authority of state plantations over native smallholders, see Dove (1999).

10. For a thorough review of variations in the treatment of "postcolonialism," see Gupta (1998). See also Abraham (2003).

11. This is not to suggest that the stakes are the same for the colonial and postcolonial state, nor are the stakes the same for the colonized people and citizens of an independent nation. However, the issues are overlapping between eras, particularly when considering the ability of local people to control access to and ownership of land. Thus, while it could be argued with equal force that the differences between the eras are noteworthy, this book focuses on the similarities.

12. For an analysis of these processes in Indonesia, see Li (1992b), and in Nepal, see Pigg (1992).

13. Escobar's (1984) analysis of the effects of development focuses on international development initiatives in the Third World in general. In this study, I do not look at the effects of international development initiatives in the Third World but, rather, on the effects of national development initiatives on peripheral groups.

14. For a similar analysis of development projects in Indonesia, see Li (1999b).

15. For other recent work on the debates surrounding globalization, see Appadurai (1996); Breckenridge (1995); Featherstone (1990, 1996); and Featherstone, Lash, and Robertson (1995).

16. See Sivaramakrishnan and Agrawal (2003) for a critical review of the scholarly literature that is engaged in this debate.

17. Other historians of Indonesia have made a similar claim, particularly illuminating "the unbroken chain of evolution that runs from colony to independent state by focusing on institutional continuity" (Lev 1985:57; see also Anderson 1990). I focus less on the institutional continuity and more on the continuity between forms of power, specifically the invention and confirmation of knowledge.

18. For recent studies exploring the relationship between cultural meaning,

social identity, community, and property rights in Southeast Asia, see Li (1996); Brosius (1997); and Dove (1986b). For similar studies in Africa, see Shipton and Goheen (1992); Peters (1994); Schroeder (1993); and Ferguson (1994). And for studies in the United States, see Rose (1994).

1 / COLLIDING DISCOURSES

1. North Borneo came under the rule of the North Borneo Chartered Company from 1877 to 1946. In 1946, it became a British colony, until Independence in 1963. I group these two colonial periods together under the rubric of "colonialism." It has been argued elsewhere that there were no significant changes in policy during the transition from Company rule to colonial rule, and, in fact, many of the administrators continued throughout both periods (Tregonning 1956:50). Additionally, in the eyes of native peoples, Company rule and colonial rule are conflated as the time of the *orang putih* (white people).

2. For an account of the cessions by Sulu and Brunei, see Tarling (1971, 1978) and Black (1983).

3. There is considerable debate considering the motives behind the Sulu cession of North Borneo. Tarling has argued that the sultan was only leasing the land to the Company and intended to reclaim it. Part of the confusion has arisen from disagreements over translations. As with the Brunei grants, the word *pajak* was used, meaning "to farm" or "to lease" rather than "to cede." The English translation of the charter, however, included the words "forever and in perpetuity" (Tarling 1978:197).

4. For accounts of British foreign policy in Southeast Asia, see Tarling (1969, 1993:21), Lea (1976:120), and Andaya and Andaya (1982:125).

5. The Royal Charter as reprinted in *The Ordinances and Rules of the State of North Borneo, 1881–1936* (Government of British North Borneo 1937:619).

6. See Sivaramakrishnan (2000) for an analogous argument with regard to discourses and practices of scientific forestry in Bengal during East India Company rule.

7. Governor Treacher's preoccupation with abolishing slavery over establishing new laws provides evidence that in the early years the Company was not solely concerned with domination and revenue production. But this moment of concern over local welfare was short-lived. By 1888, Treacher was replaced with Governor Creagh, who made land matters and the imposition of Western land laws a priority.

8. In this proclamation, the Labuan Land Ordinance, Number 2 of 1863, was adopted as law in North Borneo (Government of British North Borneo 1885:158).

9. Ibid., 158–63.

10. Ibid.

11. While Wong (1975) does not speak directly to the influence of Maxwell's writings on the formation of land laws in North Borneo, presumably his influence was

felt there as strongly as in Peninsular Malaya, since many of the Company officers had worked on the Malay Peninsula before coming to North Borneo.

12. The Torren's system of land registration was developed in the 1850s for use in South Australia. It involved title to land by registration rather than title by deed. Under the Torren's system, land registers were maintained by the government. Land in the registers needed to be accurately described, and the registers had to be kept up-to-date. In principle, a title or deed would be issued eventually to all the owners of land on the register. One of the benefits of the Torren's system from the state's perspective was that it quickly, and with the least amount of expense on the part of the state, produced revenue in the form of land taxes (see Wong 1975:16–20). Furthermore, the Torren's system was perceived as the most appropriate way to register land in a largely illiterate society. Governor Pearson of North Borneo wrote: "a man of the smallest intelligence and education can buy, sell, and mortgage land without the intervention of a lawyer. It is this fact that makes the Torren's system eminently suitable in countries where many landowners are Natives or Chinese" (Pearson, "Report on Land Administration," 1909, CO 874/796).

13. "Proclamation No. III of 1889" (Government of British North Borneo 1889:53–54).

14. It is interesting to note that the legacy of the colonial administration's inability to settle fully native claims to land has an impact in present-day Sabah. In the mid-1990s, the Lands and Survey Department had a backlog of more than 120,000 unsettled claims, and my research shows that the average waiting time for the registration of claims based on native title is ten to twenty-five years (notes from interview with the director of the Lands and Survey Department, August 12, 1996). To this day, the Lands and Survey Department is unwilling to expedite native titles because they produce little income in comparison with other classifications of landownership.

15. See "Proclamation No. IV of 1913, Land Laws," article 26 (Government of British North Borneo 1915).

16. The currency used in North Borneo at the time was the Straits Dollar, equivalent to US$0.40–US$0.60 (Kaur and Metcalfe 1999).

17. "Proclamation No. IV of 1913, Land Laws," article 57 (Government of British North Borneo 1915). This sum of Straits $1.00 for survey fees and Straits $0.50 per acre of rent was often more cash than a native agriculturist could afford. As a result, the tax books were often cluttered with debts carried over from year to year.

18. These figures were cited in the Minute by Governor Pearson to the Government Secretary, February 13, 1920 (CO 874/985). However, figures for rent and premium varied significantly over the years. They also varied according to how the land was cultivated.

19. Circular Notice to Officers, 1928, NBCA file no. 815.

20. Dane worked for more than forty years in various posts within the government of India. In 1911, the Company invited him to do a comprehensive report on the Company's administration (Black 1983:210).

21. Dane, "Report on Administration," 1911, CO 874/154, 88.
22. Annual Report on the Land Settlement Department, 1914, CO 874/797.
23. Recommendation of Governor Parr, Re: Settlement Work, February 4, 1915, CO 874/797.
24. In his book *Seeing like a State,* James Scott (1998) discusses how centralized states impose a legible property system on society. He argues that states employ schematic shorthand to organize complex property systems. This system radically abridges the customary practices of daily life, by forcing the intricacies of local tenure systems into a simplified system that facilities revenue production.
25. It was policy that each adult who paid poll tax could claim roughly three acres (Letter from Assistant District Officer Cook to the Resident of the Interior, April 30, 1913, NBCA file no. 1356.)
26. Ibid.
27. See various letters in NBCA file no. 1356.
28. Annual Report on Land Settlement, 1916, CO 874/797.
29. Ibid.
30. This process of ruling with the complicity of local social institutions is described more fully in Migdal, Kohli, and Shue (1994) as a tool of state making.
31. Letter from Pearson to the Government Secretary, October 23, 1913, CO 874/796.
32. Letter from the Assistant District Officer in Keningau to Resident Tenom. May 13, 1913, pp. 1–2, NBCA file no. 1356. I address below how the colonial administrators dealt with (or, more accurately, ignored) the issue of commonly held land.
33. While this language was ubiquitous throughout Company documents, Governor Creagh's "Report to the Chairman of the North Borneo Chartered Company," August 4, 1888 (CO 874/246), provides a good example.
34. For evidence of this logic in the colonial administration, see Letter from the Land Officer to the Government Secretary, August 25, 1919, CO 874/797, and Administrative Report for the Year 1910, CO 648/3.
35. Pearson, "Report on Land," May 11, 1909, p. 1, CO 874/283; Dane, "Report on Administration," 1911, CO 874/154.
36. Letter from Pearson to the General Secretary, October 23, 1913, CO 874/796.
37. General Return of Revenue, Expenditure, Trade, and Population for 1890–1931, NBCA file no. 579.
38. Annual Report of the Land Office, 1918, CO 648/8.
39. Annual Report of the Land Settlement Department, 1919, CO 874/797.
40. Letter from the Land Office to the Government Secretary, August 25, 1919, CO 874/797.
41. Ibid.
42. For example, in reference to revenue collected from bird nest extraction, see Daly (1888:9).
43. Minute by Governor Pearson to the Government Secretary, February 12, 1920;

Minute by Governor Pearson to the Government Secretary, February 13, 1920, CO 874/985.

44. Memorandum by A. B. C. Francis, [1920?], p. 3, CO 874/985.

45. Minute by Governor Pearson to the Government Secretary, February 13, 1920, CO 874/985.

46. Ibid.

47. Minute by Mr. C. F. Macaskie to the Government Secretary, March 17, 1920, CO 874/985.

48. Memo by W. J. W., "Land Grants to Natives," October 21, 1921, p. 3, CO 874/985.

49. For recent scholarship on colonialism, emphasizing the tensions, contradictions, and fragmentary nature of colonial rule, see inter alia Cohn (1996), Dirks (1992), Thomas (1994), John Comaroff (1989), and Cooper and Stoler (1997).

50. Letter from J. Maxwell Hall, Commissioner of Lands, to the Government Secretary, March 8, 1920, CO 874/985; emphasis added.

51. District officers have typically been defenders of the local population in the British colonies. See, e.g., Vandergeest and Peluso (1995), Sivaramakrishnan (1999), and Saberwal (1997).

52. Memorandum by A. B. C. Francis, [1920?], p. 4, CO 874/985; emphasis added.

53. Ibid., 7.

54. As cited in Minute by W. J. W., March 14, 1921, CO 874/985 (some minutes are signed only with initials).

55. Letter to the Governor, May 11, 1909, CO 874/283.

56. Memo on Rebellion in Rundum District, July 29, 1915, CO 874/834. See also Black (1983).

57. See Vandergeest and Peluso (1995) for a discussion of conflicting agendas between agricultural departments and forestry departments in Thailand and Malaysia.

58. Letter to the Pall Mall Budget, August 21, 1885, p. 679, CO 874/239.

59. Minute by M. W. E., April 11, 1920, CO 874/985. There is no evidence or documentation demonstrating whether this concern was valid.

60. Letter from the Governor to the President, June 22, 1928, p. 3, CO 874/985.

61. This question of long-term security attached to communal lands designated as native reserves is the focus of my contemporary fieldwork in the village of Govuton (see chap. 3).

62. The capital city of North Borneo, Jesselton, was renamed Kota Kinabalu after Independence in 1963.

63. Circular No. 481, Letter from the Governor to the President, August 23, 1928, NBCA microfilm no. 217/82.

64. Ibid.

65. Memorandum by A. B. C. Francis, [1920?], CO 874/985.

66. Circular No. 481, Letter from the Governor to the President, August 23, 1928,

NBCA microfilm no. 217/82. This use of the term "native reserve" by the Company appears to differ slightly from later uses of native reserve. In this context a native reserve was an area of land set aside for natives to make claims on for individual title (native title). In the case of Govuton, which is explored in chapter 3, a native reserve was a legal term imbuing the concept of village corporately held lands with legal status. Within this later use of the native reserve, individuals had use right to land but could not apply for an individual title to the land. Instead, the use of and access to land within the native reserve was supposed to be governed by local systems of property rights.

67. As seen earlier in this chapter, often natives did not respond to calls from the government to claim their land because the process of surveying was inherently disempowering. Many of the claims natives made based on customary practices were overlooked in the land settlement process and there was no effective avenue for natives to voice their concerns.

68. As referred to by the governor in Circular No. 481, Letter from the Governor to the President, August 23, 1928, NBCA microfilm no. 217/82.

69. Ibid.

70. Ibid.

71. Memo from the President of the Company to the Governor, "Development of the Interior," August 23, 1928, microfilm from the Sabah State Archive, no. 217/82.

72. As cited in ibid.

73. Ibid.

74. Treacher (1891:148), as cited in McT. Kahin (1947:57).

75. Official Regulations of the North Borneo Government, 1892, Section 7 of Land Grants Regulation.

76. Treacher (1891:148), as cited in McT Kahin (1947:57). Kaur (1998) also discusses the colonial belief that Chinese agriculturalists were the key to economic prosperity in Sarawak.

77. See Governor's Dispatch No. 259, April 30, 1928, p. 32, CO 874/985, and Circular Notice to Officers, December 24, 1931, NBCA file no. 815. According to the land commissioner, the new ordinance provided a "clearer definition of Native Land Tenure and Native Rights as derived from the old Malay theory of Customary Tenure, and is intended to confine 'Native Titles' to land used for genuine native 'homestead' occupation as opposed to commercial exploitation" (Annual Report of the Land Office, 1928, p. 1, CO 874/519).

78. Dove (1999) has shown that in Indonesia the state and its representatives often place obstacles between natives and commercial production because natives are needed as a source of labor for plantation agriculture.

79. Circular No. 481, Letter from the Governor to the President, August 23, 1928, NBCA microfilm no. 217/82.

80. Ibid.

81. Comparative Statement of Trade, 1885–1890, CO 874/89.

82. Ibid.

83. Ibid.

84. Ibid.

85. Cited in Letter from Governor Creagh to the Chairman of the British North Borneo Chartered Company, August 4, 1888, p. 40, CO 874/246.

86. Marudu Bay is on the northern coast of Borneo (see map 2).

87. Letter from Count Gelose d'Elsloo to Resident Davies, July 9, 1889, CO 874/248.

88. Letter from the Resident in Kudat to Count de Gelose, July 6, 1889, CO 874/248.

89. Ibid.

90. Ibid.

91. Ibid.

92. Letter from Resident Davies to the Government Secretary, July 9, 1889, CO 874/248.

93. Letter from the Government Secretary to Resident Davies, July 25, 1889, CO 874/248.

94. Letter from Resident Davies to the Government Secretary, July 9, 1889, CO 874/248.

95. Letter from Governor Treacher to the Chairman of the British North Borneo Chartered Company, January 18, 1883, CO 874/233.

96. *Ladang* is the Malay word for dry field agriculture.

97. Circular No. 95, August 14, 1914, NBCA file no. 284.

98. *The Ordinances and Rules of the State of North Borneo, 1881–1936* (Government of British North Borneo 1937:74).

99. I use "ideology" to denote the deeply embedded cultural values, conceptions of the world, and symbol systems that a ruling group uses to legitimize its ideas of how the world should look.

100. The Forestry Department was established in 1915 to manage the timber supply for commercial exploitation. Prior to this the administration of the forests was in the hands of the Land Office, which lacked staff trained in the scientific elements of forest management; concessions to timber rights had been granted on the basis of the financial ability of applicants to enter the timber trade rather than on their technical knowledge of forestry and forest management (Annual Report of the Forestry Department, 1915, CO 874/712). The establishment of the Forestry Department grew out of an active desire of the government to place timber on the world market (John 1974:62).

101. Memo on Shifting Cultivation [1913?], NBCA file no. 284.

102. A. C. Pearson, "Memorandum on Forestry in the Philippines, 1914," pp. 21–22, CO 874/711. This memo was written prior to the establishment of the Forestry Department in North Borneo. Governor Pearson, of North Borneo, traveled to the

Philippines to study the forestry department there and to consider the best way to form a forestry department in North Borneo. The paragraph on shifting cultivation is referring to Borneo.

103. Rutter was both a district officer and a plantation owner, which provided him with the interesting perspective that would come from being both a landowner and a state administrator.

104. Governor's Dispatch No. 194, Annual Report on the Forestry Department for 1930, p. 1, CO 874/722.

105. Letter from Smith to the General Secretary, April 12, 1931, NBCA file no. 284.

106. Minute by H. G. Keith, October 25, 1933, NBCA.

107. In 1920, the Company gave the British Borneo Timber Company exclusive rights to timber on all unalienated state land (John 1974).

108. H. G. Keith, "Explanatory Notes and Discussion of the Plan of Proposed Operations to Be in Forest Reserves," [1935?], p. 5, NBCA file no.143.

109. *Forestry Department Annual Report* (Forestry Department 1951:13). The report is unclear whether the committee is referring to current swiddens or the overall swidden cycle. I believe, because of the nature of aerial photography, it is discussing current swiddens only. However, it does not matter. If one wanted to include all land used for swidden, including the fallows, one could multiply by the average eight-to-ten-year rotation cycle. But the same could also be done for tobacco plantations because they have a similar rotation cycle.

110. I have borrowed this phrase from Migdal, Kohli, and Shue (1994:16), who argue that the colonial state, as an object of study, must be disaggregated. Instead of treating the colonial state as a hegemonic, monolithic force of change, emphasis is placed on the internal contradictions within the state's institutions. This perspective is extremely useful in that it emphasizes the limits on the state's power and draws attention to the rich social drama that also influences the direction of social change.

111. These patterns of progressive restrictions of access to resources, on the basis of class, race, or ethnicity, are not limited to the colonies in the nineteenth and twentieth centuries. Even England and the United States have a long history of perceiving the elite practice of game hunting as a noble sport, while placing strict game laws and penalties on people who hunt for subsistence purposes (MacKenzie1990; Neumann 1998; Ives 1988; Warren 1997).

2 / REDEFINING NATIVE CUSTOMARY LAW IN GOVUTON

1. The term *Dusun* is problematic for several reasons. Used by the British to describe the majority of the agricultural population living in the interior of Sabah, Dusun means "orchard," although its origin is uncertain. In colonial usage, it

merged diverse peoples who spoke similar dialects into one ethnic and linguistic group, so that ethnic and linguistic variations that were recognized at the local level were simplified.

Kadazan replaced the term Dusun in 1961, when the United National Kadazan Organization (UNKO) was formed. Donald Stephens, a timber magnate, owner of the local newspaper *Sabah Times,* and president of UNKO, argued that the ethnic name Dusun, although it was a Malay word and had been used by the British, had never been the name that local people used for themselves. Arguing that Dusun was used in a pejorative manner, Stephens claimed that Kadazan was more appropriate. But because only the people from the Penampang area called themselves Kadazan, other Dusunic-speaking people openly criticized the new term, arguing that, while Kadazan might be used in the Penampang region, Dusunic speakers in the interior and on the Kudat Peninsula considered themselves to be Dusun (Luping 1994:103–4).

Villagers in the two sites of my research considered themselves Dusun both ethnically and linguistically. They rejected the term Kadazan as an ethnic label and asserted that they spoke *bahasa Dusun* (the Dusun language). While I searched assiduously for another term, villagers maintained that they were and always have been Dusun. Therefore, I have adopted the term Dusun in my writing, aware of its contested history but confident that this is the term preferred by the people about whom I am writing.

2. Temperate vegetable crops were first introduced into this highland region just after World War II by the Department of Agriculture. First, cabbages were planted for sale to the Chinese community, particularly during the Chinese New Year, when there is a high demand for cabbage. In 1956, two Catholic brothers established a mission in Govuton. Their original objective was to increase the standard of living through tobacco cultivation. Soon they realized that highland vegetables held more promise than tobacco, so they began some experimental plots with various vegetables (field notes, interview with brother Benedict, February 18, 1996). Now the commercial vegetable market is well established, and tomatoes, cabbage, cauliflower, and onions are produced in high volume and sold to middlemen who export them regionally and to Brunei and Sarawak.

3. The term "colonial" has various meanings in Sabah's history. The North Borneo Charted Company ruled Sabah from 1881 to 1941. After World War II, from 1946 until Independence in 1963, North Borneo was a Crown colony of England. This chapter begins with the late 1950s, when North Borneo was a Crown colony. These two periods of British rule, which I collectively refer to as colonial rule, differed in subtle ways. Nevertheless, many of the administrative policies and all of the land laws instituted by the North Borneo Chartered Company remained in place under Crown rule. In fact, many of the British colonial officers who came to North Borneo to serve under the Company remained when North Borneo became a Crown colony. For the most part, the laws and the men who implemented them remained con-

stant. Other authors have noted that very few changes occurred in Sabah during the fifteen years under Crown rule (see, e.g., Ross-Larson 1976; J. Ongkili 1972; and Tregonning 1965). Thus, for the purposes of this analysis, I focus on similarities rather than variations between Company and Crown rule. Finally, from the perspective of the indigenous people, these periods were seen as the same, as *zaman orang putih,* or "the time of the white people."

4. Letter from the Director of Agriculture to the West Coast Resident, January 6, 1958, Native Court Office.

5. Letter from West Coast Resident Chisholm to other Residents, November 26, 1957, District Office Records.

6. The institution of native chief, established under colonial rule, gave state recognition to certain local leaders. Native chiefs were expected to serve as local representatives of the colonial government, collecting taxes and recording land transfers. They were also responsible for settling native disputes according to local customary laws (Kurus 1994; Phelan 1988).

7. In the interest of the villagers with whom I worked, I have chosen not to reveal the archival sources of village-level data.

8. Interview with S., December 15, 1995. While plans to gazette the native reserve began in the early 1960s, for unknown reasons the chief minister did not officially gazette the area until November 3, 1983.

9. That this concern persisted between the eras of Company rule and Crown rule demonstrates that few, if any, changes occurred in how British rulers treated natives and their land rights.

10. Circular Notice to Officers, 1928, NBCA file no. 815.

11. "Wight" is an old English word meaning "person, . . . thing, creature of unknown origin" (*Oxford Encyclopedic English Dictionary* [Oxford: Clarendon Press, 1991]).

12. Letter from the Director of Lands and Survey to all Residents, October 17, 1957, District Office Records.

13. Ibid.

14. Ibid.

15. Letter from West Coast Resident Chisholm to other Residents, November 26, 1957, District Office Records.

16. On how state management of local property rights can be seen as a strategy aimed at intensifying state control, see Li (1997).

17. For documentation of similar findings elsewhere in Southeast Asia, see Peluso and Vandergeest (2001).

18. For a seminal study that focuses on the networks formed between state agents and local people, and the influences that these networks have on the transformation of property rights, see Berry (1993).

19. Govuton is a large village and is divided into several hamlets, since each hamlet has its own headman. Therefore, as a village, Govuton has many headmen.

20. Again, in the interest of the villagers with whom I worked, I have chosen not to reveal the archival sources of village-level data.

21. Here, I am building on the insights of Tania Li, who argues that divergent and competing images of community become "culturally available points of leverage in ongoing processes of negotiation" over access to land (1996:509).

22. For more on "an indigenous labor theory of value," see ibid., pp. 511–12. For other empirical literature on relationships between individuals, communities, and the formation of property relations in Borneo, see Peluso (1996), Appell (1986, 1991b), Dove (1983, 1985), Freeman (1970), and Tsing (1993).

23. For more on the "moral economy" of peasants and the "subsistence ethic," see Thompson (1975) and Scott (1976). Neumann (1998, esp. chap. 1) provides an excellent review of the theoretical approaches to and debates on the moral economy of peasants. In my use of the phrase "moral economy" I am following Neumann (1998) and Watts (1983). I am not suggesting that villagers in Govuton did not demonstrate self-interest; rather, concerns over subsistence needs force people to place an emphasis on a different set of social relationships than in capitalist-based societies.

24. One possible explanation for why villagers place value on keeping regeneration in check, rather than on the restorative significance of allowing the forest to regrow, is that with the accessibility of inputs such as herbicides, pesticides, and fertilizers villagers now have alternative ways to enrich the soil.

25. This relationship between kin and shared ownership of durian trees is so strong that, according to one informant in Peluso's study (1996:538), "selling your durian tree is like selling your own grandfather."

26. Interview with A., June 23, 1996.

27. Interview with G., January 17, 1996.

28. Interview with I., December 1, 1995.

29. Interview with K., January 1, 1996. It is not an unusual cultural practice to move one's home after a tragic event, although usually such incidents involve illness and/or death.

30. A common complaint about the native court in Sabah is that it lacks the power to enforce its decisions. The police are responsible for upholding civil law, not native law, and therefore there is no authoritative body to ensure compliance with native court decisions. Ultimately, the native chiefs and their courts are relatively powerless in resolving village matters.

31. At the time of my research, US$1.00 was equivalent to approximately M$2.50.

32. The data in this table were collected over a three-month period in which seven households in the hamlet (30 percent of the population) kept journals in which they recorded their daily wages from labor, income from the sale of forest products, income from the sale of cultivated products, and consumption of forest products and cultivated products.

The period bridged the wet and dry seasons, before the rice was planted. During my eleven months in the field, I observed more collection of forest resources during the dry season. In particular, firewood was collected heavily during this time to be set aside for the wet months. But the gathering of vegetables and hunting for animals were consistent throughout the year. Most families have one or more persons who go into the forest several times a week. Although the sample size and time frame used to gather the data for table 2.1 provide only a snapshot of resource use, the results suggest certain trends in resource dependency that are supported by the ethnographic data from interviews and by participant observation. To develop a more nuanced description of the variations in resource use and dependency, it would be necessary to collect this type of data for the whole year and with a larger sample size.

33. According to the permanent secretary of the Ministry of Rural Development, families of five people, with an income below M$600 per month, are considered to be living below the poverty line, and families below M$300 per month are considered to be extremely poor (notes from interview, July 31, 1996).

34. "Similiu" is a pseudonym for the Forest Reserve.

35. Interview with D., July 18, 1996.

36. These conclusions support Li's (1996) findings regarding property relations in Sulawesi.

37. See Peluso (1998) for similar findings in Indonesia.

38. Interview with J. Payne, August 17, 1996.

3 / RESOURCES, IDEOLOGIES, AND NATIONALISM

1. Tania Li's 1999a article on this subject in Indonesia presents findings with striking similarities to mine. Although I did not find her work until after I had completed the initial analysis that is the basis of this chapter, I owe an intellectual debt to her. Her analysis has forced me to push mine further and has contributed significantly to this final product.

2. For similar trends in India, see Chatterjee (1993).

3. The words and intent of the phrase "Gerakan Desa Wawasan" are difficult to translate into English. In English-language newspapers from 1996 through 2003 the published translations included Vision Village Movement (*New Straits Times* 1996a), Rural Modernization Programme (*Bernama Daily Malaysian News* 2000), Rural Vision Movement (*New Straits Times* 2003a), and Visionary Rural Movement (*Bernama Daily Malaysian News* 2003b).

4. According to Francis Wah (1992:228n4), "There is no cultural group that identifies itself as 'Malay-Muslim.' However, such a category is used increasingly in official, media and academic discourse to refer to the non-Kadazan, non-Murut indigenous ethnic groups [in Sabah] who are Muslim and who closely identity themselves with Peninsular Malays, who are usually Muslim as well. These include the Suluk, Bajau, Illanun, Orang Sungai, Bisaya, Kedayan, and Brunei Malay among other groups."

5. During the ethnic riots of May 13, 1969, 196 people were killed in Kuala Lumpur, of whom only 25 were Malays, while 143 were Chinese. Unofficial reports suggest that the number of Chinese killed was much higher (Crouch 1996:24).

6. The phrases set off in quotation marks within Khoo's quote are taken directly from the *Mid-Term Review of the Fourth Malaysia Plan, 1981–1985*, 28–29, par. 82 (see Khoo 1995:194n144).

7. Shamsul Amri Baharuddin has alleged that Kemas goes so far as to gather community-level intelligence for UMNO (1986:187n36, 1989:13).

8. See Ferguson (1994, esp. chap. 9) for an explanation of how development depoliticizes political and social realities by reducing the solutions to poverty to technical ones, ignoring the need for social and political reform.

9. For a full elaboration of this and other objectives of the NEP, see *The Second Malaysia Plan 1971–1975* (Government of Malaysia n.d., 1–10).

10. Fadzilah Majid Cooke (1997) provides an alternate analysis of the timber politics in Sarawak. While she does not challenge the assertion that Malay-Muslim (*bumiputra*) elites have benefited substantially from the NEP, she finds a more nuanced sharing of control and power in Sarawak between the Malay and Chinese. She concludes that while these communities still "espouse ethnic sentiments in order to maintain electoral support of their respective communities and parties . . . [they also] effectively collaborate in the attempt to control and dominate the electorate and timber industry by way of the Ali Baba [the Bumiputra Ali and the Chinese Baba] arrangement" (1997:236).

11. This statement draws attention to the fact that religion and ethnic lines were blurred under policies aimed at facilitating Malay-Muslim domination. While some natives in Sabah have converted to Islam, they are not necessarily of Malay heritage. But the conflation of Islam with Malay ethnicity is common throughout Malaysia.

12. The PBS successfully challenged Malay-Muslim domination in Sabah between 1985 and 1994.

13. Interview with Y., July 31, 1996.

14. In 1928, the Australian Borneo Evangelical Mission began to work in Sarawak. By the 1990s, it had become one of the largest indigenous churches in Malaysia.

15. Interview with R. and K., March 21, 1996.

16. The JKKK was initiated in Sabah in 1968 as a way to institutionalize a system of community development. Its role at the village level is supposedly to give local people a voice in deciding which development projects they feel are necessary (Kitingan 1990:54).

17. When I asked other people about this program of housing assistance for people living below the poverty line, I was told that the program was a joke. It existed only during campaign years and only in villages that supported UMNO. For instance, people in Govuton never received such assistance, even though they were qualified. Interview with L. and A., February 6, 1996.

18. Excerpt from my field notes, April 8 and 15, 1996.

19. Cows roam freely in Tempulong.

20. Scott suggests that certain aspects of development have a powerful aesthetic dimension. In such cases, visual representations of modernity travel from one location to another, detached from their original mooring (Scott 1998, esp. 224–25). In the case presented above, the image of a Balinese ornamental home garden was transplanted to Borneo.

21. For a similar analysis of how development projects in Malaysia avoid confronting the real problems of rural and marginalized people, such as that of securing land ownership and access to natural resources for communities, see Ibrahim's (1995) work among the Orang Asli.

22. To protect informants, I do not identify the location of these archived letters. During the course of my fieldwork, it was not at all clear who—Sindeh or Gani—garnered more support within Tempulong. Gani clearly had a following of roughly five families, who were willing to side with him over a highly contentious land dispute. But other people described Gani as stupid (*bodoh*) and as making too much noise (*bising*) over small issues. Sindeh also had a following of five or so families, mostly those of his wife's siblings. Others criticized him for being greedy (*lapar uang*, literally, "money hungry") and untrustworthy (*tidak benar*). The remaining thirty families sided with neither man. As one woman told me, "The people in this village are not at peace. No one is willing to follow any leaders; everyone wants to follow their own path" (interview with J., March 29, 1996).

23. Tarajun's concern that Sindeh was involved in "money politics" was a constant undercurrent in all village dealings with which Sindeh was associated. I heard from many other people, on many different occasions, that Sindeh took for himself a percentage of all money earmarked for the village, that his extended family benefited from government subsidies before needier people did, and that he took bribes (interview with T., April 19, 1996).

24. Interview with T., April 10, 1996.

25. It is not unusual for national identity to be associated with government sponsorship of a single national language, religion, and culture (see, e.g., Anderson 1991; Vandergeest 1996).

26. Interview with R. and J., December 31, 1995.

27. Interview with M., June 29, 1996.

28. A regional agricultural extension officer made a similar remark to me. Commenting on the number of Muslim schoolgirls in Ranau, he said, "It seems as if the *Semenanjung* [Peninsula] is taking over Sabah. But do not worry—this will always be Datuk Pairin's state." Datuk Pairin is the ex-chief minister of the opposition party.

29. See Majid Cook (1999) for a similar analysis elsewhere in Malaysia.

30. Interview with K., April 9, 1996. The purchase of votes has a long history in Malaysia but rose to unprecedented levels in the 1994 elections. It is common knowledge throughout Sabah that the UMNO party gave hundreds of thousands of dol-

lars away to win favor among voters. Fraudulent identity cards were given to illegal immigrants in exchange for their UMNO support. Despite this, PBS still won the popular election (Khoo 1995; Luping 1994).

31. In his work on resistance in Malaysia, James Scott emphasizes the ability of "most subordinate classes, on the basis of their daily material experiences, to penetrate and demystify the prevailing ideology" (1985:317).

32. See Majid Cooke (1999) for similar findings elsewhere in Malaysia.

4 / LAND DISPUTES IN TEMPULONG

1. Out of forty-four household heads, 52 percent have wage labor jobs and the remaining 48 percent are farmers.

2. The home gardens of Tempulong are not as complex, diverse, or economically important as the Javanese home gardens. For a review of the literature pertaining to the sociopolitical aspects of home gardens in Java, see Dove (1990). For an excellent study of the ecological diversity and complexity of Javanese home gardens, see Michon and Mary (1994).

The home gardens of Tempulong farmers are more similar to some of the resource management systems in Mexico as described by Janis Alcorn (1981). Alcorn's study looks at the complex and diverse system of resource management by the Huastec. She describes how useful plants are "spared" from weeding when they are near the dooryard and how important plants, such as fruit trees, are planted from seeds that remain after a meal is completed. Home gardens do not figure prominently in my study, since they are seldom the subject of disputes over property rights, yet they warrant mentioning because they are one of many resource management strategies available to local people. Very little research has been done on the importance of home gardens in sociopolitical, agricultural, and economic cycles in Borneo.

3. The practice of forfeiting household rights to certain categories of land upon departure from the village has been documented by Dove in Indonesia (1985). Robert Harrison (1971) also notes that in the late sixties in the Ranau District, as a result of the increasing commodification of land, there was growing confusion over whether certain categories of land should be recognized as village land or as private property. In Tempulong, village house lots were also the subject of some confusion in the past, as certain individuals tried to sell their house lots when they left the village. However, before I began my fieldwork, it was decided that house lots were village property, not individual property.

4. The work in these vegetable gardens falls mostly to the women, for several reasons. First, women in Tempulong appear to be more interested than men in experimenting with new crops. Second, the labor requirement and the location of these gardens complement women's other duties, such as taking care of children and preparing meals. And, finally, women are far more likely than men to engage in small-

scale commercial sale of garden and forest resources in the local markets. Although gender is not the focus of my study, research into the linkage between property regimes, resource use, and gender in Tempulong would be interesting.

5. Interview with J., February 22, 1996.

6. Diversifying risk by planting multiple crops and by investing labor in both subsistence and cash crops is a common strategy among rural farmers. See, e.g., Hefner (1990), Padoch and Peluso (1996), and Dove (1993a).

7. Dove (1993b:136) draws attention to the composite agricultural systems, arguing that such systems "reflect the independence of . . . smallholders from external economic and political influences, which has been the key to their historical success."

8. On the concept of "ethic of access," see Peluso (1996).

9. This figure is based on my survey of June 1996.

10. This principle of investing the pioneer of the land with primary use rights has been well documented in many Borneo societies. See, e.g., Freeman (1970), Geddes (1954), Sather (1990), Appell (1965), Dove (1985), and Woolley (1953a-e, 1962a, 1962b).

11. Interview with I., February 8, 1996.

12. Interview with J., February 15, 1996.

13. Interview with K., April 15-17, 1996.

14. Michael Dove (1998) has pointed out that this ideology of exchange and reciprocity is pervasive in other Bornean societies. He also argues that Western notions of sustainability are inadequate for discussing environmental relations cross-culturally, in part because some indigenous cultures emphasize the dynamic and fluctuating relations between society and environment, whereas Western environmental concerns focus on discrete elements of nature, separating society from nature.

15. See Tsing (1993:55) and Evans (1922:67-69) for other evidence on the importance of food-oriented hospitality in Borneo.

16. I want to thank Michael Dove for drawing this parallel to my attention and George and Laura Appell for confirming the pan-Bornean nature of kempunan. For more information on kempunan, see Evans (1953). According to Ivor Evans, the Tempasuk Dusun in Sabah call this belief kopohunan. He suggests that "the root idea seems to be that if a person has not partaken of something in the way of food, drink or narcotics, when he might have done so, and regrets that he has not done so subsequently, his soul-substance is rendered weak through his unsatisfied craving and he will, therefore, have very little resistance . . . to the attacks of evil spirits in the shapes of centipedes, scorpions, or snakes" (1953:167). According to A. E. Coope (1976), kempunan is defined as "calamity, misfortune . . . owing to not having satisfied an urgent desire to eat something particular."

17. See Dove (1998:7-9) on the Kantu' belief that wealth and bounty without reciprocity bear a cost.

18. Excerpt from field notes, interview with L., March 21, 1996.

19. See Native Court records, Ranau District Office. I am extremely indebted to Shabil and Olivia, who assisted me as I read through thousands of case files from 1950 to 1995. Not only did they open their files for me, but also they took the time to explain confusing cases.

20. It is interesting to note that the native court upheld customary law in the case in Govuton against Intang in the 1990s but upheld statutory law in the 1970s in this case in Tempulong. This fluidity in viewing the validity of laws further demonstrates the ways in which property relations are really struggles over power, wealth, and meaning.

21. Native Court records, Ranau District Office.

22. Interview with J., in the Land Office, April 17, 1996.

23. Using trees as a way to assert counterclaims on land has been documented elsewhere. See, e.g., Peluso (1996).

24. This is a pseudonym for the copper mine. Villagers were afraid to cultivate this land because of the high levels of heavy metal contaminants (such as cooper, lead, and iron) in the soil that resulted from the flood (see Mohamed 1987). At the time of my fieldwork, nearly twenty years after the flood, the land still was unused.

25. Two cows had recently been stolen from Tempulong, and owners were afraid that more thefts would occur if the animals were grazed even farther away from the house lots.

26. "Katanya lebih manis daripada gula," interview with K., April 9, 1996.

27. "Dia pandai menulis surat-surat, tetapi selepas itu dia main-main saja," interview with J., March 28, 1996.

28. Interview with M., March 5, 1996.

29. Interview with J., March 5, 1996.

30. It is not my goal here to present a detailed ethnography of conservationists in Sabah. Therefore, I have lumped together many groups under the title "conservationist." These include the park officials, foreign researchers living in the park engaged in scientific studies, individuals working for the World Wide Fund for Nature, and individuals (both foreign and Malaysian) working for the "People and Plants" project (a joint initiative between Sabah Park, World Wide Fund for Nature, Unesco, and Kew Botanical Gardens). For a fascinating study of the differences between foreign and Indonesian conservationists, see Lowe (1999).

31. Interview with J., November 18, 1995.

32. Interview at the Ministry of Tourism, Environment, and Development, December 5, 1995.

33. I must thank Michael Dove for drawing this insight to my attention.

CONCLUSION

1. See *Bernama Daily Malaysian News* (2003e).
2. See ibid. (2003c, 2003d, 2003f, 2003g).

3. See ibid. (2004b); *New Strait Times* (2003b).

4. *Bernama Daily Malaysian News* (2004a).

5. The headquarters of the Sabah Forestry Department is in Sandakan, and the Sandakan District has historically been the center of Sabah's timber industry.

6. Many pharmaceutical companies do rely on ethnobotanical knowledge to identify plants for potential use in drugs, yet the forest officers whom I met did not seem to recognize this. Thus, they had only partially appropriated the discourse of the international pharmaceutical industry to their advantage.

7. Statistics on agricultural economic indicators are from the Institute of Development Studies Web site, http://www.ids.org.my/indicators/.

8. For similar findings in Zimbabwe, see D. Moore (1997:92).

BIBLIOGRAPHY

ARCHIVAL REFERENCES

A. SABAH GOVERNMENT ARCHIVES, KOTA KINABALU

1. North Borneo Company Archives on Microfilm
Circular No. 481. Letter from the Governor to the President. August 23, 1928. NBCA Microfilm no. 217/82.
Memo from the President of the Company to the Governor. "Development of the Interior." August 23, 1928. NBCA Microfilm no. 217/82.

2. North Borneo Chartered Company Archives on Paper (NBCA)
Circular No. 95. August 14, 1914. NBCA file no. 284.
Circular Notice to Officers. 1928. NBCA file no. 815.
Circular Notice to Officers. December 24, 1931. NBCA file no. 815.
General Return of Revenue, Expenditure, Trade, and Population for 1890–1931. NBCA file no. 579.
Keith, H. G. "Explanatory Notes and Discussion of the Plan of Proposed Operations to Be in Forest Reserves." [1935?]. NBCA file no. 143.
Letter from Assistant District Officer Cook to the Resident of the Interior. April 30, 1913. NBCA file no. 1356.
Letter from the Assistant District Officer in Keningau to Resident Tenom. May 13, 1913. NBCA file no. 1356.
Letter from Smith to the General Secretary. April 12, 1931. NBCA file no. 284.
Memo on Shifting Cultivation, [1913?]. NBCA file no. 284.
Minute by H. G. Keith. October 25, 1933. NBCA.

3. Personal Papers
Personal diary of W. R. Dunlop. File SP/1.

B. COLONIAL OFFICE RECORDS, PUBLIC RECORDS OFFICE, LONDON

Administrative Report for the Year of 1910. CO 648/3.
Annual Report of the Forestry Department, 1915. CO 874/712.
Annual Report of the Land Office, 1918. CO 648/8.
Annual Report of the Land Office, 1928. CO 874/519.
Annual Report of the Land Settlement Department, 1919. CO 874/797.
Annual Report on Land Settlement, 1916. CO 874/797.
Annual Report on the Land Settlement Department, 1914. CO 874/797.
Comparative Statement of Receipts, 1885–90. CO 874/89.
Comparative Statement of Trade, 1885–90. CO 874/89.
Dane, Richard. "Report on Administration." 1911. CO 874/154.
Governor's Dispatch No. 194. Annual Report on the Forestry Department for 1930. CO 874/722.
Governor's Dispatch No. 259. April 30, 1928. CO 874/985.
Letter from Count Gelose d'Elsloo to Resident Davies. July 9, 1889. CO 874/248.
Letter from Governor Creagh to the Chairman of the British North Borneo Chartered Company. August 4, 1888. CO 874/246.
Letter from Governor Treacher to the Chairman of the North Borneo Chartered Company. January 18, 1883. CO 874/233.
Letter from J. Maxwell Hall, Commissioner of Lands, to the Government Secretary. March 8, 1920. CO 874/985.
Letter from Pearson to the Government Secretary. October 23, 1913. CO 874/796.
Letter from Resident Davies to the Government Secretary. July 9, 1889. CO 874/248.
Letter from the Government Secretary to Resident Davies. July 25, 1889. CO 874/248.
Letter from the Governor to the President. June 22, 1928. CO 874/985.
Letter from the Land Office to the Government Secretary. August 25, 1919. CO 874/797.
Letter from the Resident in Kudat to Count de Gelose. July 6, 1889. CO 874/248.
Letter to the Governor. May 11, 1909. CO 874/283.
Letter to the Pall Mall Budget. August 21, 1885, p. 679. CO 874/239.
Memo by W. J. W. "Land Grants to Natives." October 21, 1921. CO 874/985.
Memo on the Rebellion in Rundum District. July 29, 1915. CO 874/834.
Memorandum by A. B. C. Francis. n.d. [1920?]. CO 874/985.
Minute by Governor Pearson to the Government Secretary. February 12, 1920. CO 874/985.

Minute by Governor Pearson to the Government Secretary. February 13, 1920. CO 874/985.
Minute by M. W. E. April 11, 1920. CO 874/985.
Minute by Mr. C. F. Macaskie to the Government Secretary. March 17, 1920. CO 874/985.
Minute by W. J. W. March 14, 1921. CO 874/985.
Pearson, A. C. "Memorandum on Forestry in the Philippines." 1914. CO 874/711.
Pearson, A. C. "Report on Land Administration." 1909. CO 874/796.
Pearson, A. C. "Report on Land." May 11, 1909. CO 874/283.
Recommendation of Governor Parr, Re: Settlement Work. February 4, 1915. CO 874/797.

C. RANAU DISTRICT OFFICE FILES

Declaration of the Native Residential Reserve, Ranau District, Land Office.
Letter from the Chairman of the JKKK to the UMNO regional office. January 4, 1995. District Office Records.
Letter from the Director of Agriculture to the West Coast Resident. January 6, 1958. Native Court Office.
Letter from the Director of Lands and Surveys to all Residents. October 17, 1957. District Office Records.
Letter from the West Coast Resident to the Chief Secretary. April 28, 1958. Native Court Office.
Letter from West Coast Resident Chisholm to Other Residents. November 26, 1957. District Office Records.

BOOKS AND JOURNAL ARTICLES

Abraham, Itty. 2003. "State, Place, and Identity: Two Stories in the Making of Region." In Sivaramakrishnan and Agrawal 2003, 404–25.
Abu-Lughod, Lila. 1990. "The Romance of Resistance: Tracing Transformations of Power through Bedouin Women." *American Ethnologist* 17 (1):41–55.
Adas, Michael. 1981. "From Avoidance to Confrontation: Peasant Protest in Precolonial and Colonial Southeast Asia." *Comparative Studies in Society and History* 23 (3):217–47.
Adewoye, Omomiyi. 1986. "Legal Practice in Ibadan." *Journal of Legal Pluralism* 24:57–76.
Agarwal, Bina. 1994a. *A Field of One's Own: Gender and Land Rights in South Asia.* Cambridge: Cambridge University Press.
———. 1994b. "Gender, Resistance and Land: Interlinked Struggles over Resources and Meanings in South Asia." *Journal of Peasant Studies* 22 (1):81–125.

Agrawal, Arun. 1995. "Dismantling the Divide between Indigenous and Scientific Knowledge." *Development and Change* 26:413–39.

———. 1997. "Community in Conservation: Beyond Enchantment and Disenchantment." Community and Development Forum Discussion Paper.

———. 1998. "The Production of Community-in Conservation: The Forest Councils of Kumaon." Paper presented at the Program in Agrarian Studies Colloquium Series, Yale University, October 2, 1998.

Agrawal, Arun, and Clark Gibson. 1999a. "Accountability in Decentralization: A Framework with South Asian and West African Cases." *Journal of Developing Areas* 33 (summer):473–502.

———. 1999b. "Enchantment and Disenchantment: The Role of Communities in Natural Resources Conservation." *World Development* 27 (4):629–49.

———, eds. 2001. *Communities and the Environment: Ethnicity, Gender, and the State in Community-based Conservation.* New Brunswick, N.J.: Rutgers University Press.

Agrawal, Arun, and K. Sivaramakrishnan. 2000. *Agrarian Environments: Resources, Representations, and Rule in India.* Durham, N.C.: Duke University Press.

Alcorn, Janis. 1981. "Huastec Noncrop Resource Management: Implications for Prehistoric Rain Forest Management." *Human Ecology* 9 (4):395–417.

Andaya, Barabara Watson, and Leonard Andaya. 1982. *A History of Malaysia.* London: Macmillan Press, Ltd.

Anderson, Benedict. 1990. "Old State, New Society: Indonesia's New Order in Comparative Historical Analysis." In *Language and Power: Exploring Political Cultures in Indonesia,* 79–93. Ithaca: Cornell University Press.

———. 1991. *Imagined Communities: Reflections on the Origin and Spread of Nationalism.* London: Verso.

Appadurai, Arjun. 1996. *Modernity at Large: Cultural Dimensions of Globalization.* Minneapolis: University of Minnesota Press.

Appell, George. 1965. "The Nature of Social Groups among the Rungus Dusun of Sabah, Malaysia." Ph.D. diss., Australian National University, Canberra.

———. 1985. "Land Tenure and Development among the Rungus of Sabah, Malaysia." In *Modernization and the Emergence of a Landless Peasantry,* ed. George Appell, 111–55. Studies in Third World Societies. Williamsburg, Va.: College of William and Mary.

———. 1986. "Kayan Land Tenure and the Distribution of Devolvable Usufruct in Borneo." *Borneo Research Bulletin* 18:119–30.

———. 1987. "Emergent Structuralism: The Design of an Inquiry System to Delineate the Production and Reduction of Social Forms." In *Choice and Morality: Essays in Honor of Derek Freeman,* ed. G. Appell and T. Madan, 43–60. Buffalo: State University of New York Press.

———. 1990. "The Jural Personality of the Village in the Societies of Borneo." Manuscript.

———. 1991a. "Errors in Borneo Ethnography." *Borneo Research Bulletin* 21:85–98.

———. 1991b. "Resource Management Regimes among the Swidden Agriculturists of Borneo: Does the Concept of Common Property Adequately Map Indigenous Systems of Ownership?" Paper presented at the International Association for the Study of Common Property Conference. University of Manitoba, Winnipeg, September 28, 1991.

———. 1992. "The History of Research on Traditional Land Tenure and Tree Ownership in Borneo." Paper presented at the Second Biennial Conference of the Borneo Research Council. Kota Kinabalu, Sabah, Malaysia, July 13–17, 1992.

———. 1995. "Community Resources in Borneo: Failure of the Concept of Common Property and Its Implications for the Conservation of Forest Resources and the Protection of Indigenous Land Rights." *Yale School of Forestry and Environmental Studies, Bulletin Series no. 98.*

Beaman, John H., and Reed S. Beaman. 1990. "Diversity and Distribution of Flora of Mount Kinabalu." In *The Plant Diversity of Melesia,* ed. P. Baas, K. Kalkman, and R Geesink. Dordrecht: Kluwer Academic Press.

Berry, Sara. 1993. *No Condition Is Permanent: The Social Dynamics of Agrarian Change in Sub-Saharan Africa.* Madison: University of Wisconsin Press.

Black, Ian. 1983. *A Gambling Style of Government: The Establishment of the Chartered Company's Rule in Sabah, 1878–1915.* Kuala Lumpur: Oxford University Press.

Blaikie, Piers. 1985. *The Political Economy of Soil Erosion in Developing Countries.* London: Longman.

Blaikie, Piers, and Harold Brookfield. 1987. *Land Degradation and Society.* London: Methuen.

Bonneuil, Christophe. 2000. "Development as Experiment: Science and State Building in Late Colonial and Postcolonial Africa, 1930–1970." In *Nature and Empire: Science and the Colonial Enterprise,* ed. Roy MacLeod, 258–81. *Osiris,* vol. 15. Ithaca: Cornell University

Bratton, Michael. 1994. "Peasant-State Relations in Postcolonial Africa: Patterns of Engagement and Disengagement." In *State Power and Social Forces: Domination and Transformation in the Third World,* ed. Joel Migdal, Atul Kohli, and Vivienne Shue, 230–54. Cambridge: Cambridge University Press.

Breckenridge, Carol, ed. 1995. *Consuming Modernity: Public Culture in a South Asian World.* Minneapolis: University of Minnesota Press.

Brookfield, Harold, and Yvon Byron, eds. 1993. *Southeast Asia's Environmental Future: The Search for Sustainability.* Tokyo: United Nations University Press; Kuala Lumpur: Oxford University Press.

Brosius, Peter. 1997. "Transcripts, Divergent Paths: Resistance and Acquiescence to Logging in Sarawak, East Malaysia." *Comparative Studies in Society and History* 39:468–510.

Brosius, Peter, Anna L. Tsing, and Charles Zerner. 1998. "Representing Communities: Histories and Polities of Community-based Natural Resource Management." *Society and Natural Resources* 11:157–68.
Bruce, John. 1993. *A Review of Tenure Terminology.* Madison: University of Wisconsin.
Bryant, Raymond. 1992. "Political Ecology: An Emerging Research Agenda in Third World Studies." *Political Geography* 11 (1):12–36.
———. 1997. *The Political Ecology of Forestry in Burma, 1824–1994.* London: London, Hurst and Company.
Bryant, Raymond, and Sinead Bailey. 1997. *Third World Political Ecology.* London: Routledge.
Burchell, Grahman, Colin Gordon, and Peter Miller. 1991. *The Foucault Effect: Studies in Governmentality with Two Lectures by and an Interview with Michel Foucault.* London: Harvester.
Burns, Peter. 1989. "The Myth of Adat." *Journal of Legal Pluralism* 28:1–127.
Case, William. 1995. "Malaysia: Aspects and Audiences of Legitimacy." In *Political Legitimacy in Southeast Asia,* ed. Muthiah Alagappa, 69–107. Stanford: Stanford University Press.
Chandran, Subash M. D. 1998. "Shifting Cultivation, Sacred Groves and Conflict in Colonial Forest Policy in Western Ghats." In Grove, Damodaran, and Sangwan 1998, 674–707.
Chanock, Martin. 1985. *Law, Custom and Social Order: The Colonial Experience in Malawi and Zambia.* Cambridge: Cambridge University Press.
Chatterjee, Partha. 1986. *Nationalist Thought and the Colonial World.* Avon: Bath Press, Zed Books for United Nations University.
———. 1993. *The Nation and Its Fragments: Colonial and Postcolonial Histories.* Princeton: Princeton University Press.
Chua, Haji Abdul Malek Chua. 1995. *YB for Sale.* Kota Kinabalu, Sabah: Zamantara Publishers.
Cleary, Mark. C. 1992. "Plantation Agriculture and the Development of Native Land Rights in British North Borneo, c. 1880–1930." *Geographical Journal* 158 (2):170–81.
Cleary, Mark, and Peter Eaton. 1992. *Borneo: Change and Development.* Singapore: Oxford University Press.
Cohn, Bernard. 1996. *Colonialism and Its Forms of Knowledge: The British in India.* Princeton: Princeton University Press.
Cohn, Bernard, and Nicholas Dirks. 1988. "Beyond the Fringe: The Nation State, Colonialism, and the Technologies of Power." *Journal of Historical Sociology* 1 (2):224–29.
Comaroff, Jean. 1985. *Body of Power, Spirits of Resistance.* Chicago: University of Chicago Press.
Comaroff, Jean, and John Comaroff. 1988. "Through the Looking Glass:

Colonial Encounters of the First Kind." *Journal of Historical Sociology* 1 (1):6–32.
Comaroff, John. 1989. "Images of Empire, Contests of Conscience: Models of Colonial Domination in South Africa." *American Ethnologist* 16:661–85.
Conklin, Harold. 1957. *Hanunoo Agriculture: A Report on an Integral System of Shifting Cultivation in the Philippines.* FAO Forestry Development Paper, no. 12. Rome: FAO.
Cooper, Frederick, and Ann Stoler. 1997. *Tensions of Empire: Colonial Culture in a Bourgeois World.* Berkeley and Los Angeles: University of California Press.
Corrigan, Philip. 1994. "State Formation." In *Everyday Forms of State Formation,* ed. Gil Joseph and David Nugent, xvii-xix. Durham, N.C.: Duke University Press.
Coope, A. E. 1976. *A Malay-English Dictionary.* Cambridge: McMilliam Publishers, Ltd.
Cowen, Michael, and Robert Shenton. 1995. "The Invention of Development." In Crush 1995, 27–43.
Cronon, William. 1998. "A Manifesto for Humanist Environmentalism." Paper presented at Yale University, November 12, 1998.
Crouch, Harold. 1992. "Authoritarian Trends, the UMNO Split and the Limits to State Power." In *Fragmented Vision: Culture and Politics in Contemporary Malaysia,* ed. Joel Kahn and Francis Wah, 21–43. Honolulu: University of Hawaii Press.
———. 1996. *Government and Society in Malaysia.* Ithaca: Cornell University Press.
Crush, Jonathan, ed. 1995. *Power of Development.* London: Routledge.
Daly, D. D. 1888. "Explorations in British North Borneo, 1883–1887." *Proceedings of the Royal Geographic Society.*
Davis, Stephen D., Vernon H. Heywood, and A.C. Hamilton. 1995. *Centers of Plant Diversity: A Guide and Strategy for Their Conservation.* Vol. 2. Washington D.C.: WWF and IUCN.
Dentan, Robert, Kirk Endicott, Albert Gomes, and M. Hooker. 1997. *Malaysia and the "Original People": A Case Study of the Impact of Development on Indigenous Peoples.* Boston: Allyn and Bacon.
Dirks Nicholas, ed. 1992. *Colonialism and Culture.* Ann Arbor: University of Michigan Press.
———. 1996. "Foreword." In *Colonialism and Its Forms of Knowledge: The British in India,* by Bernard Cohn. Princeton: Princeton University Press.
Dirks, Nicholas, Geoff Eley, and Sherry Ortner, eds. 1994. *Culture/Power/History: A Reader in Social Theory.* Princeton: Princeton University Press.
Doolittle, Amity. 1995. "Behind the Curtains of Company Rule in North Borneo: A Look at Native Resistance and Conflict within the Company." Manuscript.
———. 1998. "Historical and Contemporary Views of Legal Pluralism in Sabah, Malaysia." *Common Property Resource Digest,* vol. 47.

Dove, Michael. 1983. "Theories of Swidden Agriculture, and the Political Economy of Ignorance." *Agroforestry Systems* 1:85–99.

———. 1985. "The Kantu Land Tenure System: The Evolution of Tribal Rights in Borneo." In *Modernization and the Emergence of a Landless Peasantry,* ed. George Appell, 159–82. Studies in Third World Societies. Williamsburg, Va.: College of William and Mary.

———. 1986a. "Peasant versus Government Perceptions and Use of the Environment: A Case Study of Banjarese Ecology and River Basin Development in South Kalimantan." *Journal of Southeast Asian Studies* 17 (3):113–36.

———. 1986b. *Swidden Agriculture in Indonesia.* Berlin: Mouton.

———. 1990. "Review Article: Socio-Political Aspects of Home Gardens in Java." *Journal of Southeast Asian Studies* 21 (1):155–63.

———. 1993a. "A Revisionist View of Tropical Deforestation and Development." *Environmental Conservation* 20 (1):17–25.

———. 1993b. "Smallholder Rubber and Swidden Agriculture in Borneo: A Sustainable Adaptation to the Ecology and Economy of the Tropical Forest." *Economic Botany* 47 (2):136–47.

———. 1994. "Transition from Native Forest Rubbers to *Hevea Brasiliensis* (Euphorbiaceae) among Tribal Smallholders in Borneo." *Economic Botany* 48 (4):382–96.

———. 1998. "Living Rubber, Dead Land, and Persisting Systems in Borneo: Indigenous Representations of Sustainability." *Bijdragen* 154 (1):1–35.

———. 1999. "Representations of the 'Other' by Others: The Ethnographic Challenge Posed by Planters' Views of Peasants in Indonesia." In *Agrarian Transformations in Upland Indonesia,* ed. Tania Li, 203–26. London: Harwood Academic Publishers.

Dove, Michael, Percy Sajise, and Amity Doolittle, eds. 2005. "Introduction: The Problem of Biodiversity Maintenance." In *Conserving Nature in Culture: Case Studies from Southeast Asia,* ed. M. Dove, P. Sajise, and A. Doolittle. Southeast Asia Monograph Series, vol. 54. New Haven: Yale University, Southeast Asian Studies.

Dreyfus, Hubert, and Paul Rabinow. 1983. *Michel Foucault: Beyond Structuralism and Hermeneutics.* Chicago: University of Chicago Press.

Escobar, Arturo. 1984. "Discourse and Power in Development: Michel Foucault and the Relevance of His work to the Third World." *Alternatives* 10:377–400.

———. 1988. "Power and Visibility: Development and the Invention and Management of the Third World." *Cultural Anthropology* 3 (4):428–43.

———. 1995. "Imagining a Post-Development Era." In Crush 1995, 211–27.

Esteva, Gustavo. 1992. "Development." In *The Development Dictionary,* ed. Wolfgang Sachs, 6–25. London: Zed.

Evans. Ivor. H. 1922. *Among Primitive People in Borneo.* Philadelphia: Lippincott Co.

———. 1953. *The Religion of the Tempasuk Dusun.* Cambridge: Cambridge University Press.
Featherstone, Mike, ed. 1990. *Global Culture: Nationalism, Globalization and Modernity.* Newbury Park: Sage.
———. 1996. "Localism, Globalism, and Cultural Identity." In *Global/Local: Cultural Production and the Transitional Imaginary,* ed. Rob Wilson and Wimal Dissanayake, 46–77. Durham, N.C.: Duke University Press.
Featherstone, Mike, Scott Lash, and Roland Robertson, eds. 1995. *Global Modernities.* Thousands Oaks, Calif.: Sage.
Ferguson, James. 1994. *The Anti-Politics Machine: "Development," Depoliticization, and Bureaucratic Power in Lesotho.* Minneapolis: University of Minnesota Press.
Florini, Ann. 2003. *The Coming Democracy: Rules for Running a New World.* Washington, D.C.: Island Press.
Forestry Department. 1951. *Forestry Department Annual Report.* Sandakan: Government Publishing Office.
Fortmann, Louise. 1990. "Locality and Custom: Non-Aboriginal Claims to Customary Usufructuary Rights as a Source of Rural Protest." *Journal of Rural Studies* 6 (2):195–208.
Fortmann, Louise, and John Bruce. 1988. *Whose Trees? Proprietary Dimensions of Forestry.* Boulder: Westview Press.
Foucault, Michel. 1977. *Discipline and Punish: The Birth of a Prison.* Trans. Alan Sheridan. New York: Vintage.
———. 1980a. *The History of Sexuality.* Vol. 1: *An Introduction.* Trans. Robert Hurley. New York: Vintage/Random House.
———. 1980b. *Power/Knowledge: Selected Interviews and Other Writings, 1972–1977.* London: Harvester.
———. 1981. *Power/Knowledge.* New York: Pantheon.
———. 1982. *Power/Knowledge: Selected Interviews and Other Writings, 1972–1977.* Edited by Colin Gordon and translated by Colin Gordon et al. Pantheon: New York.
——— 1983. "The Subject of Power." In Dreyfus and Rabinow 1983, 208–26.
———. 1991a. "Governmentality." In Burchell, Gordon, and Miller 1991, 87–104.
———. 1991b. "Politics and the Study of Discourse." In Burchell, Gordon, and Miller 1991, 53–72.
Freeman, Derek. 1970. *Report on the Iban.* London: Athlone Press.
Galbraith, John. 1965. "The Chartering of the British North Borneo Company." *Journal of British Studies* 4 (2):102–26.
Gale, Bruce. 1986. "Politics at the Periphery: A Study of the 1981 and 1982 Election Campaigns in Sabah." In *Readings in Malaysian Politics,* ed. Bruce Gale, 25–53. Selangor: Pelanduk.
Gauld, Richard. 2000. "Maintaining Centralized Control in Community-based

Forestry: Policy Construction in the Philippines." *Development and Change* 31:229–54.

Geddes, William. 1954. "Land Tenure of the Land Dayaks." *Sarawak Museum Journal* 6:42–51.

Goldman, Michael. 1998. "Inventing the Commons." In *Privatizing Nature: Political Struggles for the Global Commons,* ed. Michael Goldman, 20–53. New Brunswick, N.J.: Rutgers University Press.

Government of British North Borneo. 1885. "Land Regulations, North Borneo." *JSBRAS* 15:158–63.

———. 1889. "Proclamation No. III of 1889." *North Borneo Herald and Gazette,* February 1, 53–54.

———. 1890. *Handbook of British North Borneo.* London: William Clowes and Sons, Ltd.

———. 1915. "Proclamation No. IV of 1913, Land Laws." In *The Ordinances of the State of North Borneo, 1881–1914.* Sandakan: Government Publishing Office.

———. 1937. *The Ordinances and Rules of the State of North Borneo, 1881–1936.* Sandakan: Government Printing Office.

———. 1962. "The Royal Society of North Borneo Expedition Committee, September 1962, Report to the H. E. Governor of North Borneo on the proposed National Park of Kinabalu." Manuscript. Mount Kinabalu National Park files.

Government of Malaysia. n.d. *The Second Malaysia Plan, 1971–1975.* Kuala Lumpur: Government Printers.

———. 1984. *Mid-Term Review of the Fourth Malaysia Plan, 1981–1985.* Kuala Lumpur: Government Printers.

Griffiths, John. 1986. "What Is Legal Pluralism?" *Journal of Legal Pluralism* 24:155.

Grove, Richard. 1995. *Green Imperialism: Colonial Expansion, Tropical Island Edens and the Origins of Environmentalism, 1600–1860.* Cambridge University Press: Cambridge.

———. 1997. *Ecology, Climate and Empire: Colonialism and Global Environmental History, 1400–1940.* Cambridge: White House Press.

Grove, Richard, Vinita Damodaran, and Satpal Sangwan, eds. 1998. *Nature and the Orient: The Environmental History of South and Southeast Asia.* Delhi: Oxford University Press.

Guha, Ramachandra. 1989. *The Unquiet Woods: Ecological Change and Peasant Resistance in Himalaya.* Berkeley and Los Angeles: University of California Press.

———, ed. 1995. *Nature, Culture, Imperialism: Essays on the Environmental History of South Asia.* Delhi: Oxford University Press.

Guha, Ranajit. 1963. *A Rule of Property for Bengal.* Paris: Mouton and Co.

Gupta, Akhil. 1995. "Blurred Boundaries: The Discourse of Corruption, the Culture of Politics and the Imagined State." *American Ethnologist* 22 (2):375–402.

———. 1998. *Postcolonial Developments: Agriculture in the Making of Modern India.* Durham, N.C.: Duke University Press.

Gururani, Shubhra. 2000. "Regimes of Control, Strategies of Access: Politics of Forest Use in the Uttarakhand Himalaya, India." In Agrawal and Sivaramakrishnan 2000, 170–90.

Harper, T. N. 1997. "Forest Politics in Colonial Malaya." *Modern Asian Studies* 31 (1):1–29.

Harrison, Robert. 1971. "An Analysis of the Variation among Ranau Dusun Communities of Sabah, Malaysia." Ph.D. diss., Columbia University.

Hart, Gillian, Andrew Thurton, and Benjamin White, eds. 1989. *Agrarian Transformations: Local Processes and the State in Southeast Asia.* Berkeley and Los Angeles: University of California Press.

Hay, Douglas. 1976. "Poaching, Authority and Criminal Law." In *Albion's Fatal Tree: Crime and Society in Eighteenth-Century England,* ed. D. Hay et al., 17–63. New York: Pantheon.

Hefner, Robert. 1990. *The Political Economy of Mountain Java: An Interpretive History.* Berkeley and Los Angeles: University of California Press.

Hirsch, Susan, and Mindie Lazarus-Black. 1994. "Introduction: Performance and Paradox: Exploring Law's Role in Hegemony and Resistance." In *Contested States: Law, Hegemony, and Resistance,* by Mindie Lazarus-Black and Susan Hirsch, 1–34. New York: Routledge.

Hong, Evelyen. 1989. *Natives of Sarawak: Survival in Borneo's Vanishing Forests.* Pulau Pinang: Institut Masyarakat.

Hooker, M. B. 1980. *Native Law in Sabah and Sarawak.* Singapore: Malayan Law Journal Pte. Ltd.

———. 1984. *Islamic Law in Southeast Asia.* Singapore: Oxford University Press.

Hunter, Ed. 1976. *Misdeeds of Tun Mustapha.* Hong Kong: Ed Hunter Enterprises, Ltd.

Ibrahim, Zawawi. 1995. "Regional Development in Rural Malaysia and the 'Tribal Question.'" Occasional Paper no. 28, University of Hull, Centre for South-East Asian Studies.

Institute of Development Studies (IDS). 1991. *Strategic Study on Land Matters.* Kota Kinabalu, Sabah: Institute of Development Studies.

———. 1992. *Study of Community Forestry in Sabah.* Kota Kinabalu, Sabah: Institute of Development Studies.

Ives, Edward. 1988. *George Magoon and the Down East Game War: History, Folklore, and the Law.* Urbana: University of Illinois Press.

Jackson, Cecile, and Molly Chattopadhyay. 2000. "Identities and Livelihoods: Gender, Ethnicity, and Nature in a South Bihar Village." In Agrawal and Sivaramakrishnan 2000, 147–69.

Jayasankaran S., and M. Heibert. 1997. "Malaysian Dilemmas." *Far Eastern Economic Review,* September 4.

John, David. 1974. "The Timber Industry and Forest Administration in Sabah under Chartered Company Rule." *Journal of Southeast Asian Studies* 5 (1):55–80.

John, David, and James Jackson. 1973. "The Tobacco Industry of North Borneo: A Distinctive Form of Plantation Agriculture." *Journal of Southeast Asian Studies* 4 (1):88–106.

Kahin, Audrey. 1992. "Crisis on the Periphery: The Rift between Kuala Lumpur and Sabah." *Pacific Affairs* 65 (1):30–68.

Kaur, Amarjit. 1998. "A History of Forestry in Sarawak." *Modern Asian Studies* 32 (1):117–47.

Kaur, Amarjit, and Ian Metcalfe, eds. 1999. *The Shaping of Malaysia.* London: Macmillan.

Khoo Boo Teik. 1995. *Paradoxes of Mahathirism: An Intellectual Biography of Mahathir Mohamad.* Kuala Lumpur: Oxford University Press.

Kitayama, K. 1992. "An Attitudinal Transect Study of the Vegetation on Mount Kinabalu, Borneo." *Vegetation* 102:149–71.

———. 1987. "Vegetation of Mount Kinabalu." *Review of Forest Culture* 8:103–13.

Kitingan, Jeffrey. 1984. "Political Stability and Economic Development in Malaysia." Ph.D. diss., Tufts University.

———. 1990. *Development of Administrative System in Sabah since Independence.* Kuala Lumpur: Arts Printing Works, Snd. Bhd.

Kurus, Bilson. 1994. "Review on the Role and Functions of the Local Chieftain System in Sabah." *Borneo Review* 5 (1):1–21.

Lea, William. 1976. *Southeast Asia: A History.* New York: Oxford University Press.

Leong, Cecelia. 1982. *Sabah: The First 100 Years.* Kuala Lumpur: Percetakan Nan Yang Muda Sdn. Bhd.

Lev, David 1985. "Colonial Law and the Genesis of the Indonesian State." *Indonesia* 40:57–74.

Li, Tania. 1996. "Images of Community: Discourse and Strategy in Property Relations." *Development and Change* 27 (3):501–27.

———. 1997. "Engaging State Simplifications: Community-based Resource Management, Local Processes and State Agendas in Upland Southeast Asia." Paper presented at the conference "Representing Communities: Histories and Politics of Community Based Resource Management," Unicoi Lodge, Georgia, June 1997.

———. 1999a. "Compromising Power: Development, Culture, and Rule." *Cultural Anthropology* 14 (3):295–322.

———. 1999b. "Marginality, Power and Production: Analyzing Upland Transformation." In *Agrarian Transformations in Upland Indonesia,* ed. Tania Li, 1–44. London: Harwood Academic Publishers.

———. 2001. "Boundary Work: Community, Market and State Reconsidered." In Agrawal and Gibson 2001, 157–79.

Lim, Jennfier Nyuk-Wo, and Ian Douglas. 1998. "The Impact of Cash Cropping on Shifting Cultivation in Sabah, Malaysia." *Asia Pacific Viewpoint* 39 (3):315–26.

Locke, John. [1690] 1963. "The Second Treatise of Government." In *Two Treaties of Government,* by Peter Laslett. Cambridge: Cambridge University Press.

Lowe, Celia. 1999. "Cultures of Nature: Identity, Representation and Biodiversity Conservation in the Togean Islands of Sulawesi." Ph.D. diss., Yale University.

Ludden, David. 1992. "India's Development Regime." In *Colonialism and Culture,* ed. Nicholas Dirks, 247–87. Ann Arbor: University of Michigan Press.

Luping, Herman. 1994. *Sabah's Dilemma: A Political History of Sabah (1960–1994).* Kuala Lumpur: Magnus Books.

Lynch, Owen, and Kirk Talbott. 1995. *Balancing Acts: Community-based Forest Management and National Law in Asia and the Pacific.* Washington, D.C.: World Resource Institute.

MacKenzie, John, ed. 1990. *Imperialism and the Natural World.* Manchester: Manchester University Press.

MacPherson, C. B, ed. 1978. *Property: Mainstream and Critical Positions.* Toronto: University of Toronto Press.

Majid Cooke, Fadzilah. 1997. "The Politics of 'Sustainability' in Sarawak." *Journal of Contemporary Asia* 27 (2):217–41.

———. 1999. *The Challenge of Sustainable Forests: Forest Resource Policy in Malaysia, 1970–1995.* Honolulu: Allen and Urwin

———. 2002. "Vulnerability, Control and Oil Palm in Sarawak: Globalization and a New Era?" *Development and Change* 33 (2):189–211.

Mamdani, Mahmood. 1996. *Citizens and Subject: Contemporary Africa and the Legacy of Late Colonialism.* Princeton: Princeton University Press.

———. 2001. "Beyond Settler and Native as Political Identities: Overcoming the Political Legacy of Colonialism." *Comparative Study of Society and History* 43 (4):651–64.

Mannan, Sam, and Yahya Awang. 1997. "Sustainable Forest Management in Sabah." "Sustainable Forest Management," seminar, Kota Kinabalu, Sabah, Malaysia.

Mauzy, Diane, and R. S. Milne, 1986. "The Mahathir Administration: Discipline through Islam." In *Readings in Malaysian Politics,* ed. Bruce Gale, 75–112. Petaling Jaya: Pelanduk.

Maxwell, William E. 1884. "The Law and Customs of Malays with Reference to the Tenure of Land." *JSBRAS* 13:75–220.

McHoul, Alex, and Grace, W. 2002. *A Foucault Primer: Discourse, Power and the Subject.* New York: New York University Press.

McT. Kahin, George. 1947. "The State of North Borneo, 1881–1946." *Far Eastern Quarterly* 7 (November):43–65.

Medhurst, William. [1885] 1983. "British North Borneo." In *Honorable Intentions: Talks on the British Empire in South-East Asia delivered at the Royal Colonial*

Institute. 1874–1928, ed. Paul Kratoska, 91–124. Singapore: Oxford University Press.
Meek, Charles. K. 1946. *Land Law and Custom in the Colonies.* London: Oxford University Press.
Memmi, Albert. [1965] 1991. *The Colonizer and the Colonized.* Boston: Beacon.
Menzies, Nicholas. n.d. "The Villagers' View of Environmental History in Yunnan Province." Manuscript. Ford Foundation, Beijing.
Merry, Sally E. 1988. "Legal Pluralism." *Law and Society Review* 22 (5):869–96.
———. 1991. "Law and Colonialism." *Law and Society Review* 25 (4):889–922.
Michon, G., and F. Mary. 1994. "Conversion of Traditional Village Gardens and New Economic Strategies of Rural Households in the Area of Bogor, Indonesia." *Agroforestry Systems* 25:31–58.
Migdal, Joel, Atul Kohli, and Vivienne Shue, eds. 1994. *State Power and Social Forces: Domination and Transformation in the Third World.* Cambridge: Cambridge University Press.
Mitchell, Timothy. 1990. "Everyday Metaphors of Power." *Theory and Society* 19:545–77.
———. 1991. "The Limits of the State: Beyond Statistical Approaches and Their Critics." *American Political Science Review* 85 (1):77–96.
Mohamed, M. 1987. "Impact of Copper Mining in Sabah." In *Environmental Conservation in Sabah: Issues and Strategies,* ed. S. Sani, 55–63. Proceedings of the Institute of Development Studies Seminar, January 1987.
Moniaga, Sandra. 1993. "Toward Community-based Forestry and Recognition of Adat Property Rights in the Outer Islands of Indonesia." In *Legal Frameworks for Forest Management in Asia: Case Studies of Community/State Relations,* ed. Jeff Fox, 131–50. Occasional Papers of the Programs on Government, no. 16. Honolulu: East-West Center.
Moore, Donald. 1993. "Contesting Terrain in Zimbabwe's Highlands: Political Ecology, Ethnography, and Peasant Resource Struggles." *Economic Geography* 69:390–401.
———. 1997. "Remapping Resistance: 'Ground for Struggle' and the Politics of Place." In *Geographies of Resistance,* ed. Steve Pile and Michael Keith, 87–106. New York: Routledge.
———. 1999. "The Crucible of Cultural Politics: Reworking 'Development' in Zimbabwe's Eastern Highlands." *American Ethnologist* 26 (3):645–89.
Moore, Sally Falk. 1973. "Law and Social Change: The Semi-autonomous Social Field as an Appropriate Subject of Study." *Law and Society Review* 7 (4):719–46.
———. 1986a. "Legal Systems of the World: An Introductory Guide to Classifications, Typological Interpretations, and Bibliographical Resources." In *Law and the Social Sciences,* ed. Leon Lipson and Stanton Wheeler, 11–61. New York: Russell Sage.

———. 1986b. *Social Facts and Fabrication: "Customary" Law on Kilimanjaro, 1880–1980.* Cambridge: Cambridge University Press.

———. 1987. "Explaining the Present: Theoretical Dilemmas in Processual Ethnography." *American Ethnologist* 14 (4):727–36.

———. 1992. "Treating Law as Knowledge: Telling Colonial Officers What to Say to Africans about Running 'Their Own' Native Courts." *Law and Society* 26 (1):11–46.

Neumann, Roderick P. 1998. *Imposing Wilderness: Struggles over Livelihood and Nature Preservation in Africa.* Berkeley and Los Angeles: University of California.

Nonini, David. 1992. *British Colonial Rule and the Resistance of the Malay Peasantry, 1900–1957.* New Haven: Yale University Press.

Nugent, Daniel. 1994. "Building the State, Making the Nation: The Bases and Limits of State Centralization in 'Modern' Peru." *American Anthropologist* 96 (2):333–69.

Okoth-Ogenda, H. W. 1979. "The Imposition of Property Law in Kenya." In *The Imposition of Law*, ed. Susan Burman and Barbara Harrell-Bond, 147–65. New York: Academic Press.

Ong, Aihwa. 1987. *Spirits of Resistance and Capitalist Discipline.* Albany: State University of New York Press.

———. 1999. *Flexible Citizenship: The Cultural Logics of Transnationality.* Durham, N.C.: Duke University Press.

Ongkili, James. 1972. *Modernization in East Malaysia, 1960–1970.* Kuala Lumpur: Oxford University Press.

Ortner, Sherry B. 1995. "Resistance and the Problem of Ethnographic Refusal." *Comparative Studies in Society and History* 37 (1):173–93.

Padoch, Christine, and Nancy Peluso. 1996. *Borneo in Transition: People, Forests, Conservation, and Development.* Kuala Lumpur: Oxford University Press.

Peet, Richard, and Michael Watts. 1996. "Liberation Ecology: Development, Sustainability, and Market in an Age of Market Triumphalism." In *Liberation Ecologies: Environment, Development, Social Movements,* ed. Richard Peet and Michael Watts, 1–45. London: Routledge.

Peluso, Nancy. 1983. "Markets and Merchants: The Forest Products Trade of East Kalimantan in Historical Perspective." Master's thesis, Cornell University.

———. 1992. *Rich Forests, Poor People: Resource Control and Resistance in Java.* Berkeley and Los Angeles: University of California Press.

———. 1993. "Coercing Conservation: The Politics of State Resource Control." *Global Environmental Change* 4 (2):199–218.

———. 1996. "Fruit Trees and Family Trees in an Anthropogenic Forest: Ethics of Access, Property Zones, and Environmental Change in Indonesia." *Comparative Studies in Society and History* 38:510–48.

———. 1998. "Legal Pluralism and Legacies of 'Customary Rights' in Indonesian and Malaysian Borneo." *Common Property Resource Digest* 47:10–13.

Peluso, Nancy, and Emily Harwell. 2001. "Territory, Custom, and Cultural Politics of Ethnic Wars in West Kalimantan, Indonesia." In *Violent Environments,* ed. Nancy Peluso and Michael Watts, 83–116. Ithaca: Cornell University Press.

Peluso, Nancy, and Peter Vandergeest. 2001."Genealogies of the Political Forest and Customary Rights in Indonesia, Malaysia, and Thailand." *Journal of Asian Studies* 60 (3):761–812.

Peters, Pauline. 1994. *Dividing the Commons: Politics, Policy, and Culture in Botswana.* Charlottesville: University Press of Virginia.

Petkova, Elena, and Peter Veit. 2000. Environmental Accountability beyond the Nation-State: The Implications of the Aarhus Convention." *Environmental Governance Notes.* Washington, D.C.: World Resources Institute.

Phelan, Peter. 1988. "Native Land in Sabah: Its Administrators, Headmen and Native Chiefs." *Sabah Society Journal* 8 (4):475–501.

Pierce, Jennifer. 1995. "Reflections on Fieldwork in a Complex Organization: Lawyers, Ethnographic Authority and Lethal Weapons." In *Studying Elites Using Qualitative Methods,* ed. Rosanna Hertz and Jonathan Imber, 94–110. London: Sage.

Pigg, Stacey. 1992. "Inventing Social Categories through Place: Social Representations and Development in Nepal." *Comparative Studies in Society and History* 34 (3):491–513.

Pouchepadaas, Jacques. 1995. "British Attitudes towards Shifting Cultivation in Colonial South India: A Case Study of South Canara District, 1800–1920." In *Nature, Culture, Imperialism: Essays on the Environmental History of South Asia,* ed. David Arnold and Ramachandra Guha, 123–51. Delhi: Oxford University Press.

Raffles, Hugh. 2002. *In Amazonia: A Natural History.* Princeton: Princeton University Press.

Rajan, Ravi. 1998. "Imperial Environmentalism or Environmental Imperialism? European Forestry, Colonial, Foresters and the Agendas of Forest Management in British India." In Grove, Damodaran, and Sangwan 1998, 324–72.

Ranger, Terence. 1983. "The Invention of Tradition in Colonial Africa." In *The Invention of Tradition,* ed. Eric Hobsbawm and Terrence Ranger, 211–62. Cambridge: Cambridge University Press.

Redclift, Michael. 1992. "The Meaning of Sustainable Development." *Geoforum* 23 (3):395–403.

Rhee, Steven. 2003. "*De Facto* Decentralization and Community Conflicts in East Kalimantan, Indonesia: Explanations from Local History and Implications for

Community Forestry." In *The Political Ecology of Tropical Forest in Southeast Asia: Historical Perspectives,* ed. Lye Tuck-Po, W. de. Jong, and A. Ken-ichi, 152–76. Kyoto: Kyoto University Press.

Ribot, Jesse C. 2002. *Democratic Decentralization of Natural Resources: Institutionalizing Popular Participation.* Washington, D.C.: World Resources Institute.

Roberts, Richard, and Kristin Mann. 1991. "Law in Colonial Africa." In *Law in Colonial Africa,* ed. Kristin Mann and Richard Roberts, 3–57. Portsmouth: Heinemann.

Rocheleau, Diane, Barbara Thomas-Slayter, and Ester Wangari. 1996. *Feminist Political Ecology: Global Issues and Local Experience.* New York: Routledge.

Roff, Margaret. 1974. *The Politics of Belonging: Political Change in Sabah and Sarawak.* Kuala Lumpur: Oxford University Press.

Rose, Carol. 1994. *Property and Persuasion: Essays on the History, Theory, and Rhetoric of Ownership.* Boulder: Westview Press.

Roseberry, William. 1989. *Anthropologies and Histories: Essays in Culture, History and Political Economy.* New Brunswick, N.J.: Rutgers University Press.

Ross-Larson, Bruce. 1976. *The Politics of Federalism: Syed Kechik in East Malaysia.* Singapore: Bruce Ross-Larson.

Rutter, Owen. 1922. *British North Borneo: An Account of Its History, Resources and Native Tribes.* London: Constable and Company, Ltd.

———. 1929. *The Pagans of North Borneo.* London: Hutchinson.

Saberwal, Vasant. 1997. "Pastoral Politics: Bureaucratic Agendas, Shepherds' Land Use Practices and Conservation Policy in Himachal Pradesh, India, 1986–1994." Ph.D. diss., Yale University.

———. 2000. "Environmental Alarm and Institutionalized Conservation in Himachal Pradesh, 1865–1994." In Agrawal and Sivaramakrishnan 2000, 68–106.

Said, Edward. 1979. *Orientalism.* New York: Vintage.

Sangren, P. Steven. 1995. "'Power' against Ideology: A Critique of Foucaultian Usage." *Cultural Anthropology* 10 (1):3–40.

Sather, Clifford. 1990. "Trees and Tree Tenure in Paku Iban Society: The Management of Secondary Forest Resources in a Long-Established Iban Community." *Borneo Review* 1 (1):16–44.

Schroeder, Richard. 1993. "Shady Practices: Gender and the Political Ecology of Resource Stabilization in Gambia Garden/Orchards." *Economic Geography* 69 (4):349–65.

Scott, James. 1976. *The Moral Economy of the Peasant: Subsistence and Rebellion in Southeast Asia.* New Haven: Yale University Press.

———. 1985. *Weapons of the Weak: Everyday Forms of Peasant Resistance.* New Haven: Yale University Press.

———. 1990. *Domination and the Arts of Resistance: Hidden Transcripts.* New Haven: Yale University Press.

———. 1998. *Seeing like a State: How Certain Schemes to Improve the Human Condition Have Failed.* New Haven: Yale University Press.

Shamsul Amri Baharuddin. 1986. *From British to Bumiputra Rule: Local Politics and Rural Development in Peninsular Malaysia.* Singapore: Institute of Southeast Asian Studies.

———. 1989. "Village: The Imposed Social Construct in Malaysia's Developmental Initiatives." Working Paper no. 115, Faculty of Sociology, Sociology of Development Research Centre, University of Bielefeld.

———. 1998. "Debating about Identity in Malaysia: A Discourse Analysis" In *Cultural Contestations: Mediating Identities in a Changing Malaysian Society,* ed. Zawawi Ibrahim, 17–50. London: ASEAN Academic Press.

Shipton, Parker, and Mitzi Goheen. 1992. "Understanding African Land-Holdings: Power, Wealth and Meaning." *Africa* 62 (3):307–25.

Sihombing, Judith. 1989. *Malaysian Torrens System.* Kuala Lumpur: Dewan Bahasa dan Pustaka Kementerian Pendidikan Malaysia.

Sivaramakrishnan, K. 1999. *Modern Forests: Statemaking and Environmental Change in Colonial Eastern India.* Stanford: Stanford University Press.

———. 2000. "State Sciences and Development Histories: Encoding Local Forestry Knowledge in Bengal." *Development and Change* 31:61–89.

Sivaramakrishnan K., and Arun Agrawal, eds. 2003. *Regional Modernities: The Cultural Politics of Development in India.* New York: Oxford University Press.

Skaria, Ajay. 2000. "Cathecting the Natural." In Agrawal and Sivaramakrishnan 2000, 265–76.

Sonnenfeld, David, and Arthur Mol. 2002. "Globalization and the Transformation of Environmental Governance." *American Behavioral Scientist* 45 (9):1318–39.

———. 2002. "Ecological Modernization, Governance and Globalization: Epilogue." *American Behavioral Scientist* 45 (2): 1456–61.

Spurr, David. 1993. *The Rhetoric of Empire: Colonial Discourse in Journalism, Travel Writing and Imperial Administration.* Durham, N.C.: Duke University Press.

Starr, June, and Jane Collier, eds. 1989. *History and Power in the Study of Law: New Directions in Legal Anthropology.* Ithaca: Cornell University Press.

Stoler, Ann. 1985. *Capitalism and Confrontation in Sumatra's Plantation Belt: 1870–1979.* New Haven: Yale University Press.

———. 1992. "Rethinking Colonial Categories." In *Colonialism and Culture,* ed. Nicholas Dirks, 319–52. Ann Arbor: University of Michigan Press.

Stott, Philip, and Sian Sullivan, eds. 2000. *Political Ecology: Science, Myth and Power*. London: Arnold.

Suryanata, K. 1994. "Fruit Trees under Contract: Tenure and Land Use Change in Upland Java." *World Development* 22 (10): 1567–78.

Synder, Francis. 1981. "Colonialism and Legal Form: The Creation of 'Customary Law' in Senegal." *Journal of Legal Pluralism* 19:49–90.

Tangau, Wilfred, and Geoffrey, Tanakinjal. 2000. "Poverty and Rural Development: Prospect and Challenges Beyond the Year 2000." In *Sabah and Beyond 2000: Development Challenges and the Way Forward*, ed. Mohd. Yaakub Hj. Johari and Bilson Kurus, 203–27. Kota Kinabalu, Sabah: Percetakan tedasjaya Sendriian Berhad.

Tarling, Nicholas. 1969. *British Policy in the Malay Peninsular and Archipelago, 1824–1871*. Kuala Lumpur: Oxford University Press.

———. 1971. *Britain, the Brookes and Brunei*. Kuala Lumpur: Oxford University Press.

———. 1978. *Sulu and Sabah*. Kuala Lumpur: Oxford University Press.

———. 1993. *The Fall of Imperial Britain in South-East Asia*. Singapore: Oxford University Press.

Thomas, Nicholas. 1994. *Colonialism's Culture: Anthropology, Travel and Government*. Princeton: Princeton University Press.

Thompson, Edward P. 1975. *Whigs and Hunters: The Origins of the Black Act*. New York: Pantheon.

Treacher, William. 1890. "British Borneo: Sketches of Brunai, Sarawak, Labuan and North Borneo." *JSBRAS* 21:19–122.

———. 1891. *British Borneo*. Singapore.

Tregonning, K. C. 1956. *Under Chartered Company Rule*. Singapore: University of Malaya Press.

———. 1965. *A History of Modern Sabah*. Singapore: University of Malaya Press.

Tsing, Anna. 1993. *In the Realm of the Diamond Queen: Marginality in an Out-of-the-Way Place*. Princeton: Princeton University Press.

———. 1998. "Notes on Culture and Natural Resource Management." Paper presented at the University of California, Berkeley, Environmental Politics Seminar, December 11.

Tucker, Richard. 1998. "Non-Timber Forest Products Policy in the Western Himalayas under British Rule." In Grove, Damodaran, and Sangwan 1998, 459–83.

Vandergeest, Peter. 1996. "Real Villages: National Narratives of Rural Development." In *Creating the Countryside: The Politics of Rural and Environmental Discourse*, ed. E. Melanie DuPuis and Peter Vandergeest, 279–302. Philadelphia: Temple University Press.

Vandergeest, Peter, and Nancy Peluso. 1995. "Territorialization and State Power in Thailand." *Theory and Society* 24:385–426.

Wah, Francis. 1992. "Modernisation, Cultural Revival and Counter-Hegemony: The Kadazans of Sabah in the 1980s." In *Fragmented Vision: Culture and Politics in Contemporary Malaysia*, ed. Joel Kahn and Francis Wah, 225–51. Honolulu: University of Hawaii Press.

Warner, Jeroen. 2000. "Global Environmental Security: An Emerging 'Concept of Control'?" In *Political Ecology: Science, Myth and Power*, ed. Philip Stott and Sian Sullivan, 247–65. London: Arnold.

Warren, Louis. 1997. *The Hunter's Game: Poachers and Conservationists in Twentieth-Century America*. New Haven: Yale University Press.

Watts, Michael. 1983. *Silent Violence: Food, Famine, and Peasantry in Northern Nigeria*. Berkeley and Los Angeles: University of California Press.

———. 1992. "Idioms of Land and Labor." In *Land Tenure in Africa*, ed. T. Bassett, 157–93. Madison: University of Wisconsin Press.

———. 1995. "A New Deal in Emotions: Theory and Practice and the Crisis of Development." In Crush 1995, 44–61.

———. 2002. "Green Capitalism, Governance, and the Environment." *American Behavioral Scientist* 45 (9):1331–12.

———. 2003. "Development and Governmentality." *Singapore Journal of Tropical Geography* 24 (1):6–34.

West, L. 1897. "British North Borneo." *Asiatic Quarterly Review*, vol. 1.

Western, David, and Michael Wright. 1994. *Natural Connections: Perspectives in Community-based Conservation*. Washington, D.C.: Island Press.

Williams, Thomas. R. 1965. *The Dusun: A North Borneo Society*. New York: Holt, Rinehart and Winston.

Wong, David. 1975. *Tenure and Land Dealings in the Malay States*. Singapore: Singapore University Press.

Woolley, G. C. 1953a. "Tuaran Adat," *Native Affairs Bulletin*, no. 2. Kota Kinabalu, Sabah: North Borneo Government Printer.

———. 1953b. "Murut Adat." *Native Affairs Bulletin*, no. 3. Kota Kinabalu, Sabah: North Borneo Government Printer.

———. 1953c. "Dusun Adat." *Native Affairs Bulletin*, no. 4. Kota Kinabalu, Sabah: North Borneo Government Printer.

———. 1953d. "Dusun Adat." *Native Affairs Bulletin*, no. 5. Kota Kinabalu, Sabah: North Borneo Government Printer.

———. 1953e. "Kwijau Adat." *Native Affairs Bulletin*, no. 6. Kota Kinabalu, Sabah: North Borneo Government Printer.

———. 1962a. "The Timoguns." *Native Affairs Bulletin*, no. 1. Kota Kinabalu, Sabah: North Borneo Government Printer.

———. 1962b. "Dusun Customs in Putatan District." *Native Affairs Bulletin*, no. 7. Kota Kinabalu, Sabah: North Borneo Government Printer.

Worboys, Michael. 1990. "The Imperial Institute: The State and the Development of the Natural Resource in the Colonial Empire, 1887–1964." In *Imperialism and the Natural World,* ed. John MacKenzie. Manchester: Manchester University Press.

Yahya Bin Mohamad. 1990. *Perkembangan Ugama Kristian di Sabah Setelah Meredeka* [Development of Christianity in Sabah before Independence]. Universiti Kebangsaan Malaysia, Bangi.

Zerner, Charles. 1994. "Through a Green Lens: The Construction of Customary Environmental Law and Community in Indonesia's Maluku Islands." *Law and Society Review* 28 (5):1079–1121.

NEWSPAPER ARTICLES

Berita Harian (Kuala Lumpur). 1996. "Gerakan Desa Wawasan: Ke Arah Transformasi Kedua Luar Bandar." July 4.

Bernama Daily Malaysian News. 2000. "Rural Dwellers Must Adopt Competitive Attitude, Says Azmi." June 11.

———. 2002. "Half of Villages in GDW Programme Fail to Achieve Objective." September 11.

———. 2003a. "The Rural Development Ministry Will Restructure 'Gerakan Desa Wawasan.'" February 24.

———. 2003b. "Help Promote Biodiversity, Rural Community Total." April 29.

———. 2003c. "Urgent Need to Venture Aggressively into Agricultural Sector." June 28.

———. 2003d. "Agriculture Sector Has Potential to Better 1.5 Percentage Growth Target." July 21.

———. 2003e. "Sabah to Tighten Conditions for Native Certificate." November 3.

———. 2003f. "Helping Rural Dwellers through Rubber Settlements." December 9.

———. 2003g. "Sabah Foundation to Venture into Oil Palm Plantation Next Year." December 12.

———. 2004a. "Urgent Need for Large Scale Forest Plantations in Sabah." March 6.

———. 2004b. "Don't Doubt Government's Agriculture Programmes." May 26.

Idrus, R. 1998. "Towards a Better Life for Villagers." *New Straits Times,* August 10.

Mokhtar, Nor Ashmah. 1994. "Government Agencies Play Vital Role in Changing Values." *Business Times,* December 29.

New Straits Times. 1996a. "Help Realise Vision 2020, Rural Folks Told." June 1.

———. 1996b. "Start Adopting Modern Technology, PM Advises Farmers." July 5.

———. 1997. "Anwar: Carry out Islamic Laws Wisely, Objectively." July 27.

———. 2001. "Community Involvement in Plan 'Still Lacking.'" May 11.

———. 2003a. "Changing the Mindset of Rural Populations." February 25.

———. 2003b. "Addressing Status of Minority Bumis in Sabah, Sarawak." November 20.

Sawatan, Jackson. 2002. "When the Poor Become Landless." *Bernama Daily Malaysian News,* March 4.

Visvanathan, T. 1997. "Proud Moment for Most Beautiful Village in Malaysia." *New Straits Times,* October 11.

INDEX

A

Aarhus Convention, 163–64
Adat (custom): colonial obligations to, 34; and land appropriation, 138; and land claims, 143; and natural resource management, 136; and reciprocity, 133; and redistributive feasts, 143. *See also under* Borneo Evangelical Mission; Headman; Hunting
Agrawal, Arun, viii; on community, 160; on critique of development, 102, 172n.16; on modernity and development, 19, 20, 21, 150
Agricultural cycle, 69; and fallows, 80–81, and property rights, 41, 125, 150
Agriculturalists, European, 45, 57–58, 60. *See also* Plantation agriculture; Rutter, Owen; Tobacco plantations
Agriculture: and colonialism, 31; commercial, 53, 69, 80–82; complexity of native, 35, 123, 127, 182–83n.32; and development, 51–54, 65, 71, 152; and economy, 69–70, 82, 127, 152; and gender, 186n.4; in Indonesia, 101; and inputs, 125, 152, 182n.24; and irrigation, 87; permanent, 42–43, 47, 80–81, 96; and risk, 187n.6; sharecropping, 82, 150; subsistence, 53, 69, 70, 155, 157; and state land, 151. *See also* Chinese; Gardens; Plantation agriculture; Shifting cultivation; *Tanah kampong*; Tobacco plantations
Agroforestry. *See* Buffer zone; Fruit orchards
Anderson, Benedict, 18, 172n.17, 185n.25
Appell, George N., ix; on native land rights under colonialism, 45; on property rights, 84, 101, 182n.22, 187n.10
Archives, colonial, 5, 70, 71, 73; regional, 131

B

Berry, Sara, 13, 25, 181n.17
Birch, Governor Ernest, 42. *See also* Governors of North Borneo
Black, Ian: on colonialism in North Borneo, 13, 32, 34, 35, 46, 173n.2
Blaikie, Piers, 5–6, 25
Borneo Evangelical Mission, 108, 112, 184n.14; and conflicts with *adat*, 143
Brooke regime, 47, 50
Brookfield, Harold, 5–6, 25
Brosius, Pete, 146, 158, 172–73n.18
Brunei, 180n.2. *See also* Sultan, of Brunei
Bryant, Raymond, 47
Buffer zone, 4, 161; and agroforestry, 145
Bukit Hempuan, 3–4, 10, 94, 137, 171n.2
Bumiputra (sons of the soil), 105–8, 118, 155, 184n.10

C

Capitalism: and colonial policy, 17, 38, 55, 64–65; and natives, 74; and postcolonialism, 100; and property rights, 172n.8; and tobacco plantations, 58–59
Chambers, Robert, 101
Chinese: and agriculture, 51–54, 69, 177n.76; and ethnic riots, 103, 184n.5; and land administration, 35, 48, 51–53; and land revenue, 53–54; merchants, 130, 139; and New Economic Plan, 104
Christianity, 106. *See also* Borneo Evangelical Mission
Circular 14 of 1920, 47–48
Colonial law: and control over natives, 41; enforcement of, 42; as a technology of rule, 10–11, 15, 21, 31, 66, 101. *See also* Land revenue; Native customary land rights; Power
Colonial rule, 15; and appropriation of native lands, 70–71, 75; and conservation, 5, 65; and discourse of "backward" natives, 18, 31, 39–40; and economic rationality, 17, 38, 55, 58–59, 64–65, 104; and native chiefs, 13; and native courts, 12; and native land rights, 29–66 passim; and paternalism, 1, 41, 49–50, 56, 64, 74, 141; and property rights, 35, 75–76, 89, 100, 181n.16; resource exploitation, 3–5, 6, 17; rights to land, 140; and science, 55, 59, 62. *See also under* Property rights
Community: and identity, 24, 97–98; and rights of access, 77–78, 80, 96, 133, 140; stratification of, 92
Community-based natural resource management, 144, 146, 160–62, 164–65
Community forestry, 155
Conservation, 5, 97, 188n.30, 78; and "backward" natives, 146; coerced, 160; community based, 98; ethic of, 160–61; failure of, 160; and fruit trees, 145; and markets, 161; and natural resource management, 144; and property rights, 137; and rafflesia, 137–38; rhetoric of, 153, 155; and science, 154
Cows. *See* Livestock, free-ranging
Creagh, Governor Charles, 56; and land laws, 173n.7; and land settlement, 39, 178n.85; and land "squatters," 175n.33. *See also* Governors of Borneo
Customary law, 77. *See also* Moore, Sally Falk; Native customary land rights; Zerner, Charles

D

Dane, Sir Richard, 42, 46, 175n.21
Decentralization, and natural resources, 27, 162–64
Dent, Alfred and Edward, 31–32
Development, 5; and aesthetics, 110–13, 114–15, 116–17; blueprints, 101–2; bottom-up, 116–17; and control over natural resources, 22, 99; "failures," 116, 118, 119; funds, 115; gifts of, 103; in Indonesia, 103, 116, 172n.14; instrument-effect, 102; international, 172n.13; and Islam, 99, 107, 116; and knowledge, 19, 40, 100; large-scale, 144; and marginal people, 19, 20–21, 119–20, 185n.21; and material benefits, 118; and money politics, 113, 117; and normalization, 99, 112; obstacles to, 119–20; poststructural critique of, 19–21; and property rights, 22; rejection of, 118; and Robert Chambers, 101; side effects of, 20; spectacle of, 116–17; and state rule, 99–121 passim. *See also* Ferguson, James; Gerakan Desa Wawasan; Islamic values; Kemas; Money politics; Wawasan 2020
Discourse: of "backward" natives, 18, 31, 39–40, 74–75, 119–21, 142, 151, 154; and development, 99, 102, 118–20, 141; of indigeneity, 117; and land appropriation, 84; and land use, 134; of modernity, 100–116, 119, 141, 157; natural resource management, 12; and power, 8–9, 25, 103, 144; and property relations, 151; and state rule, 5, 7, 22; and tradition, 141, 144, 151. *See also* Ethic of access; Politics; Power
District officer Dusing, 73, 130, 139; and land acquisition, 140; and land settlement, 38, 40, 46–48, 52, 56, 64; and native disputes, 83, 84; and native people, 176n.51; opposition to governors, 49, 51, 60–61
Dove, Michael R., viii; on agriculture and biodiversity, 161; on community and identity, 172–73n.18; on home gardens, 186n.2; on land tenure, 42, 182n.22, 186nn.2–3; 187n.10; on passive resistance, 43; on reciprocity, 187nn.16–17; on shifting cultivation, 62, 101; on smallholders, 146, 187nn.6–7; on state plantations and smallholders, 172n.9, 177n.78, 188n.33
Dusing, John. *See* District Officer Dusing
Dusun, 3, 179n.1; ethnicity, 68, 73, 103, 179–80n.1; language, xi, 129. *See also* Ethnic groups

E

East India Company, 13–14, 31, 32, 173n.6
Escobar, Arturo: on development, 19, 20, 172n.13; on postcolonialism, 18; on property rights, 129; on state-society relations, 9
Ethic of access, 137, 187n.8; and agriculture, 128; and durians, 81–82; to fallows, 82, 96, 127, 149; and forest resources, 127–28, 132, 149–50; and sharecropping, 150; and shifting cultivation, 129. *See also Kepunya'an hutan*; Moral economy of peasants
Ethnic groups: and discourse, 132–33; Dusun, 68, 73, 103, 129; Kadazan, 180n.1, 183n.4; Murut, 52, 103, 183n.4; *orang asli*, 74. *See also Bumiputra*
Ethnic identity, and nationalism, 103

European planters. *See* Plantation agriculture

F

Fallows. *See* Land, fallow
Ferguson, James: on community and identity, 172–73n.18; on critique of development, 19–21, 101–3, 184n.8; on development failures, 119; on state power, 99
Forest reserve. See *Hutan simpan*
Forest resources, 186–87n.4; and "ethic of access," 127; and native reserve, 73, 93; and reciprocity, 133; and state rule, 146. See also *Kepunya'an hutan*; Nontimber forest products
Forestry Department, vii; and claims on native reserves, 92–96; and lack of forest skills, 153–54; and state plantations, 156. *See also* Community forestry
Fortmann, Louise, 23
Foucault, Michel, on power, 14, 15–16, 22, 25, 108
Fruit orchards, 70, 123; in buffer zones, 145; income from, 125; native customary rights to, 49; and property rights, 125, 144
Fruit trees: and *adat*, 78 (table 2.1), 127 (table 4.2), 136; as cash crops, 127, 150; compensation for, 45; and conservation, 145; and fallows, 150; in home gardens, 123; and kin, 182n.25; and land settlement, 46; and native reserve, 77–78; and pioneer of the land, 134; and private property, 127–28, 150; rights to, 40, 41; shared access, 136; wild, 135, 137

G

Gardens: income from, 91 (table 2.2), 124 (table 4.1), 150; and property rights, 125, 128, 139, 147; and *Tanah kampong*, 71, 80, 82–84, 87, 89, 127. *See also* Gardens, vegetable
Gardens, vegetable, 70, 87 (fig), 115, 123, 127 (table 4.2), 183n.32; as cash crops, 127, 149; commercialization of, 180n.2; and moral economy, 135; and *Tanah kampong*, 71, 80, 82–84, 87, 89
Gerekan Desa Wawasan, 99–121 passim; and agriculture, 101; and "Malaysization," 113; project launch, 109; translation of, 183n.3; and UMNO, 120
Gisil. *See* Native chief Gisil
Globalization, 160, 172n.15
Governance: and civil society, 113, 162–63; and transparency, 156, 163–64
Governmentality, 6–7, 22; and colonialism, 17; and development, 108, 112; and postcolonialism, 120; and property relations, 158
Governors of North Borneo, 35, 39 (table 1.2), 64
Grazing reserve: and land claims, 127 (table 4.2), 143; and money politics, 142; and native reserve, 78 (table 2.1); and shifting cultivation, 144
Grove, Richard, 64, 65

H

Hamlet, 68
Hay, Douglas, 14
Headman: and *adat* (custom), 113; and

colonialism, 43, 51, 65, and land administration, 74, 76, 109, 123, 130; and land claims, 141, 143–44
Hegemony, 14–15, 49, 179n.109
History, oral, 70, 71, 73, 129
Home gardens, 122, 123; in Java, 186n.2
House lots, and usufruct rights, 123, 142
Humphreys, Governor John: and opening up of native reserves, 51–54. *See also* Governors of North Borneo
Hunting, 12; and *adat*, 133, and agricultural cycle, 183n.32; colonial views of, 29; and cultural norms, 135; in forest reserves, 154; game, 154–55, 179n.111; in Kinabalu Park, 4; in native reserves, 71, 78, 96; and property boundaries, 78 (table 2.2), 127 (table 4.2), 134; subsistence, 3–4, 69, 125
Hutan simpan (forest reserve), 79 (map), 81 (fig); access to, 89–90, 94, 131; daily use, 90–92; dependence on, 91; development of, 82–83; and firewood, 90–91; forest department prohibitions in, 93–94; and hunting, 154; and native reserves, 77, 78 (table 2.1), 81 (fig); and wild vegetable, 90–91

I

Independence, Malaysian, 73, 120, 151
Ideology, of development: and economic growth, 101; and state power, 99, 117, 157. *See under* Islamic values; Kemas; Malay-Muslim
India, 64, 183n.2
Indigenous knowledge, 83, 155; representations of, 11, 117

Indirect rule, 12–13, 38, 65
Inheritance: of land, 78, 83, 85, 96; of usufruct rights, 86
Islamic values, 104; and development, 107, 113, 116–18; and politics, 103–5; and poverty alleviation, 107. *See also* Malay-Muslim; Money politics; Politics

J

Jesselton, 52, 176n.62. *See also* Kota Kinabalu
JKKK chairman (*Jawatankuasa Kemajuan dan Keselamatan Kampung*, Village Authority for Development and Safety): and development politics, 109, 113, 114, 119; and land claims, 141

K

Kadazan, 106, 180n.1, 183n.4; and nationalism, 106; political control in Sabah, 106, 114. *See also* Ethnic groups
Kemas, 184n.7; and development, 104, 107–8, 113, 115–16
Kempunan, 135–36, 187n.16. *See also* Reciprocity
Kepunya'an hutan: and hunting, 133; and nontimber forest products, 134, 136, 137; and private property, 136
Kinabalu Park, 69, 83, 122; boundaries, 2–4, 123; and rafflesia, 137. *See also* Buffer zone
Kinship, 68, 82; and access to land, 78, 81–82, 132; and fruit trees, 182n.25

Knowledge. *See under* Power
Kota Kinabalu, 67, 70. *See also* Jesselton

L

Labor, wage, 69, 70, 80, 110, 113, 130, 186n.1; and dependence on forest reserve, 90–92; and property rights, 139
Labuan Land Ordinance, 173n.8
Ladang, defined, 178n.96
Ladang Ordinance, 59, 61. *See also* Shifting cultivation; Tobacco plantations
Land: abandoned, 86–87, 140; access to, 14, 172n.11; classification of, 78; as collateral, 85, 88; as a commodity, 29, 34, 36, 74, 121, 186n.3; compulsory acquisition of, 71, 156; degradation of, 152; and economics, 29; and gender, 186n.3; idle, 12, 152; improvement, 45, 139; inheritance of, 14; and native areas, 52; and native profiteering, 47–48, 51; native prohibition to sell, 40; privatization of, 81, 84; redistribution, 140; and shortage, 110, 129, 131; squatters, 45, 156; unclaimed, 131; waste, 42, 140
Land, fallow, 123; access to, 78–81; ecological function of, 80; and ethic of access, 82, 96, 127, 149; and insecure property rights to, 41, 42, 96, 152; use rights to, 132, 139
Land alienation, 93
Land boundaries, 74, 188n.23
Land claims: appropriation through use, 134, 139; and common property, 141; and ethic of access, 144; and fruit trees, 139; and grazing reserves, 141; and labor theory, 86; and modernity, 141–42; by pioneer of land, 129, 139
Land classification, 78 (table 2.1), 127 (table 4.2)
Land disputes: and abandoned land, 130; between Forestry Department and native reserve, 92–96; legacy of colonialism, 70, 181n6; and native courts, 88; in native reserves, 83–88; and politics, 141; and property relations, 131; use of customary law in, 88; use of statutory law in, 140. *See also under* Politics; Wealth
Land Law of 1913, 37 (table 1.1), 40, 47, 48
Land Law of 1953, 73
Land laws: implementation of, 41, 42, 118, 131; Western, 11, 13, 24, 173n.7. *See also* Colonial law; Labuan Land Ordinance; Land Law of 1913; Land Law of 1953; Land Proclamation of 1885; Proclamation of December 23, 1881; Proclamation III of 1889
Land Proclamation of 1885, 35
Land registration. *See* Land settlement
Land revenue, 29–66 passim; and Chinese immigrants, 53–54; and native chiefs, 13; and native holdings, 42, 46–51, 75; and shifting cultivation, 139
Landscape mosaics, 123
Land settlement, 13, 42–66, 70, 127; areas omitted, 49; completion of, 46–47; confusions over complex rights, 51; and land laws, 35–66; native resistance to, 43, 46, 52, 56, 177n.67; and tobacco plantations, 55. *See also under* Native customary land rights; Property, common; Property, private
Land survey. *See* Land settlement
Land taxes. *See* Land revenue

Land tenure. *See* Property rights
Land use. *See* Agriculture; Discourse; Fruit orchards; Gardens; House lots; Hunting; *Hutan simpan*; Land; Plantation agriculture; Shifting cultivation; *Tanah kampong*; Tobacco plantations
Law. *See* Colonial law
Legal pluralism, 5, 15, 24, 34, 70, 123, 149
Li, Tania Murray, viii; on community action, 114; on community and identity, 172–73n.18; on conservation, 161; on development discourse, 20, 102–3, 116–17, 119, 172nn.12, 14; on modernity, 143; on property relations, 24, 25, 77–78, 87, 88, 181n.16, 183n.36; on state power over peripheries, 22, 102–3, 162–63, 183n.1
Livestock, free-ranging, 110, 122, 123, 185n.19, 188n.25; and discourse of modernity, 142; and native reserves, 77–78, 89; and state land, 127 (table 4.2). *See also* Grazing reserve
Locke, John: on property rights, 11, 172n.8

M

Mahathir Mohamed, 101, 102, 103
Majid Cooke, Fadzilah: on the Brooke regime, 47; on nationalism, 99, 185n.29; on state-society relations, 9, 10, 186n.32; and timber politics, 184n.10
Malay-Muslim, 20, 21–22, 109, 183n.4, 184nn.11–12; domination of, 117; ideology of, 99, 107, 120. *See also* Development; Islamic values; Politics
Mamdani, Mahmood, 18, 36, 100, 106

Maps: of land use in Govuton's native reserve, 79; of North Borneo, 1878, 30; of overlapping boundaries between Govuton's native reserve and Similiu forestry reserve, 94; of Sabah with residencies, 44; of Sabah with districts, 72; of status of property in Tempulong, 126
Marx, Karl, 7
Maxwell, Resident W. E., 36
Merry, Sally, 11, 23
Modernity: and appropriate resource use, 147; and land claims, 141, 144; local views of, 117; models of, 116; in opposition to traditional, 143, 153–54; and politics, 142; and science, 154, 155; and sloganeering, 115; and state rule, 10, 118, 148–49, 155, 157. *See also under* Discourse
Money politics: and development, 113, 116, 117–19; and grazing reserve, 142; and UMNO, 105, 114, 117–18, 185n.23
Moore, Donald, 23, 120, 189n.8
Moore, Sally Falk, 12, 13, 15, 23, 25, 149
Moral economy of peasants, 78; and access to resources, 137, 140; and gardens, 135; and land use, 133–34, 140; and management of natural resources, 135; and shifting cultivation 135
Mount Kinabalu, viii, 68 (fig), 69, 154, 171n.1
Murut, 52, 103, 183n.4. *See also* Ethnic groups

N

Nationalism, 99, 185n.25; and development, 108, 118; and ethnicity, 106; and modernization, 100, 103

Native Chief Gisil, 73–74; and indirect rule, 38, 64–65; and land disputes, 88; and land revenue, 13, 42, 47, 181n.6; and land settlement, 45, 56; and native courts, vii, 81, 87, 181n.6, 182n.30, 188nn.20, 22; and native reserves, 51, 73–74, 76, 82

Native customary land rights: and abandoned land, 87; access to, 3–5, 13, 15, 26, 71–98, 129, 146, 188n.20; agricultural development, 83; classification of, 75, 78 (table 2.1); codification of, 12, 14–15, 54, 70, 88, 92; colonial confusion over, 41–42; compensation for, 38, 56; criminalization of, 4, 23–24; debates over, 35–66; durability of, 137; and fruit trees, 11–12, 38, 40, 41, 45, 46; invention of, 12, 13 23; and land settlement, 29–66, 73, 140; obstacles to development, 34–66; and postcolonialism, 121; reinvigoration of, 26, 97, 141; romanticization of, 26; and royal charter, 34; selling of, 96; and social change, 67–98; and state control, 137; static image of, 95–97; and statutory law, 76–77, 127, 132, 137–38, 148, 158, 177n.77; and tobacco plantations, 56–58; and village land, 73. *See also* Garden; *Hutan simpan;* Land disputes; Land laws; Property, private; Property rights; Shifting cultivation; *Tanah kampong*

Native people: dependency of, 120; and ethic of conservation, 160; and identity, 100; and Islam, 155; as obstacles to conservation, 145, 165; as obstacles to development, 119–20, 152; and resource degradation, 121, 152–53; romanticization of, 69; and science, 120, 155. *See also* Headman; Indigenous knowledge; Indirect rule; Native Chief Gisil

Native reserves, 51, 76, 176–77n.66; abolished, 53; and access to abandoned land, 87; access to forest resources, 89–90; and cash crops, 87; classification of land in, 78 (table 2.1); dependence on forest reserve, 91; development of, 83; and fallows, 149; and firewood, 90–91; and Forestry Department, 92–95; and insecure tenure to land, 51; land cultivation in, 89; and livestock, 89; opening for settlement, 52–53; privatization of land in, 84–85, 88, 92, 96; restrictions on selling land in, 88, 96; in statutory law, 70–98; and usufruct rights, 89; and vegetable gardens, 91; and wild vegetables, 90–91. *See also Hutan simpan;* Native customary land rights; Property rights; *Tanah kampong*

Natural resources: access to, 131–33, 138; colonial exploitation of, 33; commercialization of, 39, 132, 154; and cultural values, 90, 132; and decentralization, 26, 162–64; and injustices, 165; landscape-level management, 145, 161; and long-term management, 163; management of, 135, 146; and neoliberal economics, 163; ownership of, 17, 24, 64; and power, 132; state control over, 5, 23, 145, 159–60; and state-society relations, 158, 162; and subsistence needs, 90, 123. *See also* Community-based natural resource management; Moral economy of peasants; Nontimber forest products; Reciprocity

Native title, 73, 85, 131, 152; conflicts with Forestry Department, 157; and lack of security, 156; restrictions on selling, 74–75; selling, 74, 88, 89; statutory law and, 88. *See also* Land settlement; Native customary land rights

NEP (New Economic Plan), 105

Neumann, Roderick, 23, 62, 64, 65, 179n.111; on coerced conservation, 160; on moral economy, 182n.22

Nontimber forest products: access to, 139; collection, 3–4, 12, 69, 71, 96, 11 (fig), 123, 125; and conflict, 137; economic value of, 47, 69, 136; and fruit trees, 138–39; income from, 124 (table 4.1); medicinal plants, 153–54, 155; and moral economy, 140; and native reserves, 77; rights to, 29, 40, 41, 73, 78 (table 2.1), 127 (table 4.2), 132; trade in, 31; wild vegetables, 78, 133, 138, 183n.32. *See also* Forest resources; *Hutan simpan*; *Kepunya'an hutan*, Native reserves; Rafflesia, Rattan

Normalization: and development, 99, 103, 116; and law, 46; and technology of rule, 8, 20, 29–30, 64

North Borneo, 30 (map); as a colony, 180–81n.3. *See also* Maps

North Borneo Chartered Company: founders of, 16; the establishment of, 31–33; Royal charter of, 34

O

Ong, Aihwa, 155

Orang asli, 74, 106. *See also* Ethnic groups

Ortner, Sherry, 9, 92, 158

P

Parr, Governor, 175n.23. *See also* Governors of North Borneo

PBS (*Parti Bersatu Sabah*, United Party of Sabah), 106, 114, 118

Pearson, Governor Aylmer: and land revenue, 50–51, and land settlement, 175nn.31, 35, 36; and native land title, 47–48, 175–76n.43; and shifting cultivation, 178n.102. *See also* Governors of North Borneo

Peluso, Nancy, vii, viii; on coercive conservation, 160; on colonial land administration, 11, 13, 18, 47, 181n.17; on colonial rule, 176nn.51, 57; on ethic of access, 82, 182n.25, 187n.8; on ethnic violence, 163; on passive resistance, 43, 158; on property rights, 23, 24, 25, 140, 182n.22, 183n.37; on usufruct rights in Java, 36; on trade, 101

Peninsular Malay, under colonialism: and Chinese agriculturalists, 53; control over regions, 32–33; and land revenue, 42; and native land tenure, 36, 48; and native agriculturalists, 54; and paternalism, 74. *See also* Torrens system

Peninsular Malaysia: and state-federal politics, 105–6, 108, 117, 183n.4, 185n.28; and race riots, 103

Peters, Pauline: on property rights in Africa, 25, 172–73n.18

Pigg, Stacey, 19, 172n.12

Plantation agriculture, 42, 54, 62; and colonial land laws, 34; and native fruit trees, 45; and native land rights, 71; and oil palm, 152, 155–56; and rubber 152; and revenue, 29. *See also*

Plantation agriculture *(continued)* Agriculture; Agriculturalists; Tobacco plantations

Political ecology, defined, 5–6

Political patronage, 99

Politics: and conversion to Islam, 104; and land disputes, 88, 141; and Malay-Muslim elite, 104, 106, 117; transformation of property rights, 92, 96. *See also* Money politics; Timber

Postcolonialism, 172n.11; defined as, 18, 171n.10; and colonialism, 100, 120, 157; and development, 21–22; and discourse of "backward" natives, 119–21, 142, 151, 154; and governmentality, 120, 155. See also *Bumiputra;* Colonial rule; Development; Modernity; Money politics; Power; UMNO

Poststructuralism, critique of development, 19, 65, 102, 172n.16

Poverty, 107, 108, 120, 183n.33; rural, 99–121 passim

Power: consolidation of, 157; and control over people, 40, 64, 99–100; and control over resources, 5, 14, 99–100, 132, 137; and development discourse, 99, 103; and ideology, 99; and indirect rule, 13; and knowledge, 6–11, 15, 35, 100, 121, 157, 172n.17; and local government, 122–51 passim; and social networks, 84; theories of, 6

Proclamation of December 23, 1881, 35, 37 (table 1.1)

Proclamation III of 1889, 37 (table 1.1), 38, 40, 42, 56–58

Property, common: and access to resources, 135; and fallows, 138; and forest products, 125, 132; and land security, 176n.61; and land settlement, 11–12, 45, 46–47; and land use, 80–86; in native reserves, 70–71, 73, 75–76, 127, 176–77n.66; and state rule, 95; in statutory law, 51; and temporary gardens, 125. *See also* Ethic of access; *Hutan simpan; Tanah kampong*

Property, private: and community access, 136; and customary law, 127 (table 4.2), 138; and fruit trees, 125, 127; and John Locke, 11; and land commercialization, 121; and land settlement, 14, 45, 51, 130, 131–32, 176–77n.66. *See also* Property rights

Property and social relations, 23–24, 77, 131, 146, 172–73n.18; changes in, 92, 147; and cultural idioms, 132, 146; and economic change, 70; and state-society relations, 147, 158; unpredictability of, 161

Property of the forest. See *Kepunya'an hutan*

Property rights: and agricultural cycle, 125, 150; and capitalism, 171n.8; and cash crops, 84; classification of, 78 (table 2.1), 127 (table 4.2); and colonial rule, 35, 132, 149; and complexity of, 70, 95, 144; de facto, 77, 87, 96, 134, 161–62; and development, 22; and gender, 25, 186n.3; and identity, 25; insecure, 110, 146, 161; and landscape, 129; limited by custom, 132; multiplicity of, 127; and pioneer of the land, 78, 129, 134, 139, 142; and political networks, 73; and power, 6, 25, 158, 157; simplifications of, 13, 77, 95; and social change, 69, 82, 96; state power, 95; transformation of, 147, 151. *See also* Agriculture; Ethic of access; *Kepunya'an hutan;* Kinship; Land, fallow; Native customary land rights; Native reserves; Native title; Property, common; Property, private; Property and social relations; Usufruct rights

R

Raffles, Sir Hugh, 36
Rafflesia, 137–38
Rattan, 3, 69, 71; and conservation, 146; and property rights, 138
Rebellion, 49–51, 54; in Rundum, 176n.56
Reciprocity: cultural norms of, 85, 133, 135–36; and hunting, 135; and land use, 89, 133; and natural resource management, 135; and property, 132, 137; and redistribution of wealth, 136, 187nn.14, 17. See also *Kempunan*
Resistance, 7, 158; everyday, 9–10; and land claims, 143–44; and land distribution, 3–5, 25; to land settlement, 43, 58; and state-society relations, 27, 144
Resource degradation, 6, 121, 144, 152–53; blaming local people for, 146, 151, 153, 155, 165
Rutter, Owen, 33, 60, 179n.103

S

Sabah, 44 (residence map), 72 (district map). See also Maps
Sarawak, 47, 50, 54, 177n.76, 180n.2; and *bumiputra*, 105
Schroeder, Richard, 6, 24, 25, 150, 172–73n.18
Science: and colonial rule, 55, 59, 62; and modernity, 104, 154, 155; and native people, 120, 155; and resource control, 145; and tobacco plantations, 55, 59, 62

Scott, James, viii; on high modernism, 155; on moral economy 133, 182n.22; on resistance, 14, 43, 186n.31; on state simplifications, 13, 77, 95, 185n.20
Secondary forest, 80
Shifting cultivation, 78 (table 2.1), 86 (fig), 127 (table 4.2); amount of land under, 61; and cash crops, 82; and customary law, 139; cycle of, 79–81; forest destruction, 59–62, 93, 155; and insecure tenure, 152; Kinabalu Park, 4, 161; and moral economy, 134; and native reserves, 78, 79 (map); present-day, 69, 124, 129, 179n.109; and property rights, 125, 127–28, 144; rights to fallow, 84, 88; and tobacco plantations, 58; wasteful practice, 58. See also Land, fallow; *Ladang* Ordinance
Sivaramakrisnan, K., viii; on colonialism, 14, 173n.6, 176n.51; on critique of development, 65, 102, 172n.16; on modernity and development, 19, 20, 21
Slavery, 32, 35, 173n.7
State rule, 99–121 passim
Sultan, of Brunei, 31–32, 173n.3
Swidden. *See* shifting cultivation

T

Tanah kampong (village land), 79 (map), 80 (fig); classification of, 77–78 (table 2.1); and shifting cultivation, 77, 129; and vegetables, 80, 81 (fig)
Tarling, Nicholas, 31, 173nn.2–3
Tax: collection of, 181n.6; poll, 175n.25. See also Land revenue
Thompson, Edward, 14; on moral economy, 182n.23

Timber, concessions, 33, 178n.100; commercial, 155, 189n.5; loss of, 58–60; native lands 49; on plantations, 57, 62; politics, 105, 184n.10; and reforestation, 152; rights, 4, 179n.107

Tobacco, 55, 59. *See also* Tobacco plantations

Tobacco plantations, 55; and Count Gelose d'Elsoo, 56–58, 178nn.87–88; and *Ladang* Ordinance, 59; and science, 55, 59; similarities to native shifting cultivation, 58–62 (table 1.3), 63. *See also* Plantation agriculture

Torrens system, 36, 38

Tourism, 122

Treacher, Governor William Hood: and acquisition of North Borneo, 32; and Chinese agriculturalist, 53, 177n.76; and slavery, 35, 173n.7; and tobacco plantations, 58, 178n.95. S*ee also* Governors of North Borneo

Tsing, Anna, 24, 101, 182n.22, 187n.15

U

UMNO (United Malaysian National Organization), 184n.17, 185–86n.30; electoral support for, 117; and rural development, 103–8, 113–14, 117–18, 120

Usufruct rights, 36, 77–79, 86; and agriculture, 129, 131–32; and house lots, 123, 142; and land pioneer, 129; limits of, 89; native customary rights, 127 (table 4.2), 142; on private property, 127 (table 4.2); purchase of, 86; selling, 85, 89. *See also under* Land, fallow; Native reserves; Property rights

V

Vandergeest, Peter, vii; on colonial land administration, 11, 13, 18, 47, 181n.17; on colonial rule, 176nn.51, 57; on nationalism, 185n.25; on resistance, 43; on usufruct rights in Java, 36

Village land. See *Tanah kampong*

Vision 2020. *See* Wawasan 2020

von Overbeck, Baron, 31–32

W

Watts, Michael, 6, 8, 11, 25; on environmental management, 159–60, 163; on moral economy, 182n.22; on oil and violence, 162

Wawasan 2020, 101, 103

Wealth, 82–83; and land disputes, 84–88; and transformation of property rights, 92, 96

Woolley, G. C., 42, 54, 187n.10

Z

Zamindar class, 13–14

Zerner, Charles, 12, 13, 23, 24

LIBRARY OF CONGRESS CATALOGING-IN-PUBLICATION DATA

Doolittle, Amity Appell.
Property and politics in Sabah, Malaysia :
native struggles over land rights/
Amity A. Doolittle. — 1st ed.
p. cm. — (Culture, place, and nature)
Includes bibliographical references and index.
ISBN 0-295-98539-9 (hardback : alk. paper)
1. Land tenure—Law and legislation—Malaysia—Sabah.
2. Customary law—Malaysia—Sabah.
I. Title. II. Series.
KPH66.3D66   2005   340. 5'259'3—dc22   2005008068

AMITY A. DOOLITTLE is program director of the Tropical Resources Institute at the Yale School of Forestry and Environmental Studies.

(Photo of author interviewing a Dusan woman ©1996 by Michael J. Doolittle)